WE ONLY FIND THEM WHEN THEY'RE DEAD

Book One: The Seeker

Published by

BOOM!
STUDIOS

Ross Richie CEO & Founder
Joy Huffman CFO
Matt Gagnon Editor-in-Chief
Filip Sablik President, Publishing & Marketing
Stephen Christy President, Development
Lance Kreiter Vice President, Licensing & Merchandising
Bryce Carlson Vice President, Editorial & Creative Strategy
Kate Henning Director, Operations
Spencer Simpson Director, Sales
Scott Newman Manager, Production Design
Elyse Strandberg Manager, Finance
Sierra Hahn Executive Editor
Jeanine Schaefer Executive Editor
Dafna Pleban Senior Editor
Shannon Watters Senior Editor
Eric Harburn Senior Editor
Sophie Philips-Roberts Associate Editor
Amanda LaFranco Associate Editor
Jonathan Manning Associate Editor
Gavin Gronenthal Assistant Editor
Gwen Waller Assistant Editor
Allyson Gronowitz Assistant Editor

Ramiro Portnoy Assistant Editor
Kenzie Rzonca Assistant Editor
Shelby Netschke Editorial Assistant
Michelle Ankley Design Lead
Marie Krupina Production Designer
Grace Park Production Designer
Chelsea Roberts Production Designer
Samantha Knapp Production Design Assistant
José Meza Live Events Lead
Stephanie Hocutt Digital Marketing Lead
Esther Kim Marketing Lead
Breanna Sarpy Live Events Coordinator
Amanda Lawson Marketing Assistant
Morgan Perry Retail Sales Lead
Holly Aitchison Digital Sales Coordinator
Megan Christopher Operations Coordinator
Rodrigo Hernandez Operations Coordinator
Zipporah Smith Operations Coordinator
Jason Lee Senior Accountant
Sabrina Lesin Accounting Assistant
Lauren Alexander Administrative Assistant

WE ONLY FIND THEM WHEN THEY'RE DEAD Vol. 1, May 2021.
Published by BOOM! Studios, a division of Boom Entertainment,
Inc. We Only Find Them When They're Dead is ™ & © 2021 Al Ewing
& Simone Di Meo. Originally published in single magazine form
as WE ONLY FIND THEM WHEN THEY'RE DEAD No. 1-5. ™ & ©
2020, 2021 Al Ewing & Simone Di Meo. All rights reserved. BOOM!

BOOM! Studios, 5670 Wilshire Boulevard, Suite 400, Los Angeles, CA, 90036-5679. Printed in
Canada. First Printing.

ISBN: 978-1-68415-677-1, eISBN: 978-1-64668-162-4

Discover Now Edition:
ISBN: 978-1-68415-683-2

Forbidden Planet Exclusive Edition:
ISBN: 978-1-68415-766-2

Written by **Al Ewing**
Illustrated by **Simone Di Meo**
with Color Assists by **Mariasara Miotti**
Lettered by **AndWorld Design**

Cover by **Simone Di Meo**

Discover Now Edition Cover by **Toni Infante**

Forbidden Planet Exclusive Edition Cover by **Jenny Frison**

Series Designer **Grace Park**

Collection Designer **Chelsea Roberts**

Assistant Editor **Gwen Waller**

Editor **Eric Harburn**

We Only Find Them When They're Dead created by **Al Ewing + Simone Di Meo**

To my mother,
who taught me to
look at the stars.
1967-2020

—Simone Di Meo

Chapter One

Eight Bells, All's Well

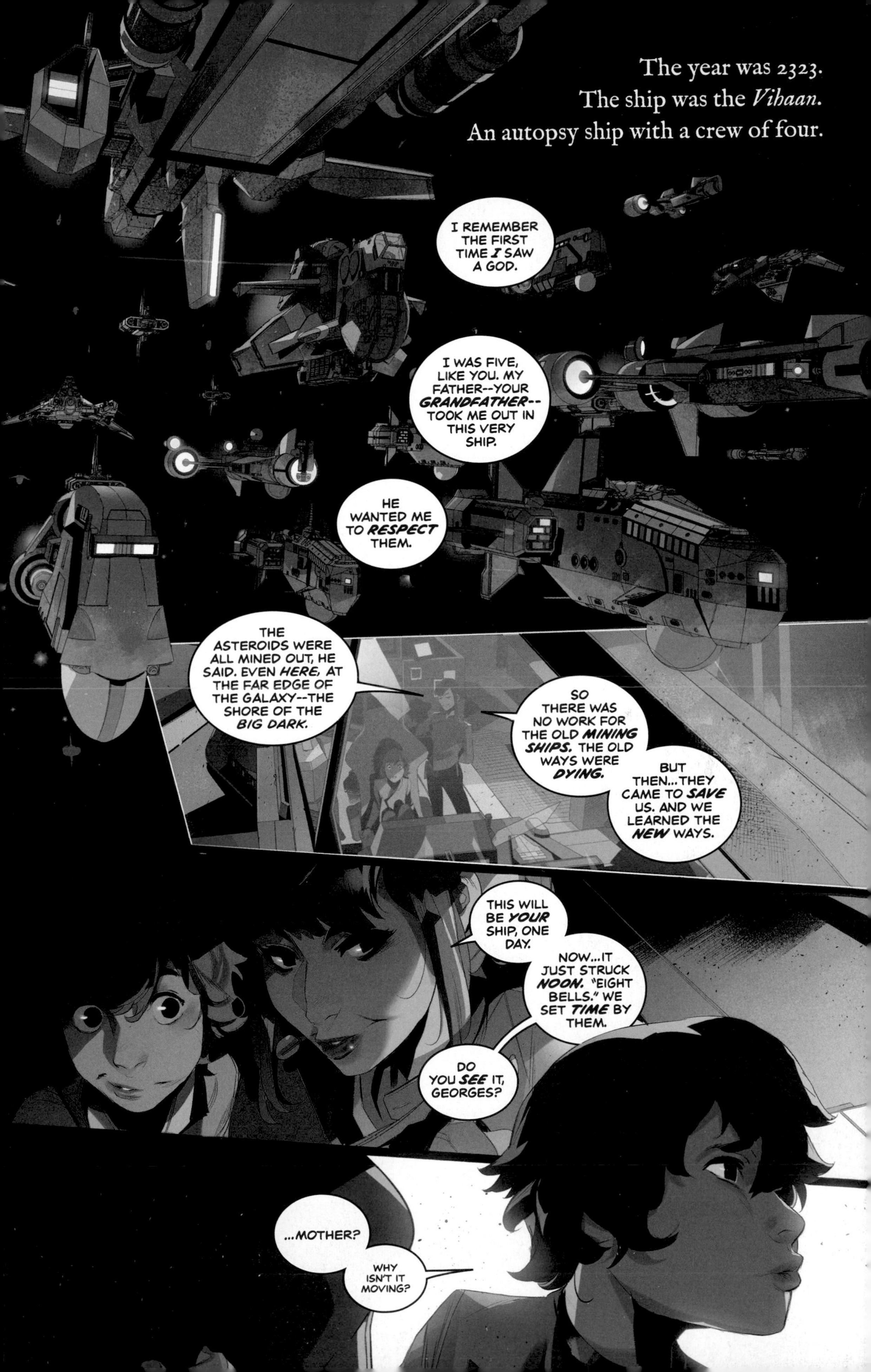
The year was 2323.
The ship was the *Vihaan*.
An autopsy ship with a crew of four.
I REMEMBER THE FIRST TIME *I* SAW A GOD.
I WAS FIVE, LIKE YOU. MY FATHER--YOUR *GRANDFATHER*--TOOK ME OUT IN THIS VERY SHIP.
HE WANTED ME TO *RESPECT* THEM.
THE ASTEROIDS WERE ALL MINED OUT, HE SAID. EVEN *HERE,* AT THE FAR EDGE OF THE GALAXY--THE SHORE OF THE *BIG DARK.*
SO THERE WAS NO WORK FOR THE OLD *MINING SHIPS.* THE OLD WAYS WERE *DYING.*
BUT THEN...THEY CAME TO *SAVE* US. AND WE LEARNED THE *NEW* WAYS.
THIS WILL BE *YOUR* SHIP, ONE DAY.
NOW...IT JUST STRUCK *NOON.* "EIGHT BELLS." WE SET *TIME* BY THEM.
DO YOU *SEE* IT, GEORGES?
...MOTHER?
WHY ISN'T IT MOVING?

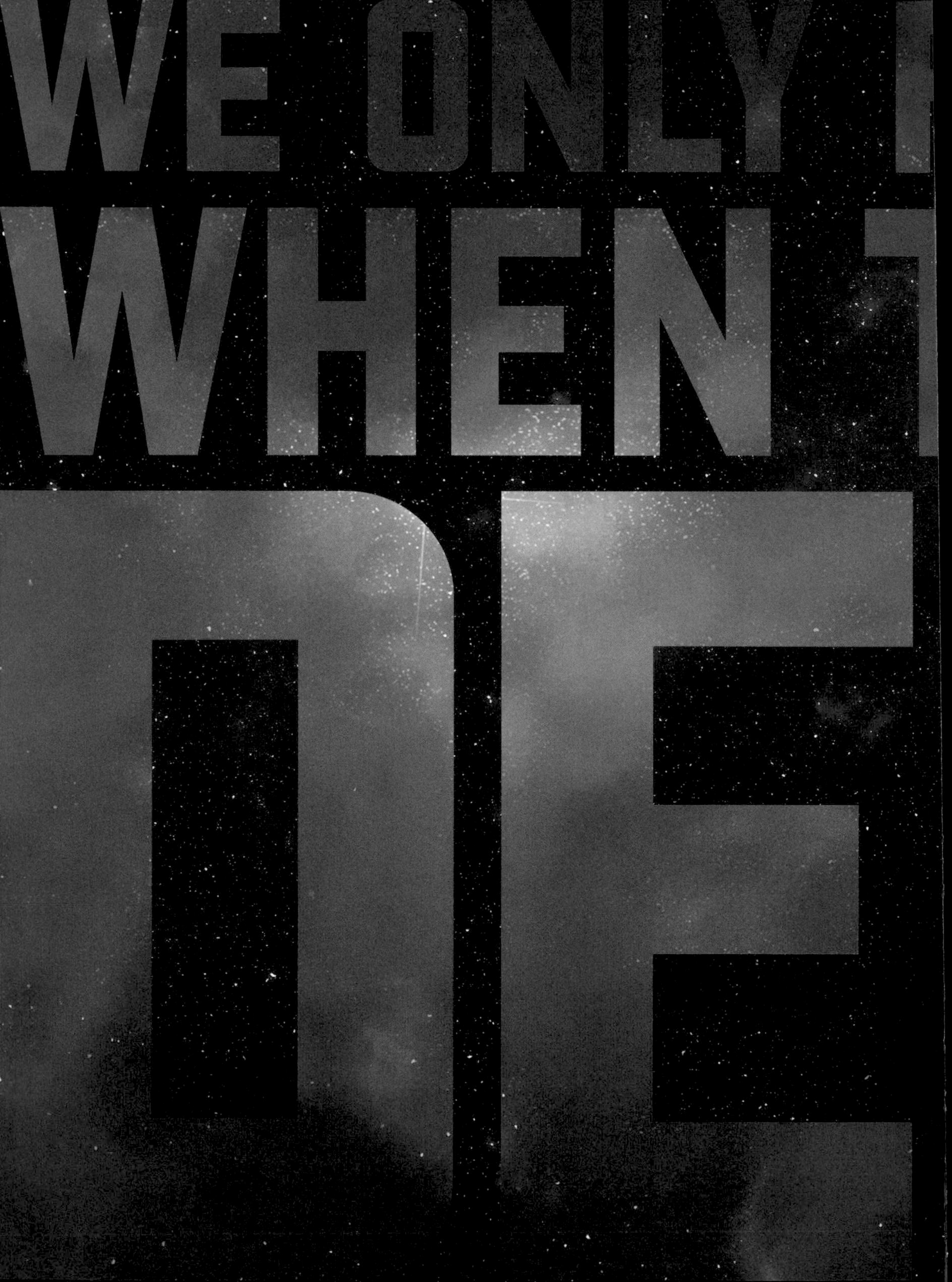
WE ONLY
WHEN

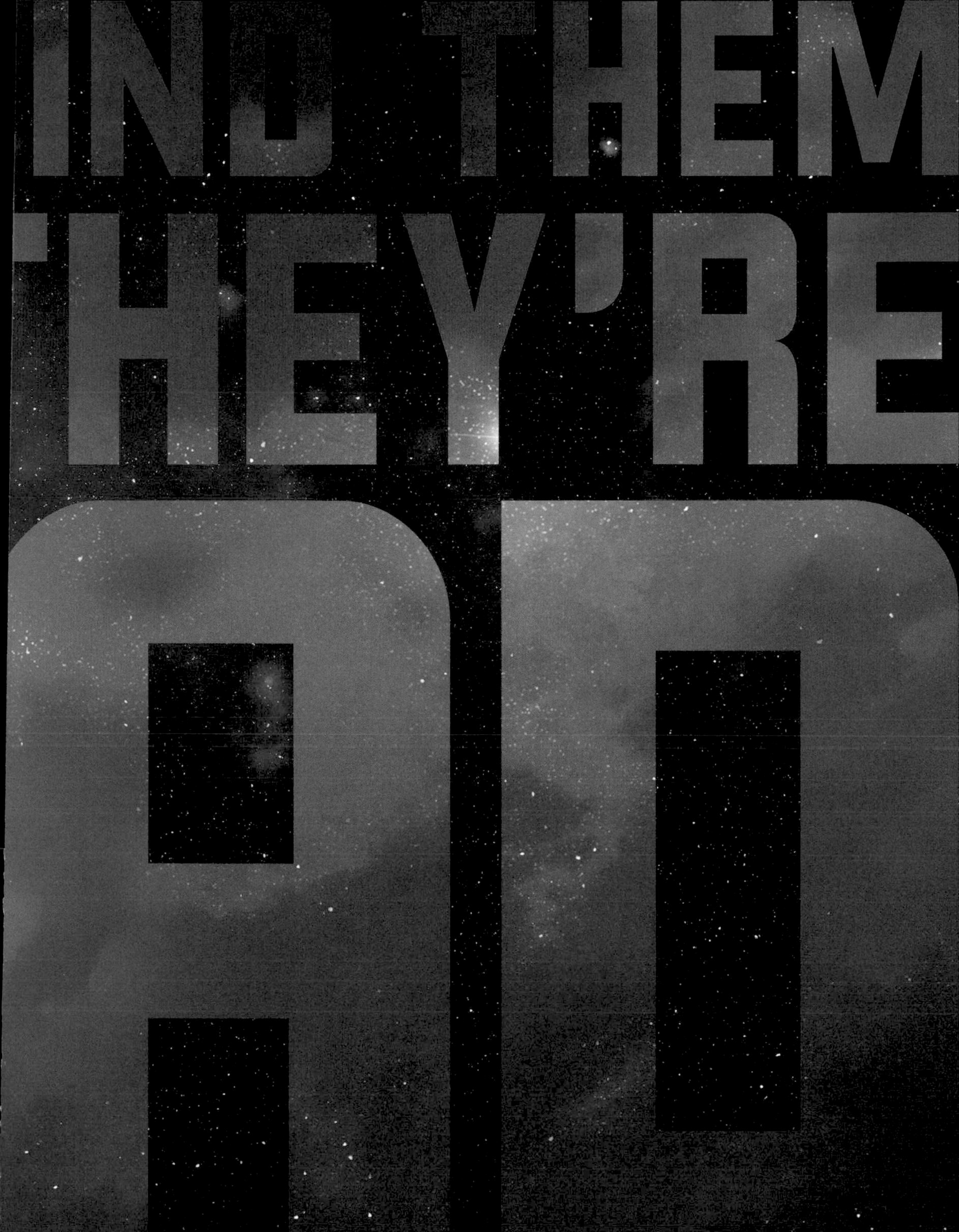
IND THEM
HEY'RE

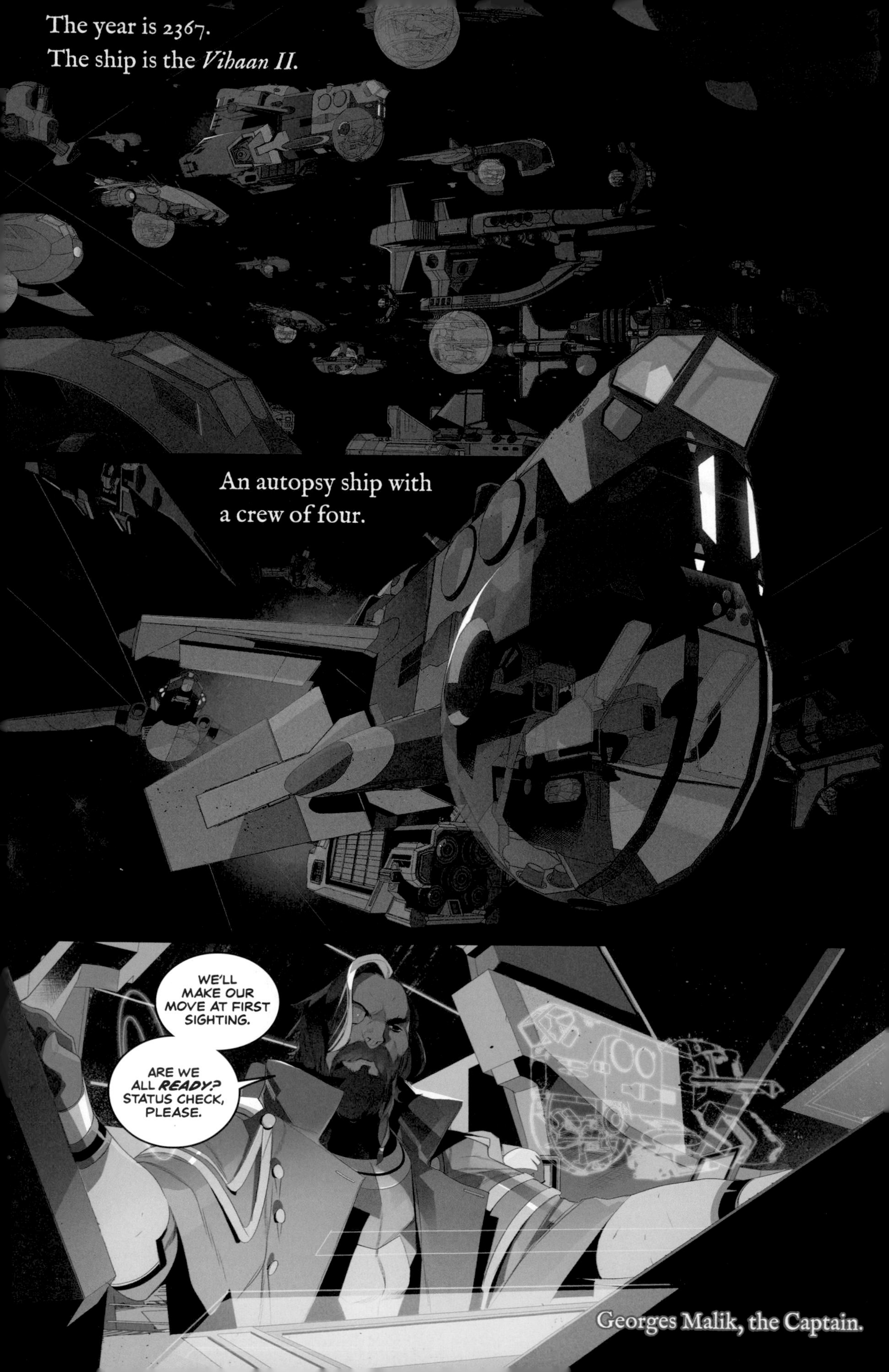

The year is 2367.
The ship is the *Vihaan II.*
An autopsy ship with a crew of four.
WE'LL MAKE OUR MOVE AT FIRST SIGHTING.
ARE WE ALL ***READY?*** STATUS CHECK, PLEASE.
Georges Malik, the Captain.

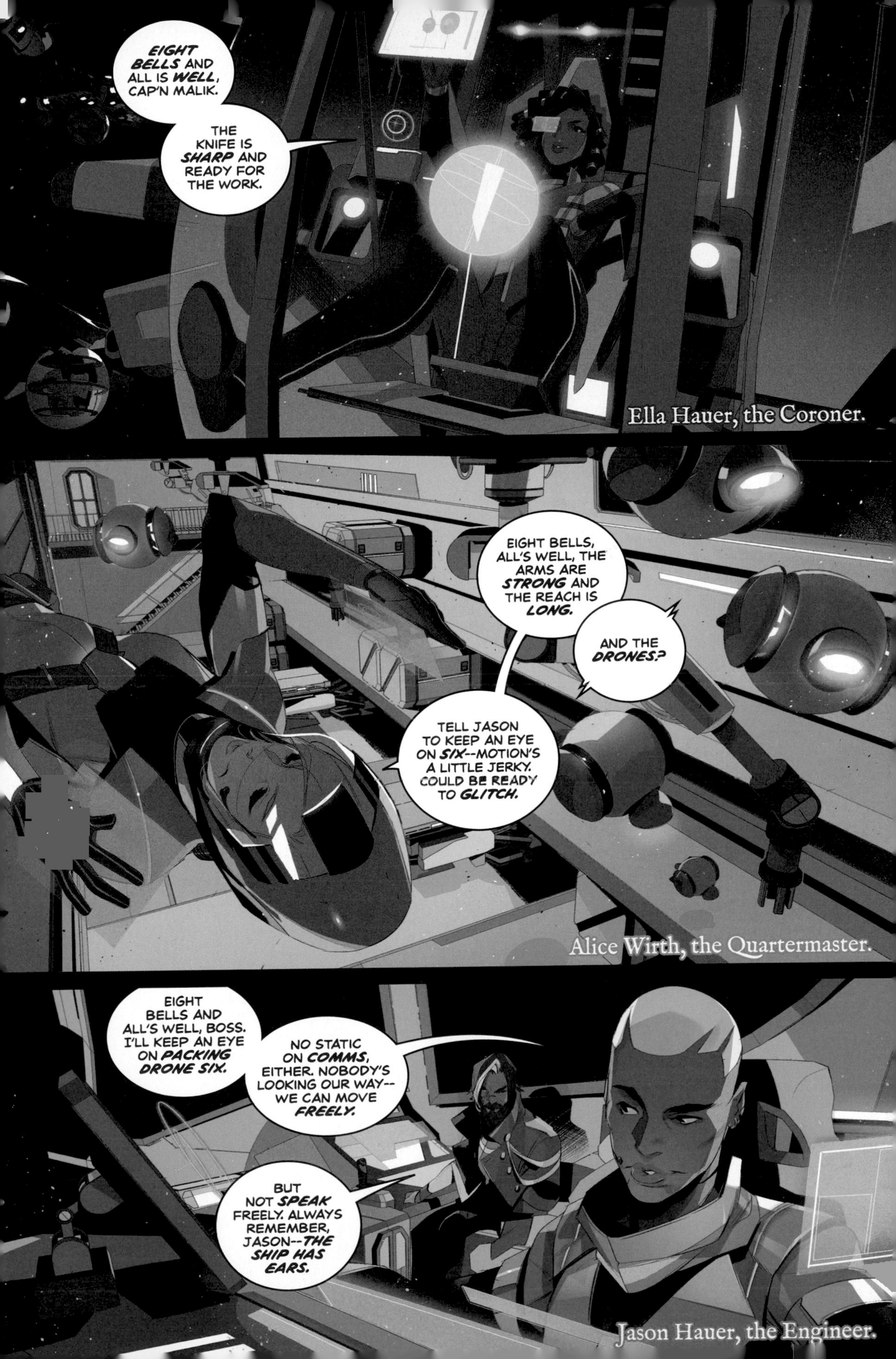
EIGHT BELLS AND ALL IS WELL, CAP'N MALIK.
THE KNIFE IS SHARP AND READY FOR THE WORK.
Ella Hauer, the Coroner.
EIGHT BELLS, ALL'S WELL, THE ARMS ARE STRONG AND THE REACH IS LONG.
AND THE DRONES?
TELL JASON TO KEEP AN EYE ON SIX--MOTION'S A LITTLE JERKY. COULD BE READY TO GLITCH.
Alice Wirth, the Quartermaster.
EIGHT BELLS AND ALL'S WELL, BOSS. I'LL KEEP AN EYE ON PACKING DRONE SIX.
NO STATIC ON COMMS, EITHER. NOBODY'S LOOKING OUR WAY--WE CAN MOVE FREELY.
BUT NOT SPEAK FREELY. ALWAYS REMEMBER, JASON--THE SHIP HAS EARS.
Jason Hauer, the Engineer.

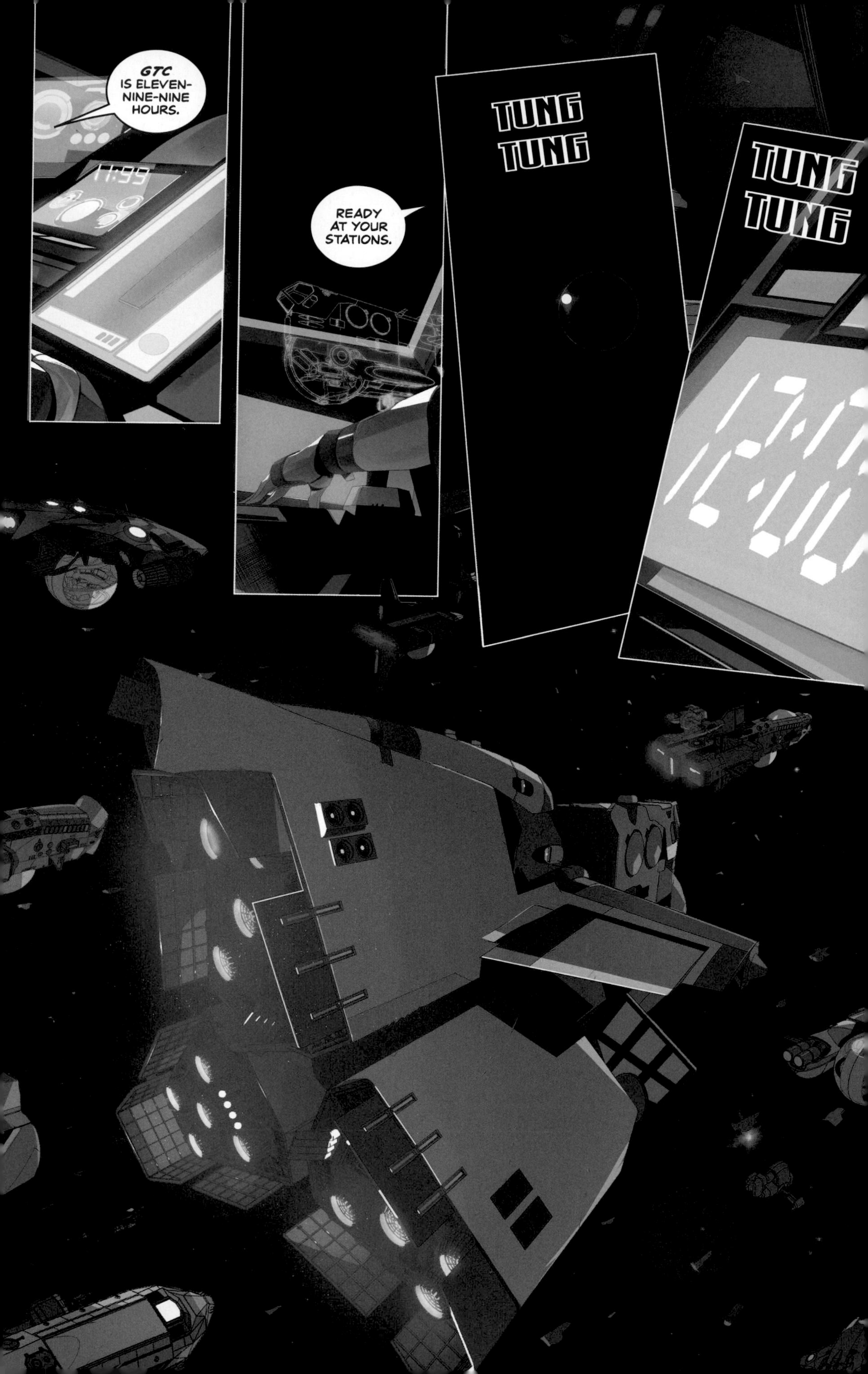
GTC IS ELEVEN-NINE-NINE HOURS.
11:59
READY AT YOUR STATIONS.
TUNG
TUNG
TUNG
TUNG

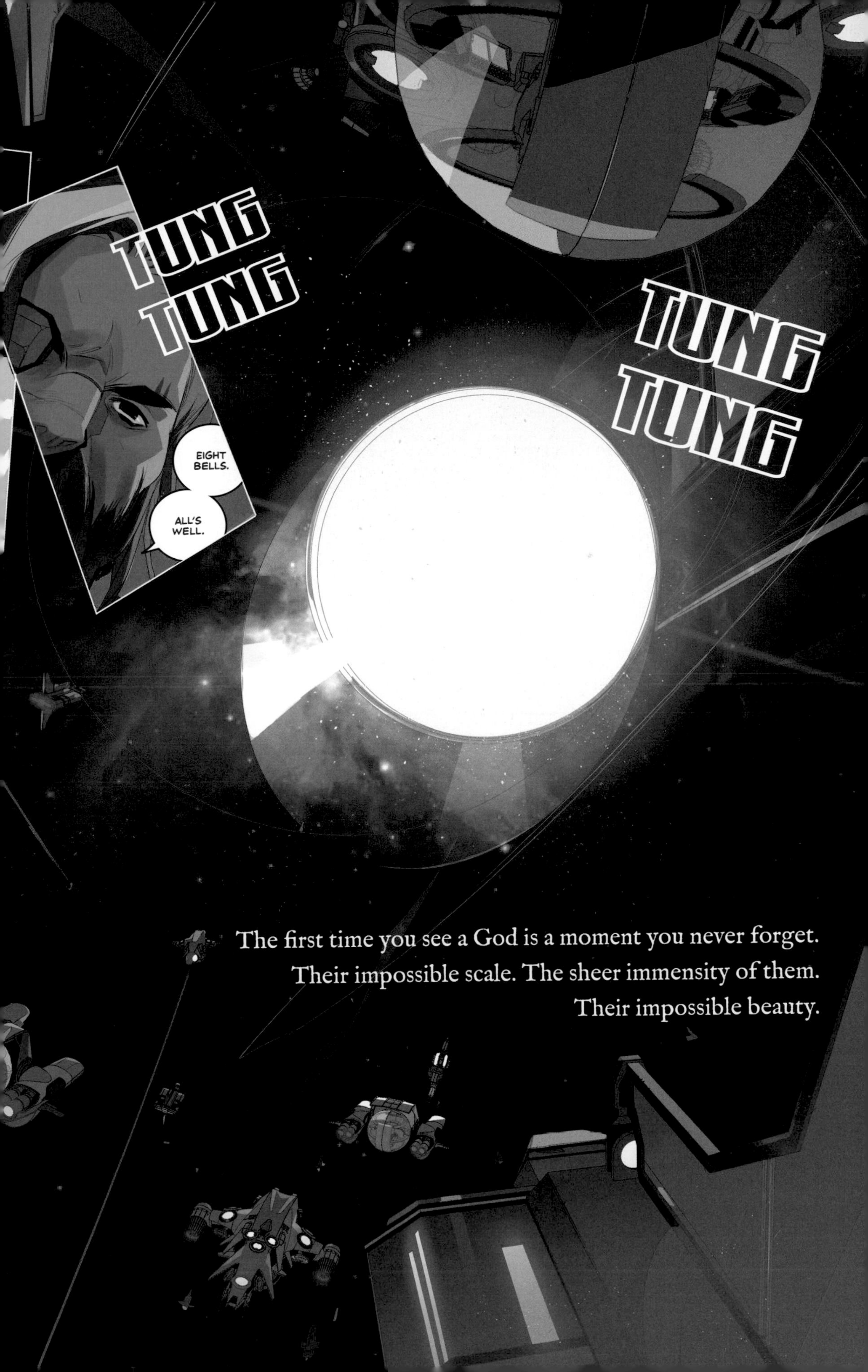
TUNG TUNG
EIGHT BELLS.
ALL'S WELL.
TUNG TUNG
The first time you see a God is a moment you never forget.
Their impossible scale. The sheer immensity of them.
Their impossible beauty.

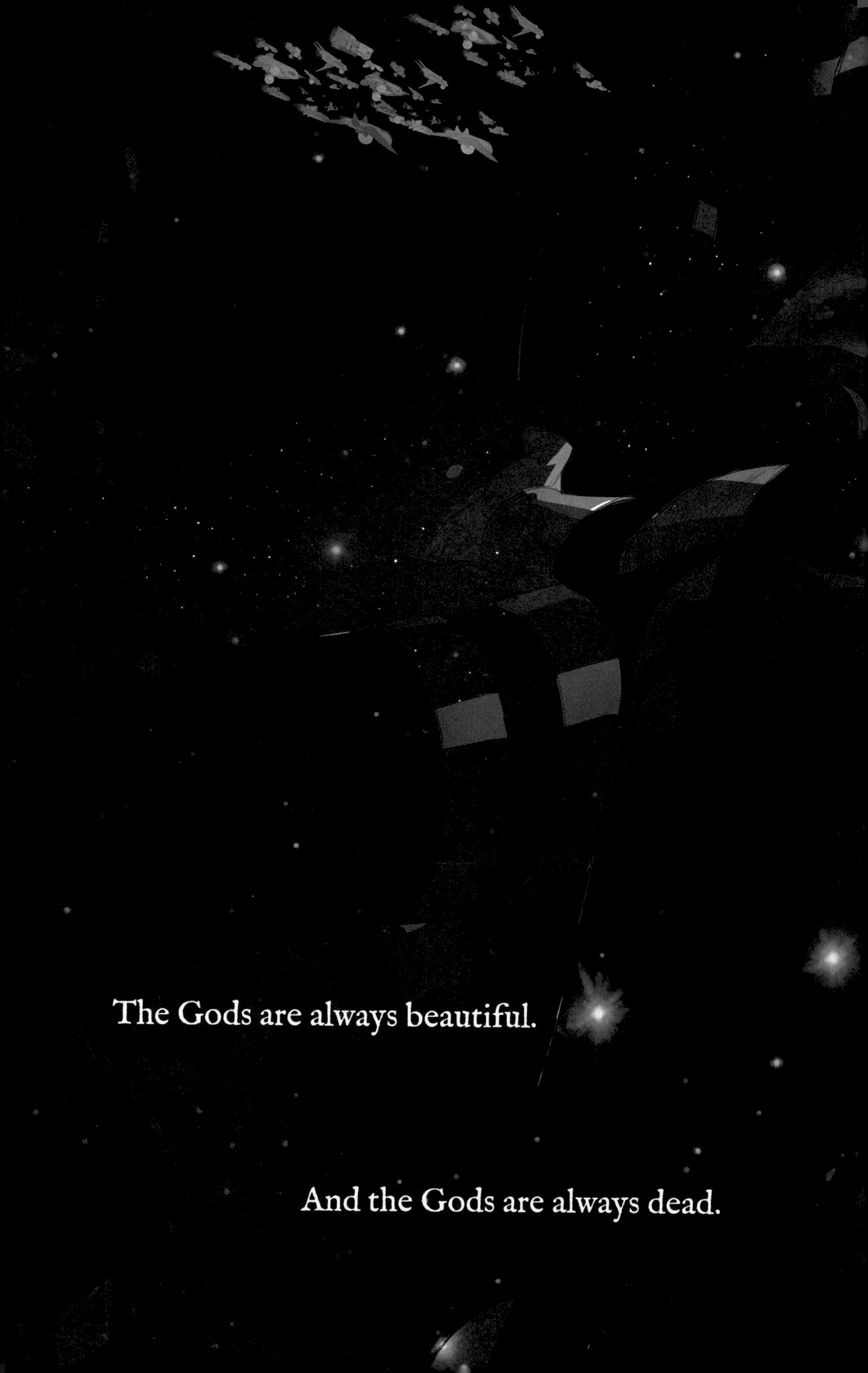
The Gods are always beautiful.
And the Gods are always dead.

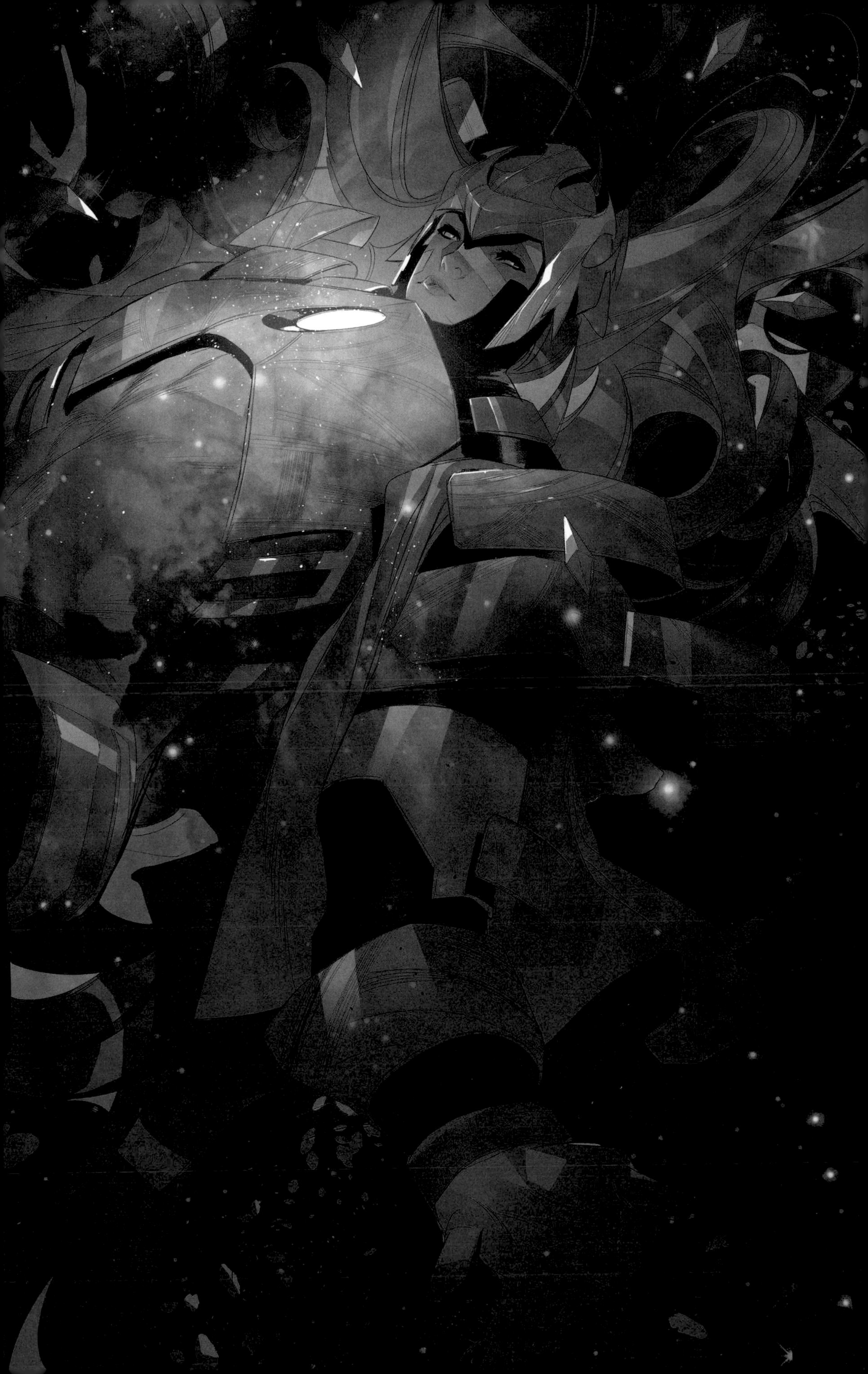

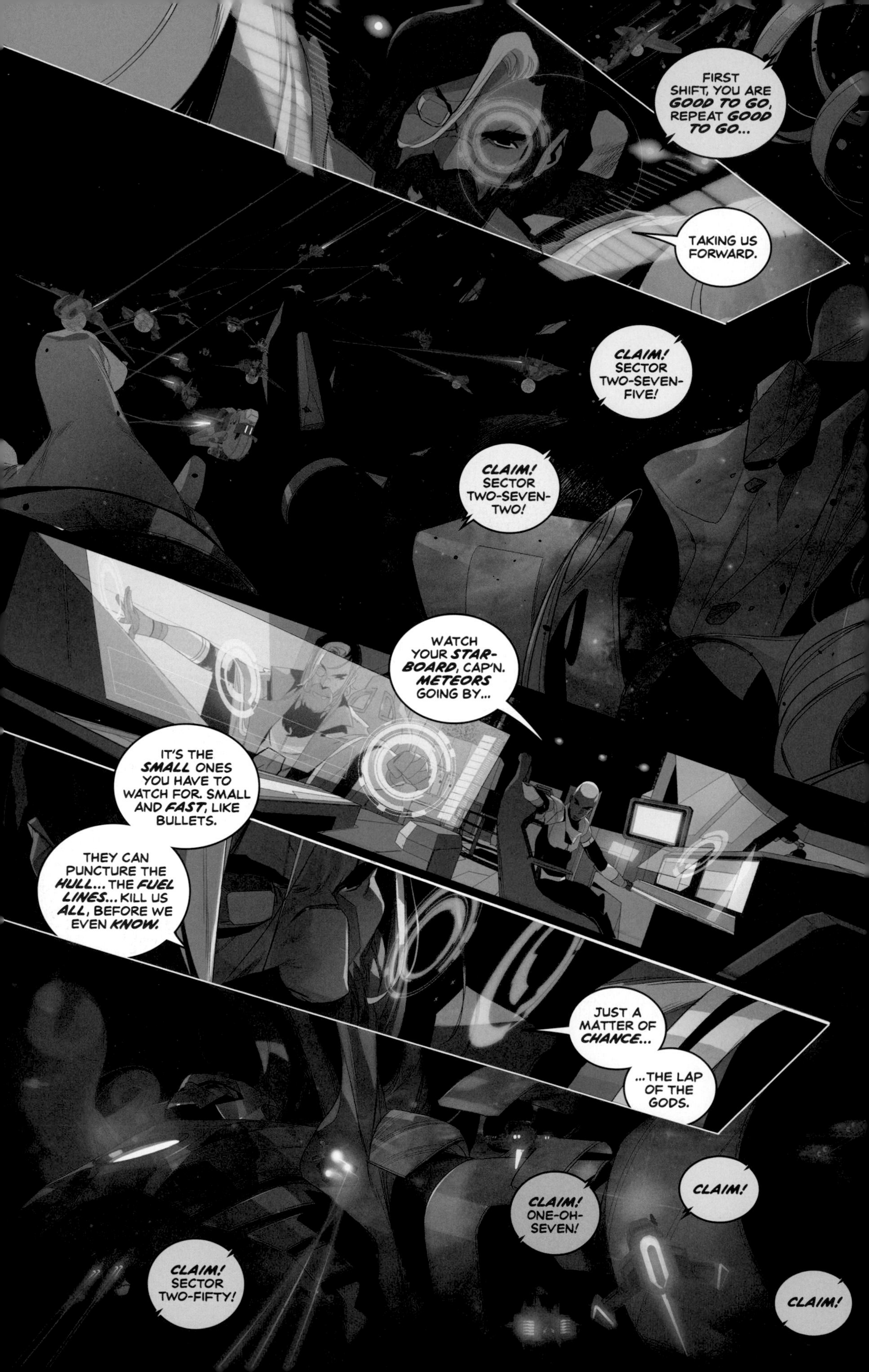

FIRST SHIFT, YOU ARE GOOD TO GO, REPEAT GOOD TO GO...
TAKING US FORWARD.
CLAIM! SECTOR TWO-SEVEN-FIVE!
CLAIM! SECTOR TWO-SEVEN-TWO!
WATCH YOUR STARBOARD, CAP'N. METEORS GOING BY...
IT'S THE SMALL ONES YOU HAVE TO WATCH FOR. SMALL AND FAST, LIKE BULLETS.
THEY CAN PUNCTURE THE HULL... THE FUEL LINES... KILL US ALL, BEFORE WE EVEN KNOW.
JUST A MATTER OF CHANCE...
...THE LAP OF THE GODS.
CLAIM! ONE-OH-SEVEN!
CLAIM!
CLAIM! SECTOR TWO-FIFTY!
CLAIM!

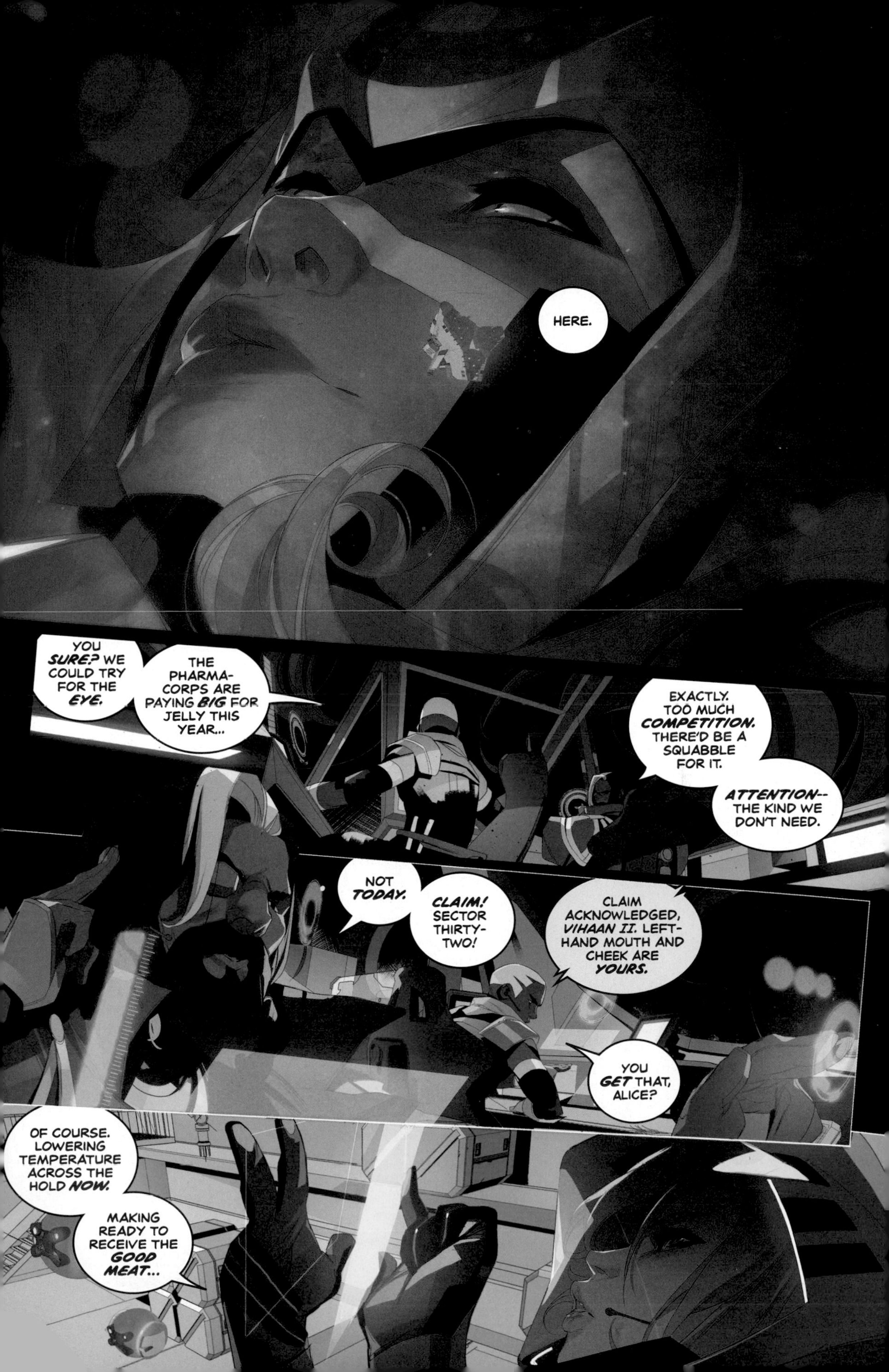
HERE.
YOU SURE? WE COULD TRY FOR THE EYE.
THE PHARMA-CORPS ARE PAYING BIG FOR JELLY THIS YEAR...
EXACTLY. TOO MUCH COMPETITION. THERE'D BE A SQUABBLE FOR IT.
ATTENTION-- THE KIND WE DON'T NEED.
NOT TODAY.
CLAIM! SECTOR THIRTY-TWO!
CLAIM ACKNOWLEDGED, VIHAAN II. LEFT-HAND MOUTH AND CHEEK ARE YOURS.
YOU GET THAT, ALICE?
OF COURSE. LOWERING TEMPERATURE ACROSS THE HOLD NOW.
MAKING READY TO RECEIVE THE GOOD MEAT...

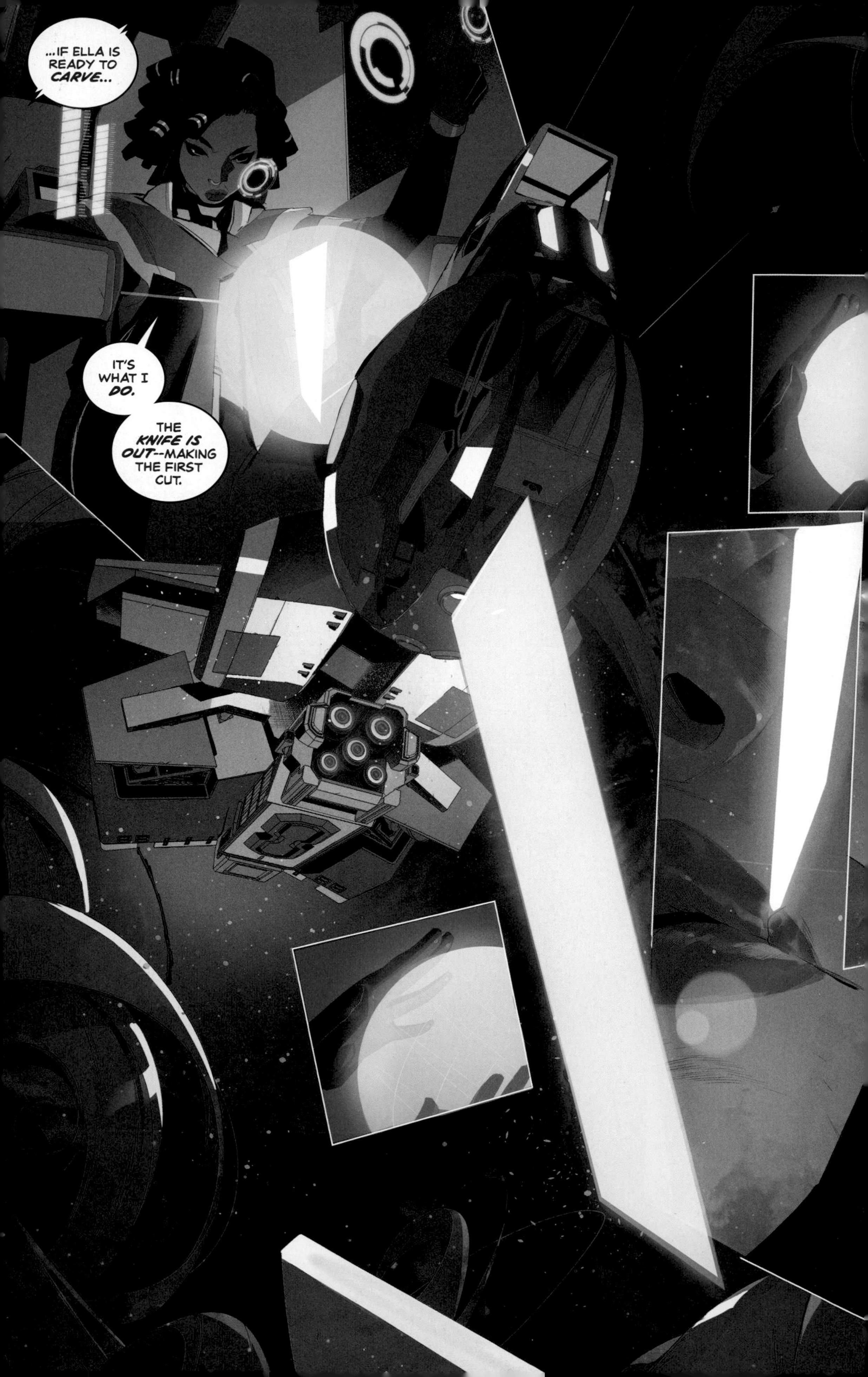
...IF ELLA IS READY TO CARVE...
IT'S WHAT I DO.
THE KNIFE IS OUT--MAKING THE FIRST CUT.

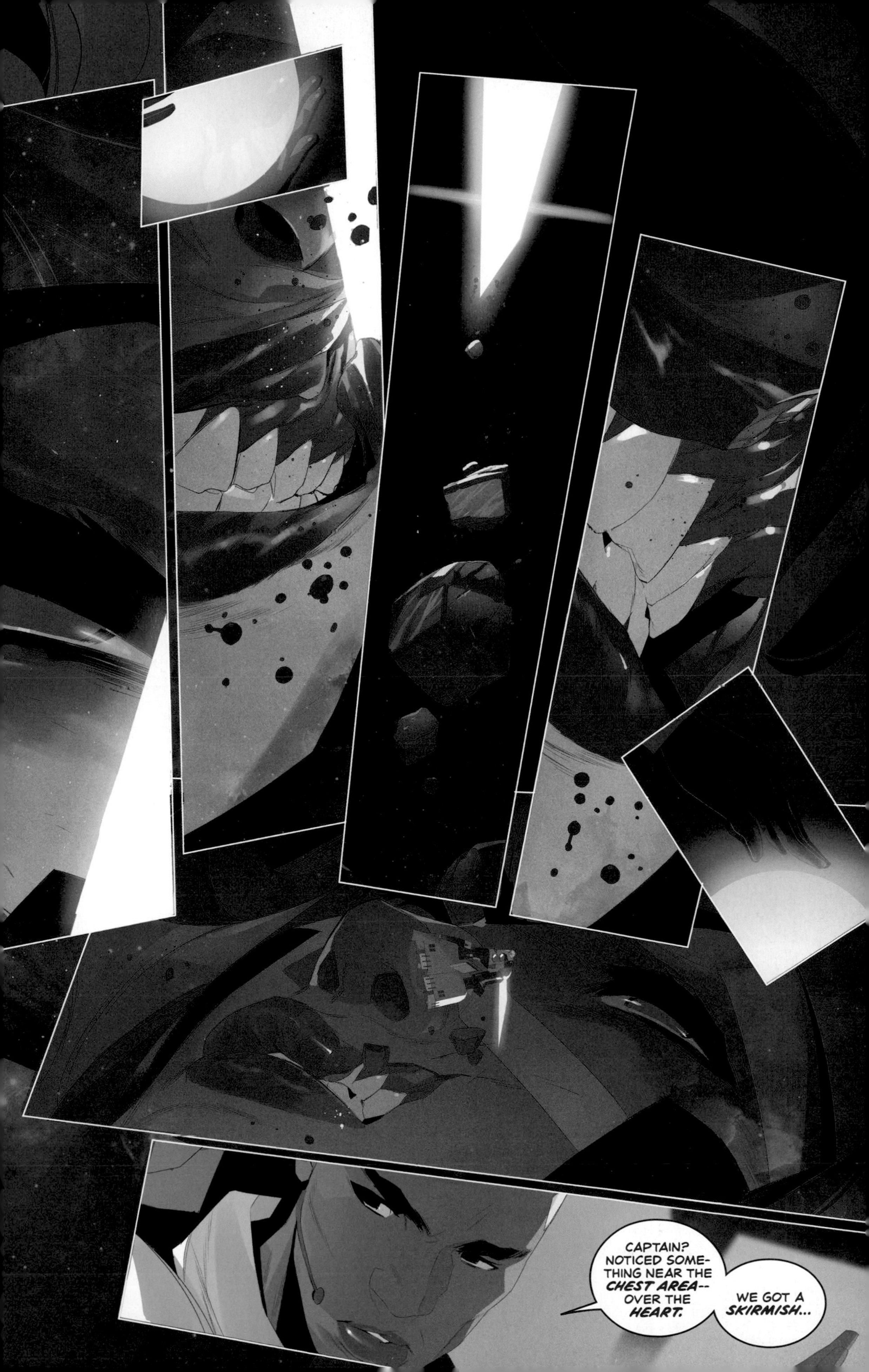
CAPTAIN? NOTICED SOMETHING NEAR THE CHEST AREA-- OVER THE HEART.
WE GOT A SKIRMISH...

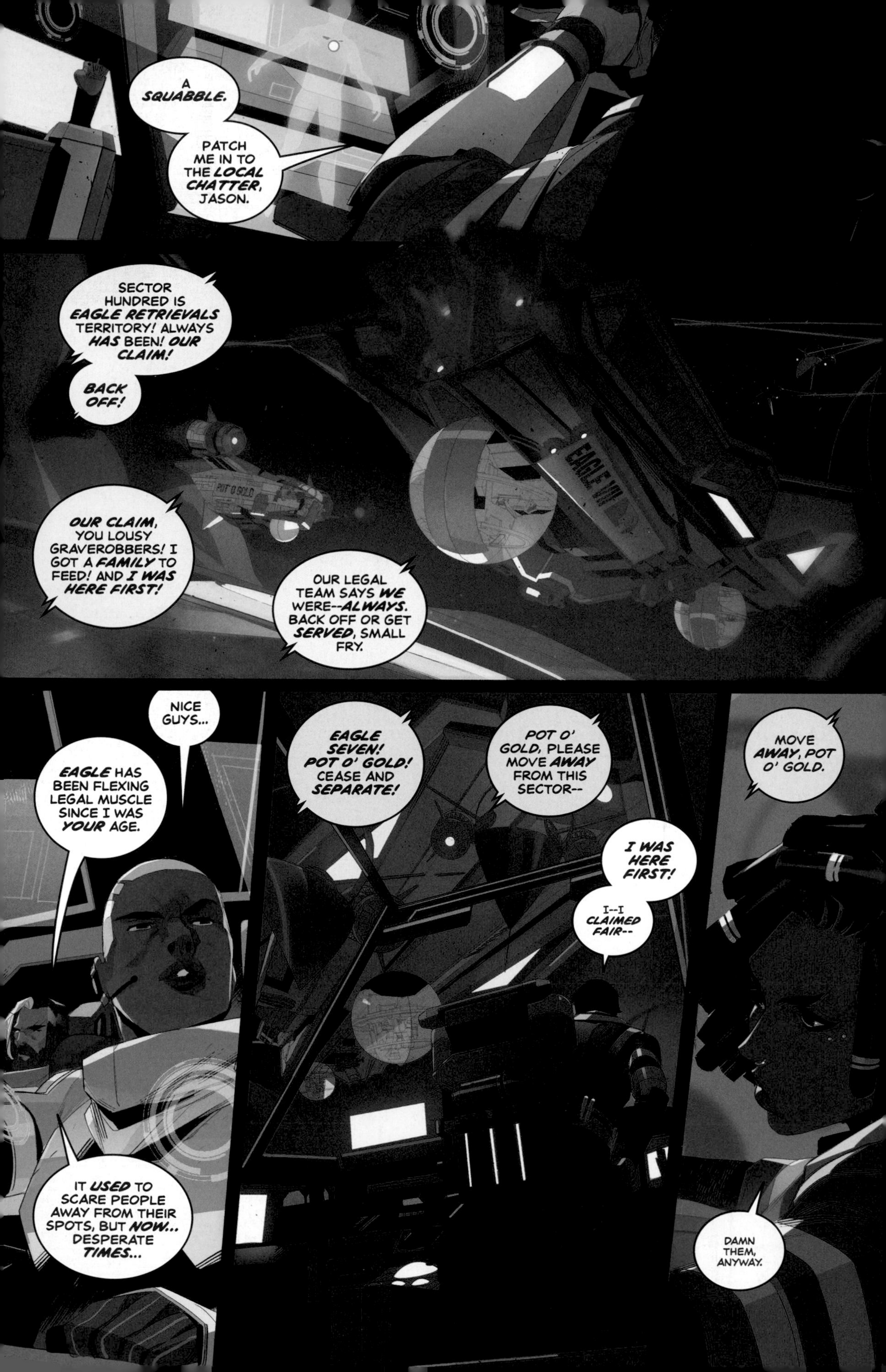
A SQUABBLE.
PATCH ME IN TO THE LOCAL CHATTER, JASON.
SECTOR HUNDRED IS EAGLE RETRIEVALS TERRITORY! ALWAYS HAS BEEN! OUR CLAIM!
BACK OFF!
POT O GOLD
EAGLE VII
OUR CLAIM, YOU LOUSY GRAVEROBBERS! I GOT A FAMILY TO FEED! AND I WAS HERE FIRST!
OUR LEGAL TEAM SAYS WE WERE--ALWAYS. BACK OFF OR GET SERVED, SMALL FRY.
NICE GUYS...
EAGLE HAS BEEN FLEXING LEGAL MUSCLE SINCE I WAS YOUR AGE.
IT USED TO SCARE PEOPLE AWAY FROM THEIR SPOTS, BUT NOW... DESPERATE TIMES...
EAGLE SEVEN! POT O' GOLD! CEASE AND SEPARATE!
POT O' GOLD, PLEASE MOVE AWAY FROM THIS SECTOR--
I WAS HERE FIRST!
I--I CLAIMED FAIR--
MOVE AWAY, POT O' GOLD.
DAMN THEM, ANYWAY.

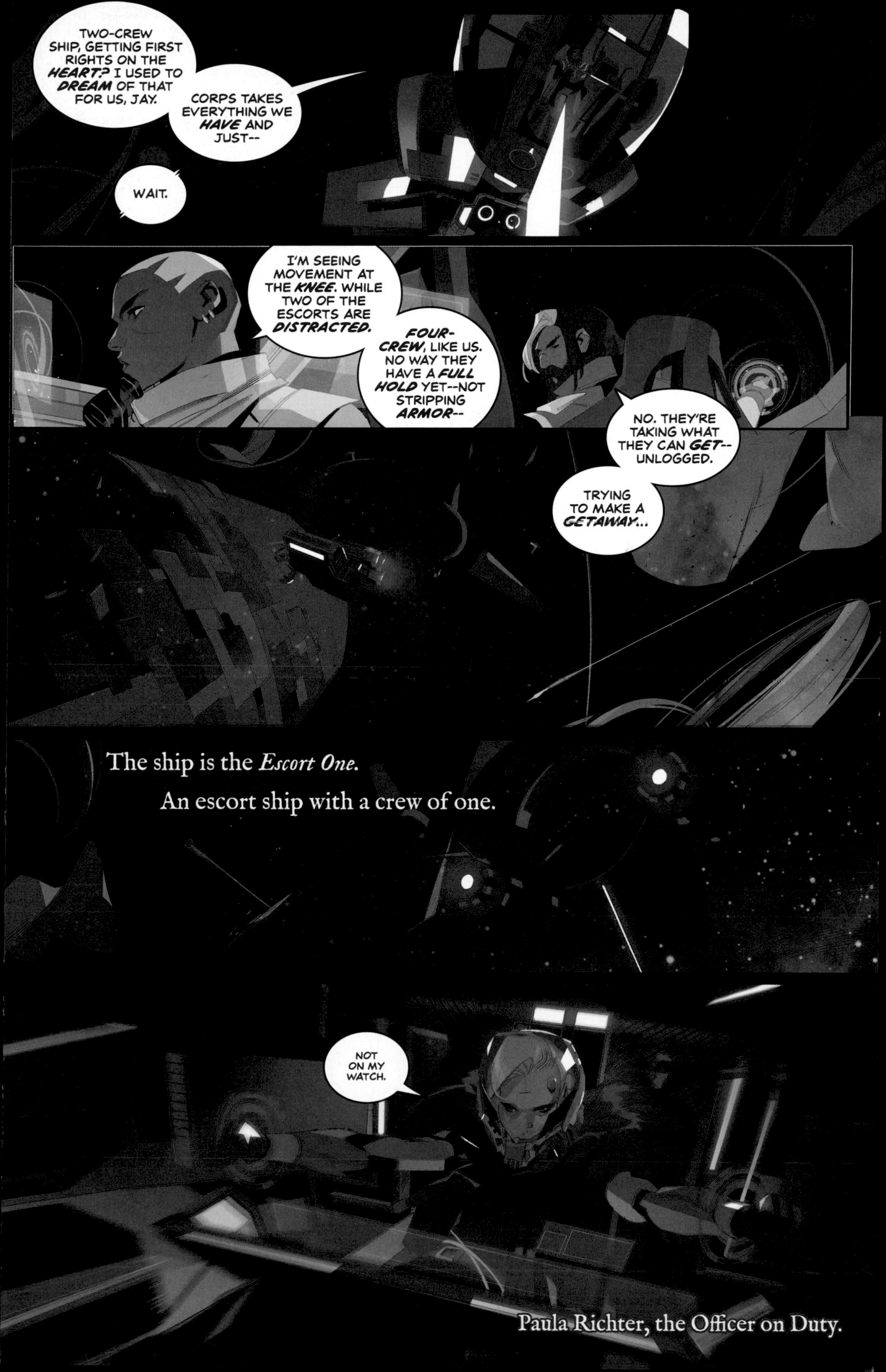
TWO-CREW SHIP, GETTING FIRST RIGHTS ON THE HEART? I USED TO DREAM OF THAT FOR US, JAY.
CORPS TAKES EVERYTHING WE HAVE AND JUST--
WAIT.
I'M SEEING MOVEMENT AT THE KNEE. WHILE TWO OF THE ESCORTS ARE DISTRACTED.
FOUR-CREW, LIKE US. NO WAY THEY HAVE A FULL HOLD YET--NOT STRIPPING ARMOR--
NO. THEY'RE TAKING WHAT THEY CAN GET--UNLOGGED.
TRYING TO MAKE A GETAWAY...
The ship is the Escort One.
An escort ship with a crew of one.
NOT ON MY WATCH.
Paula Richter, the Officer on Duty.

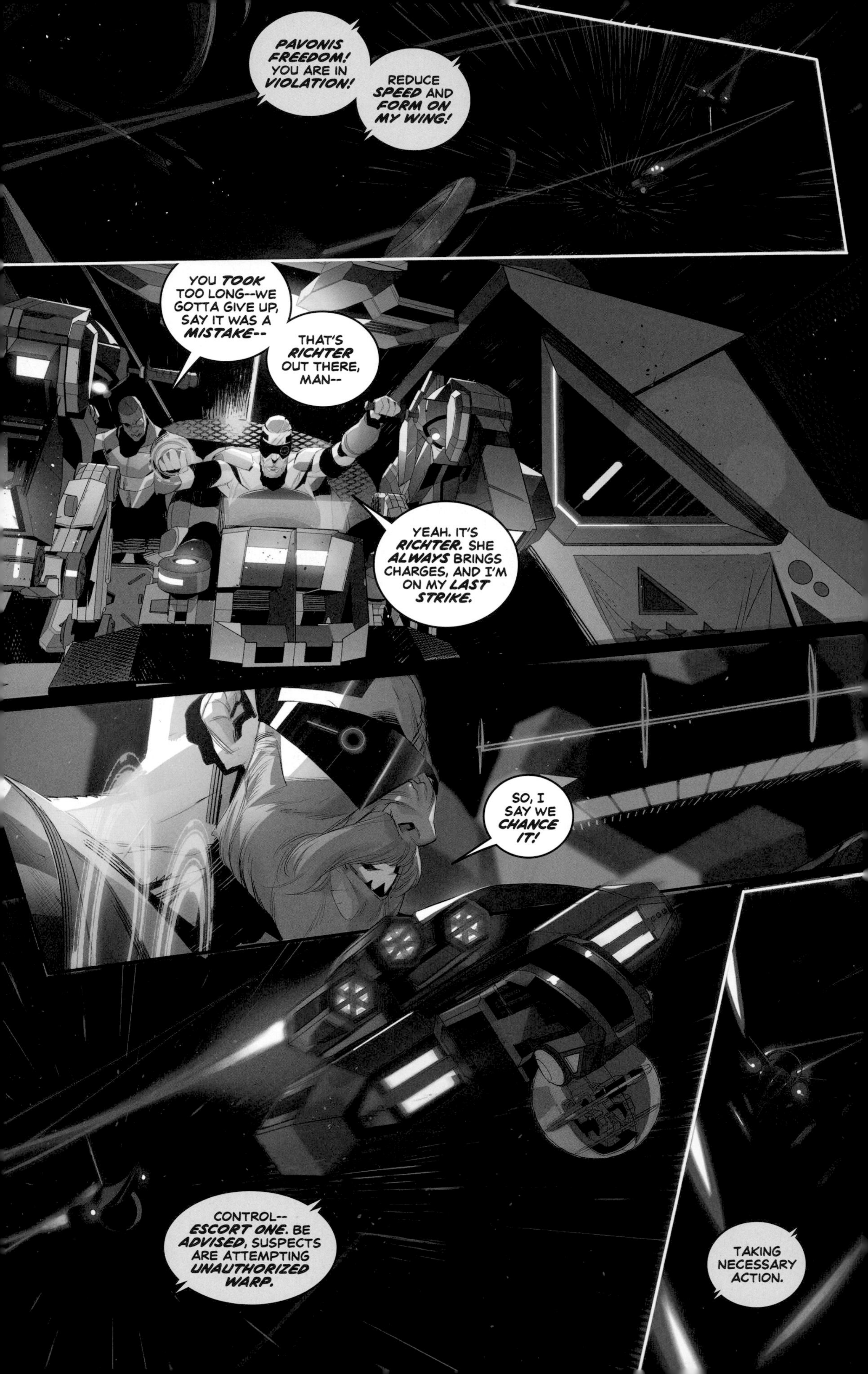
PAVONIS FREEDOM! YOU ARE IN VIOLATION!
REDUCE SPEED AND FORM ON MY WING!
YOU TOOK TOO LONG--WE GOTTA GIVE UP, SAY IT WAS A MISTAKE--
THAT'S RICHTER OUT THERE, MAN--
YEAH. IT'S RICHTER. SHE ALWAYS BRINGS CHARGES, AND I'M ON MY LAST STRIKE.
SO, I SAY WE CHANCE IT!
CONTROL-- ESCORT ONE. BE ADVISED, SUSPECTS ARE ATTEMPTING UNAUTHORIZED WARP.
TAKING NECESSARY ACTION.

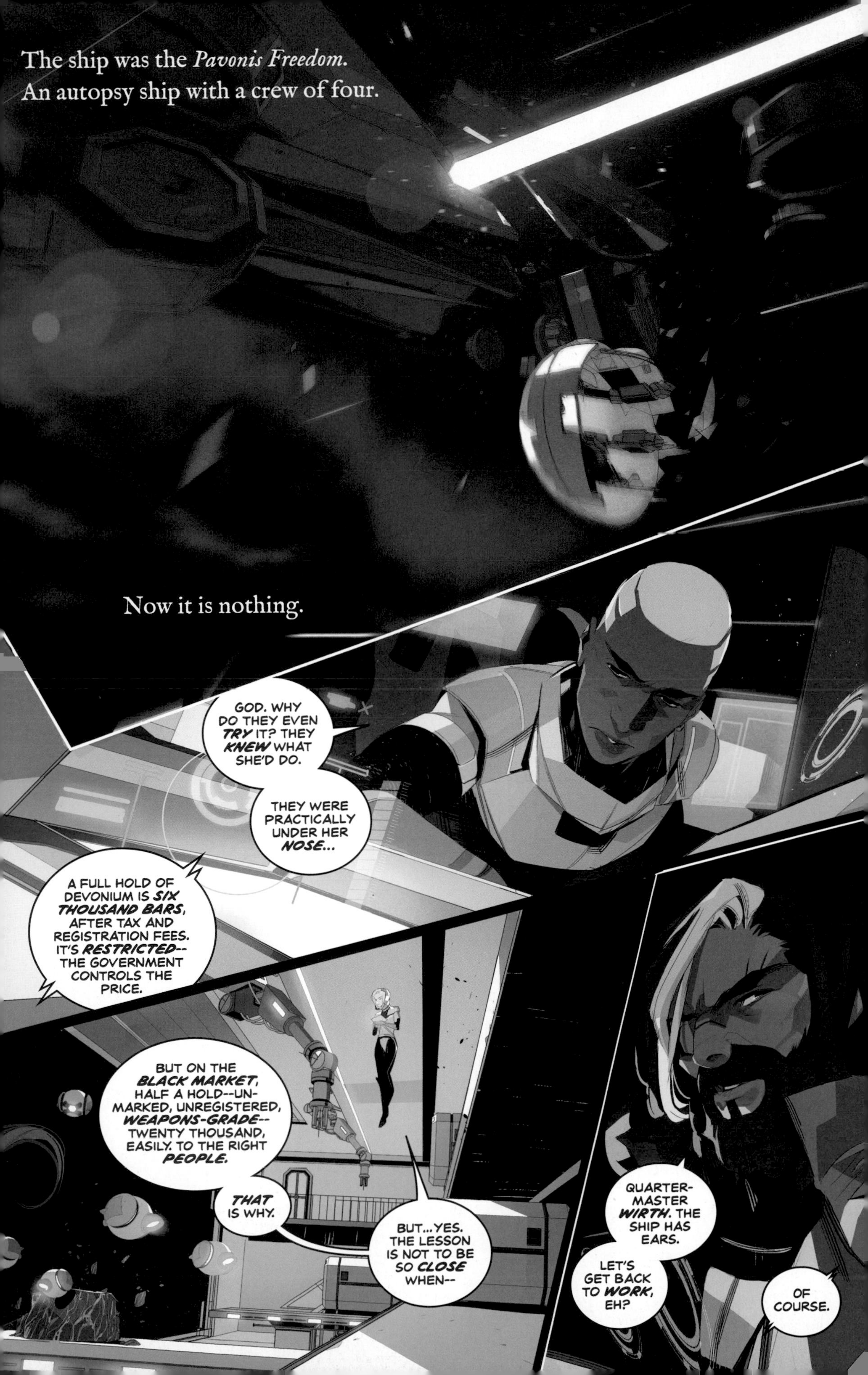
The ship was the *Pavonis Freedom*.
An autopsy ship with a crew of four.
Now it is nothing.
GOD. WHY DO THEY EVEN *TRY* IT? THEY *KNEW* WHAT SHE'D DO.
THEY WERE PRACTICALLY UNDER HER *NOSE*...
A FULL HOLD OF DEVONIUM IS *SIX THOUSAND BARS*, AFTER TAX AND REGISTRATION FEES. IT'S *RESTRICTED*-- THE GOVERNMENT CONTROLS THE PRICE.
BUT ON THE *BLACK MARKET*, HALF A HOLD--UN-MARKED, UNREGISTERED, *WEAPONS-GRADE*-- TWENTY THOUSAND, EASILY. TO THE RIGHT *PEOPLE*.
THAT IS WHY.
BUT...YES. THE LESSON IS NOT TO BE SO *CLOSE* WHEN--
QUARTER-MASTER *WIRTH*. THE SHIP HAS EARS.
LET'S GET BACK TO *WORK*, EH?
OF COURSE.

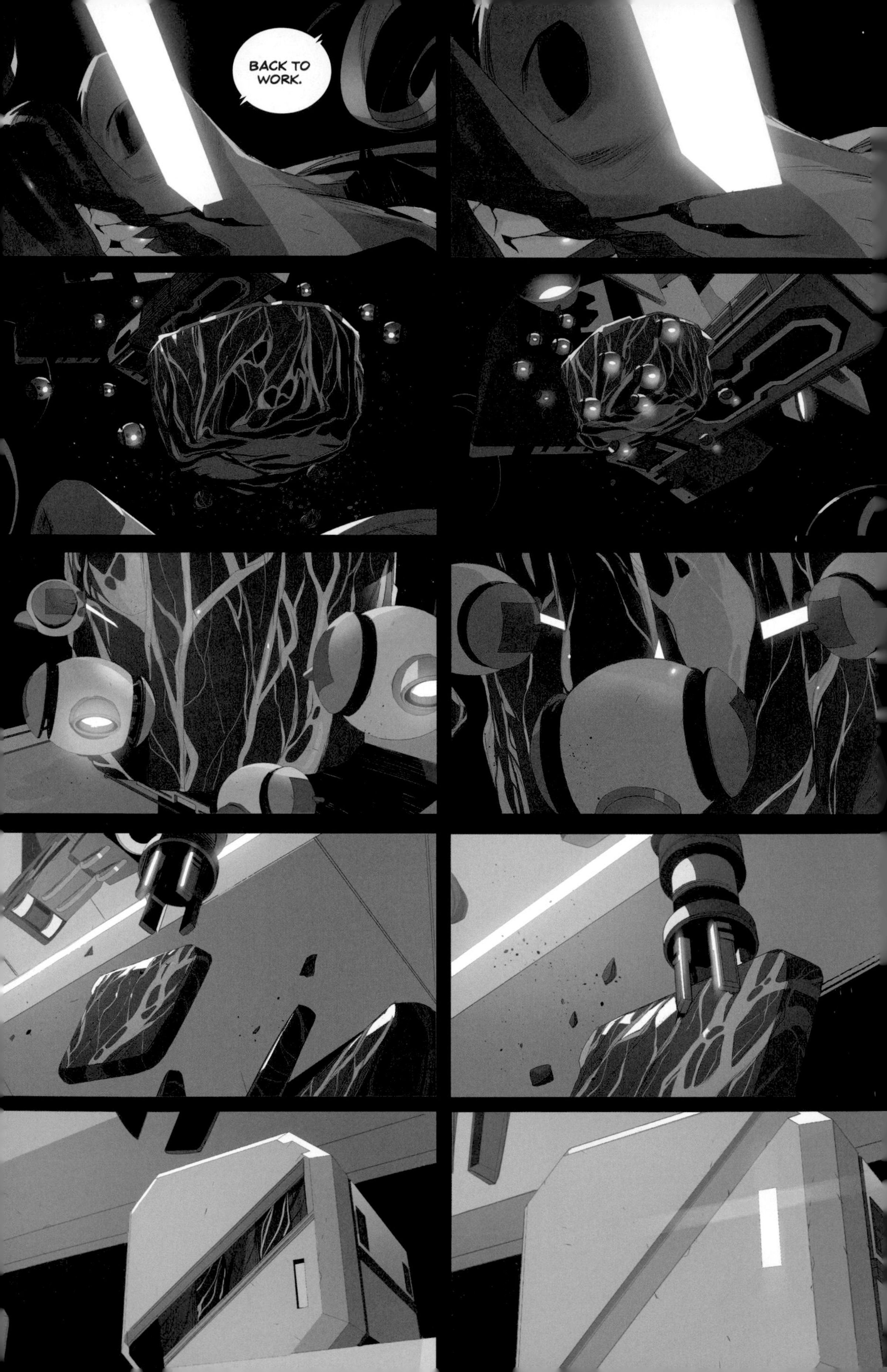
BACK TO WORK.

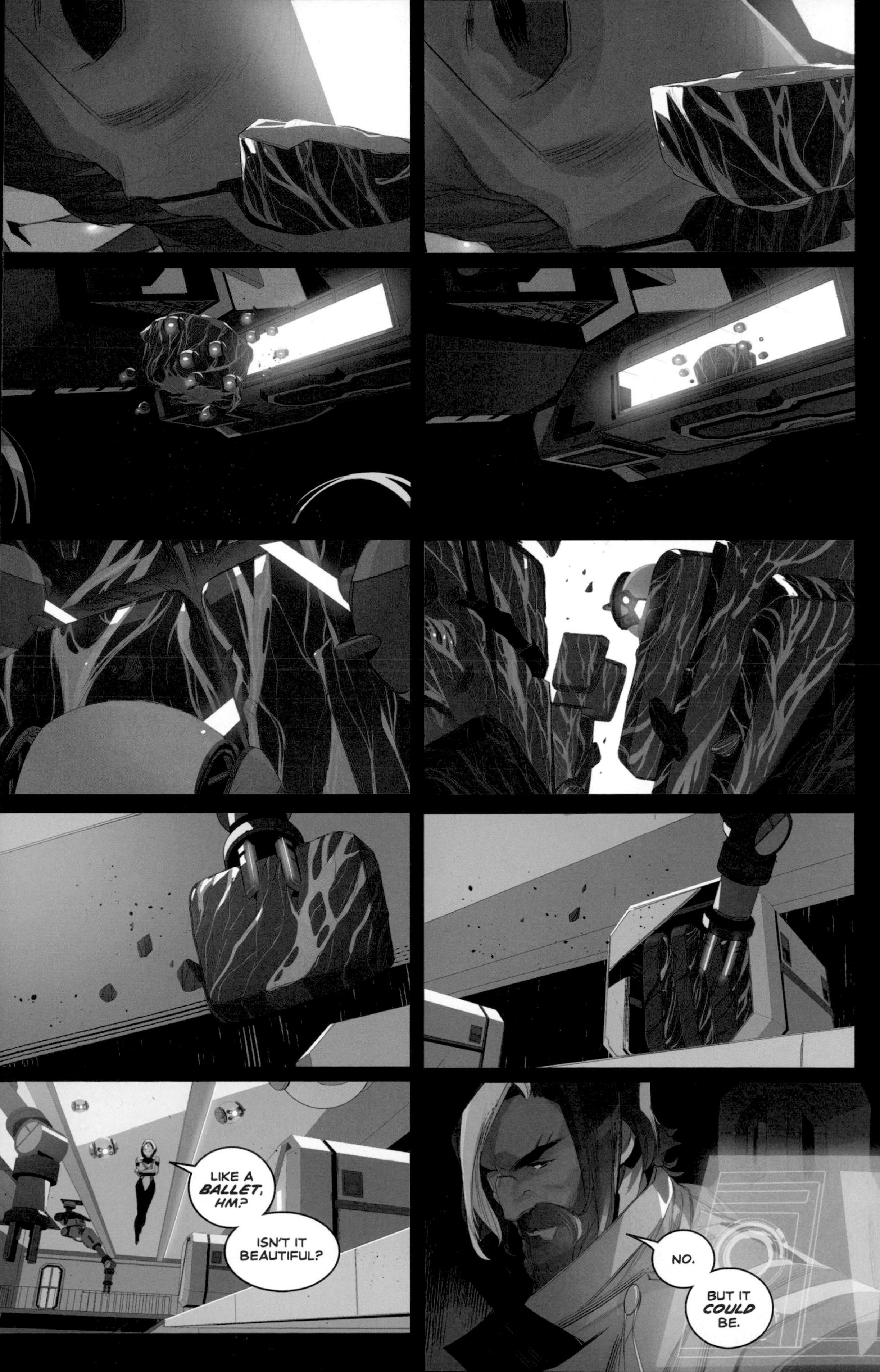
LIKE A *BALLET*, HM?
ISN'T IT BEAUTIFUL?
NO.
BUT IT *COULD* BE.

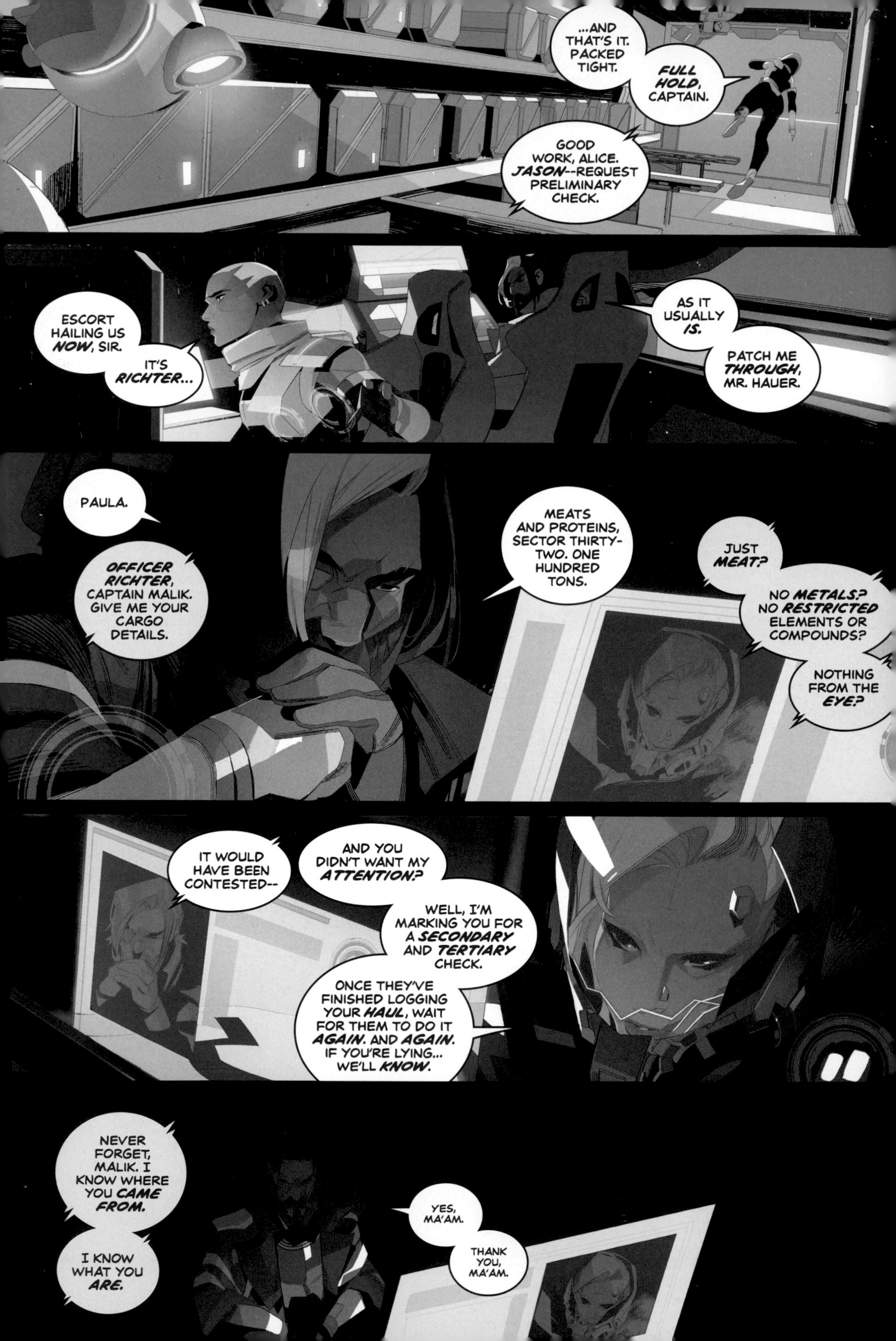
...AND THAT'S IT. PACKED TIGHT.
FULL HOLD, CAPTAIN.
GOOD WORK, ALICE. JASON--REQUEST PRELIMINARY CHECK.
ESCORT HAILING US NOW, SIR.
IT'S RICHTER...
AS IT USUALLY IS.
PATCH ME THROUGH, MR. HAUER.
PAULA.
OFFICER RICHTER, CAPTAIN MALIK. GIVE ME YOUR CARGO DETAILS.
MEATS AND PROTEINS, SECTOR THIRTY-TWO. ONE HUNDRED TONS.
JUST MEAT?
NO METALS? NO RESTRICTED ELEMENTS OR COMPOUNDS?
NOTHING FROM THE EYE?
IT WOULD HAVE BEEN CONTESTED--
AND YOU DIDN'T WANT MY ATTENTION?
WELL, I'M MARKING YOU FOR A SECONDARY AND TERTIARY CHECK.
ONCE THEY'VE FINISHED LOGGING YOUR HAUL, WAIT FOR THEM TO DO IT AGAIN. AND AGAIN. IF YOU'RE LYING... WE'LL KNOW.
NEVER FORGET, MALIK. I KNOW WHERE YOU CAME FROM.
I KNOW WHAT YOU ARE.
YES, MA'AM.
THANK YOU, MA'AM.

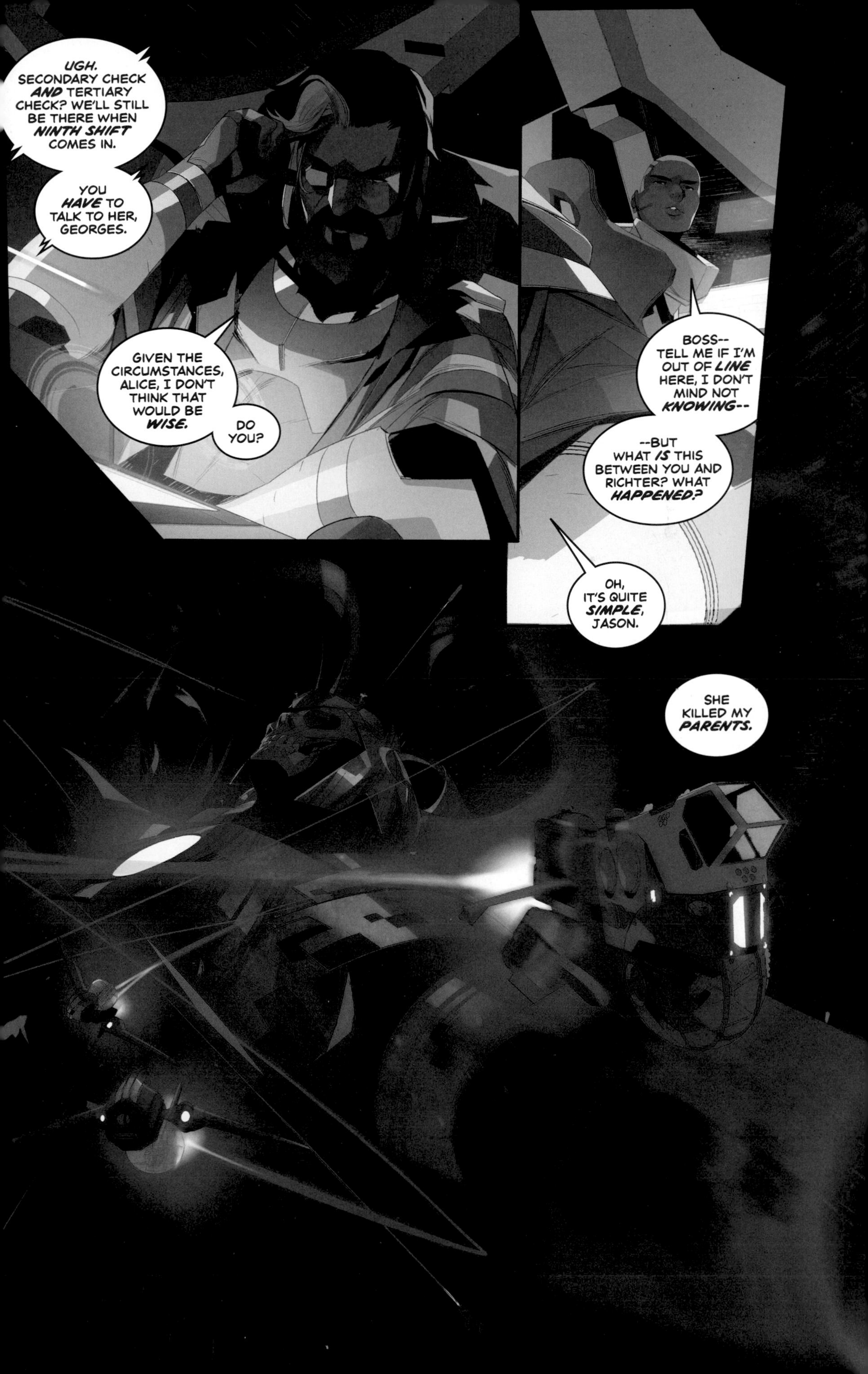
UGH. SECONDARY CHECK AND TERTIARY CHECK? WE'LL STILL BE THERE WHEN NINTH SHIFT COMES IN.
YOU HAVE TO TALK TO HER, GEORGES.
GIVEN THE CIRCUMSTANCES, ALICE, I DON'T THINK THAT WOULD BE WISE.
DO YOU?
BOSS-- TELL ME IF I'M OUT OF LINE HERE, I DON'T MIND NOT KNOWING--
--BUT WHAT IS THIS BETWEEN YOU AND RICHTER? WHAT HAPPENED?
OH, IT'S QUITE SIMPLE, JASON.
SHE KILLED MY PARENTS.

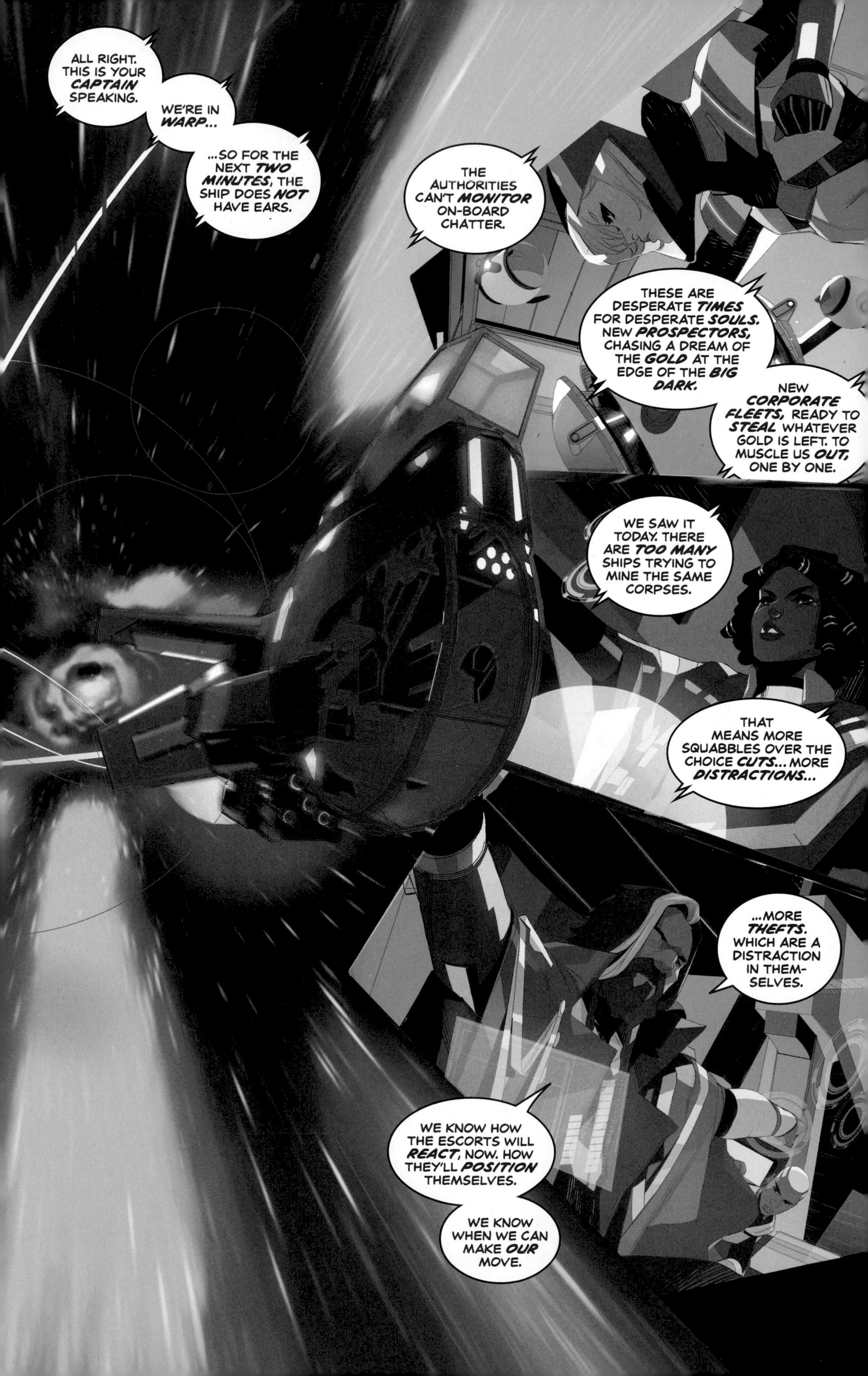

ALL RIGHT. THIS IS YOUR CAPTAIN SPEAKING.
WE'RE IN WARP...
...SO FOR THE NEXT TWO MINUTES, THE SHIP DOES NOT HAVE EARS.
THE AUTHORITIES CAN'T MONITOR ON-BOARD CHATTER.
THESE ARE DESPERATE TIMES FOR DESPERATE SOULS. NEW PROSPECTORS, CHASING A DREAM OF THE GOLD AT THE EDGE OF THE BIG DARK.
NEW CORPORATE FLEETS, READY TO STEAL WHATEVER GOLD IS LEFT. TO MUSCLE US OUT, ONE BY ONE.
WE SAW IT TODAY. THERE ARE TOO MANY SHIPS TRYING TO MINE THE SAME CORPSES.
THAT MEANS MORE SQUABBLES OVER THE CHOICE CUTS... MORE DISTRACTIONS...
...MORE THEFTS. WHICH ARE A DISTRACTION IN THEM-SELVES.
WE KNOW HOW THE ESCORTS WILL REACT, NOW. HOW THEY'LL POSITION THEMSELVES.
WE KNOW WHEN WE CAN MAKE OUR MOVE.

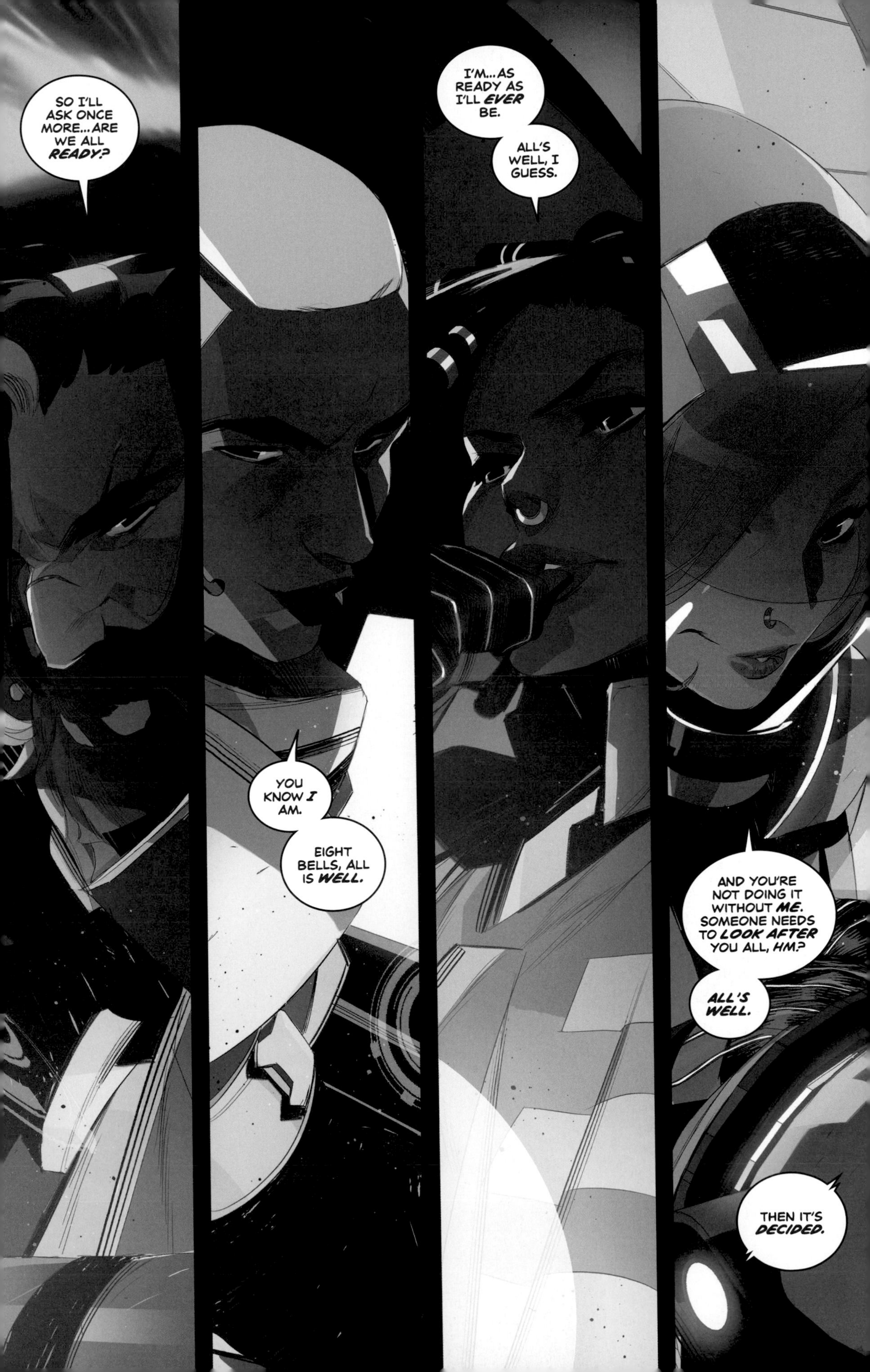
SO I'LL ASK ONCE MORE...ARE WE ALL READY?
YOU KNOW I AM.
EIGHT BELLS, ALL IS WELL.
I'M...AS READY AS I'LL EVER BE.
ALL'S WELL, I GUESS.
AND YOU'RE NOT DOING IT WITHOUT ME. SOMEONE NEEDS TO LOOK AFTER YOU ALL, HM?
ALL'S WELL.
THEN IT'S DECIDED.

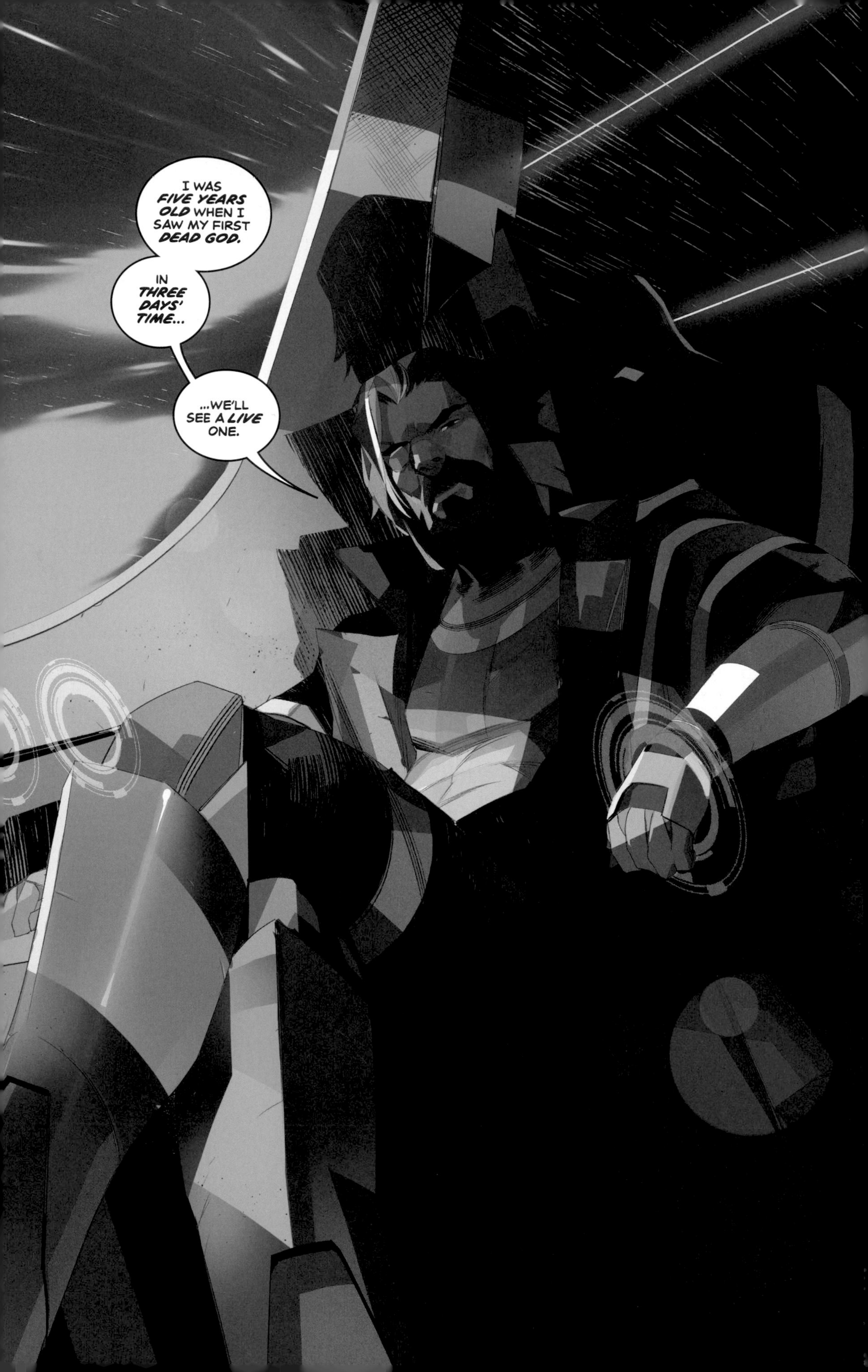
I WAS *FIVE YEARS OLD* WHEN I SAW MY FIRST *DEAD GOD.*
IN *THREE DAYS' TIME...*
...WE'LL SEE A *LIVE* ONE.

Chapter Two

What's So Important

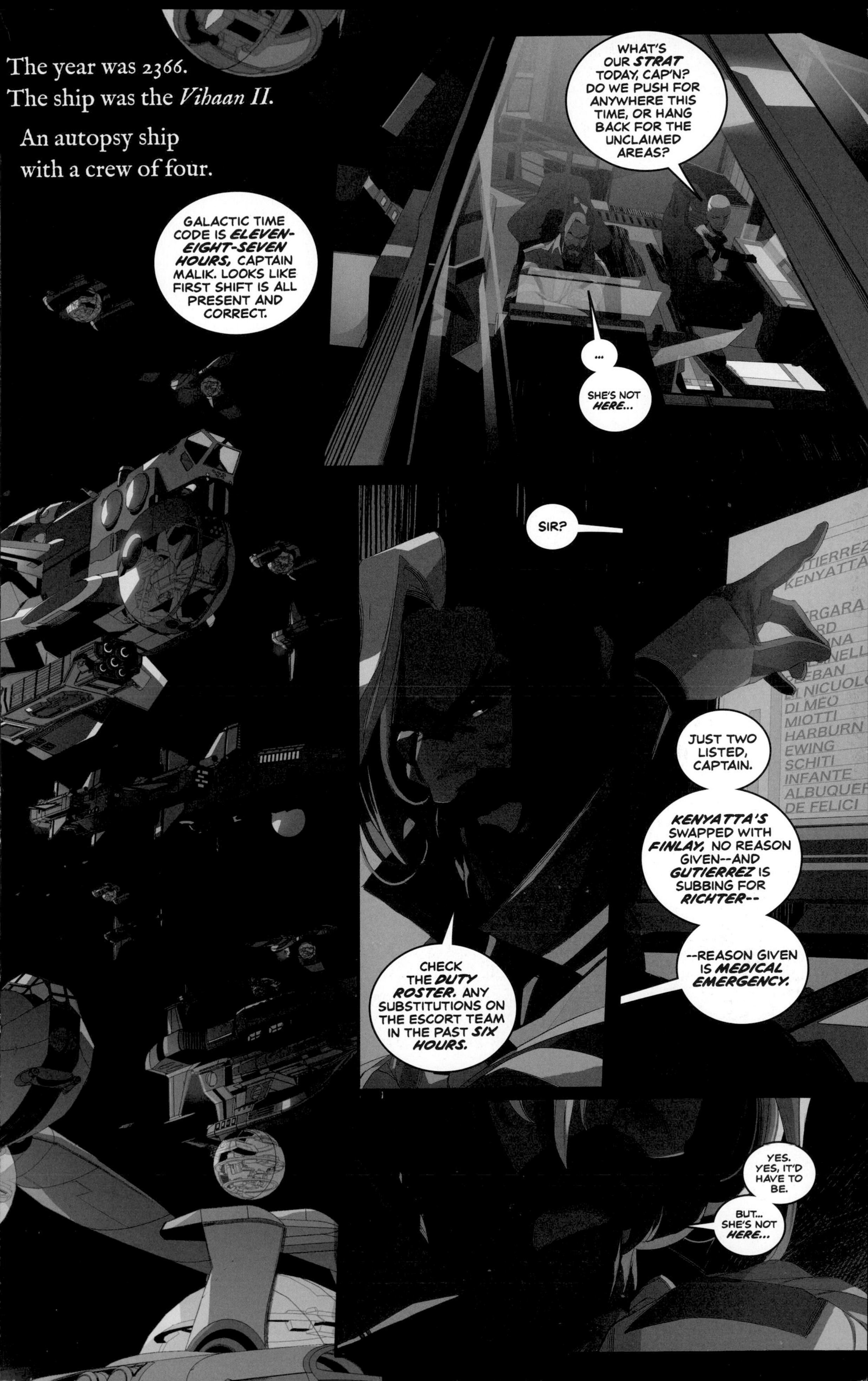

The year was 2366.
The ship was the *Vihaan II*.
An autopsy ship with a crew of four.
GALACTIC TIME CODE IS ELEVEN-EIGHT-SEVEN HOURS, CAPTAIN MALIK. LOOKS LIKE FIRST SHIFT IS ALL PRESENT AND CORRECT.
WHAT'S OUR STRAT TODAY, CAP'N? DO WE PUSH FOR ANYWHERE THIS TIME, OR HANG BACK FOR THE UNCLAIMED AREAS?
...
SHE'S NOT HERE...
SIR?
CHECK THE DUTY ROSTER. ANY SUBSTITUTIONS ON THE ESCORT TEAM IN THE PAST SIX HOURS.
JUST TWO LISTED, CAPTAIN.
KENYATTA'S SWAPPED WITH FINLAY, NO REASON GIVEN--AND GUTIERREZ IS SUBBING FOR RICHTER--
--REASON GIVEN IS MEDICAL EMERGENCY.
KENYATTA
DI MEO
MIOTTI
HARBURN
EWING
SCHITI
INFANTE
DE FELICI
YES. YES, IT'D HAVE TO BE.
BUT... SHE'S NOT HERE...

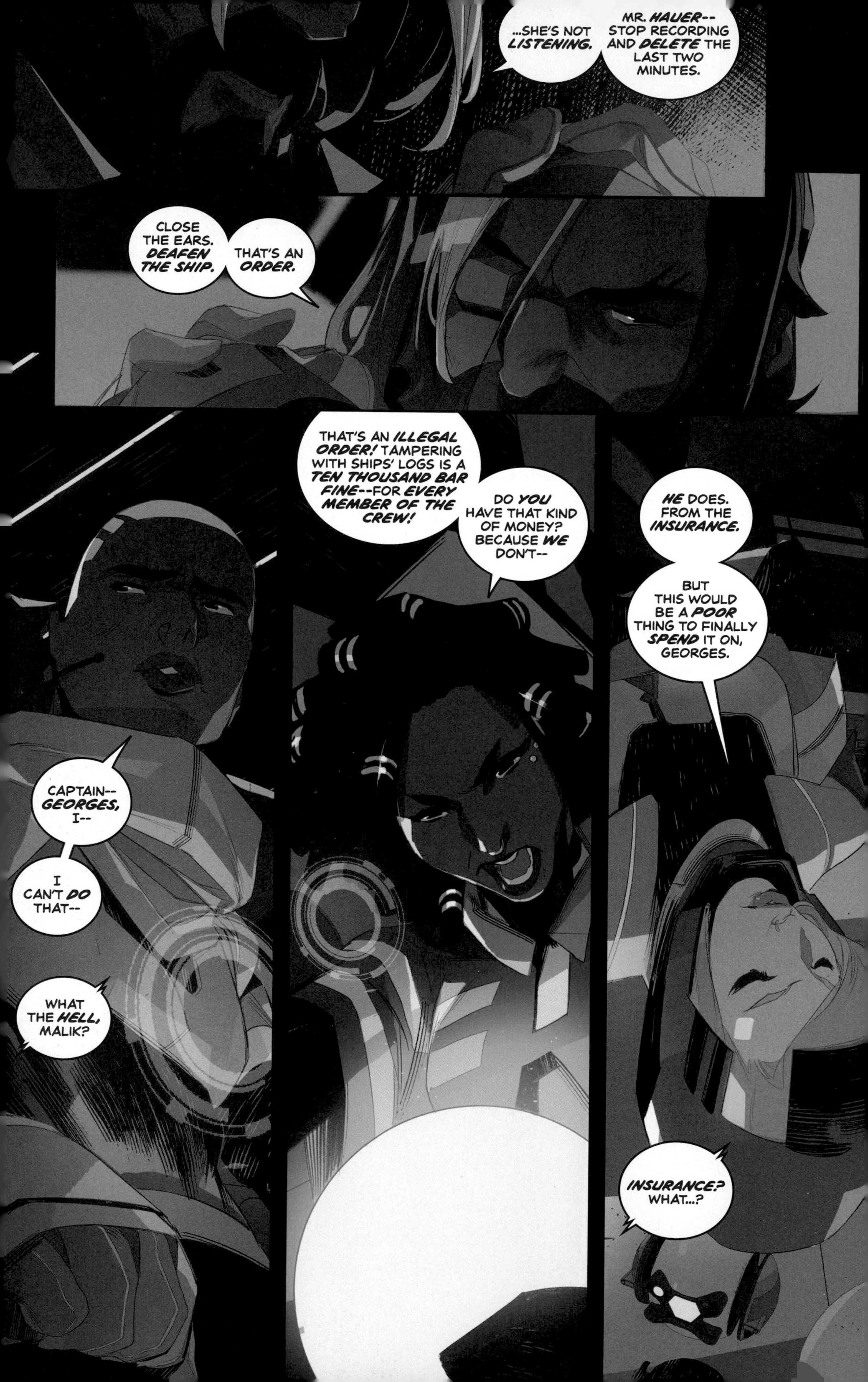
...SHE'S NOT LISTENING.
MR. HAUER-- STOP RECORDING AND DELETE THE LAST TWO MINUTES.
CLOSE THE EARS. DEAFEN THE SHIP.
THAT'S AN ORDER.
THAT'S AN ILLEGAL ORDER! TAMPERING WITH SHIPS' LOGS IS A TEN THOUSAND BAR FINE--FOR EVERY MEMBER OF THE CREW!
DO YOU HAVE THAT KIND OF MONEY? BECAUSE WE DON'T--
HE DOES. FROM THE INSURANCE.
BUT THIS WOULD BE A POOR THING TO FINALLY SPEND IT ON, GEORGES.
CAPTAIN-- GEORGES, I--
I CAN'T DO THAT--
WHAT THE HELL, MALIK?
INSURANCE? WHAT...?

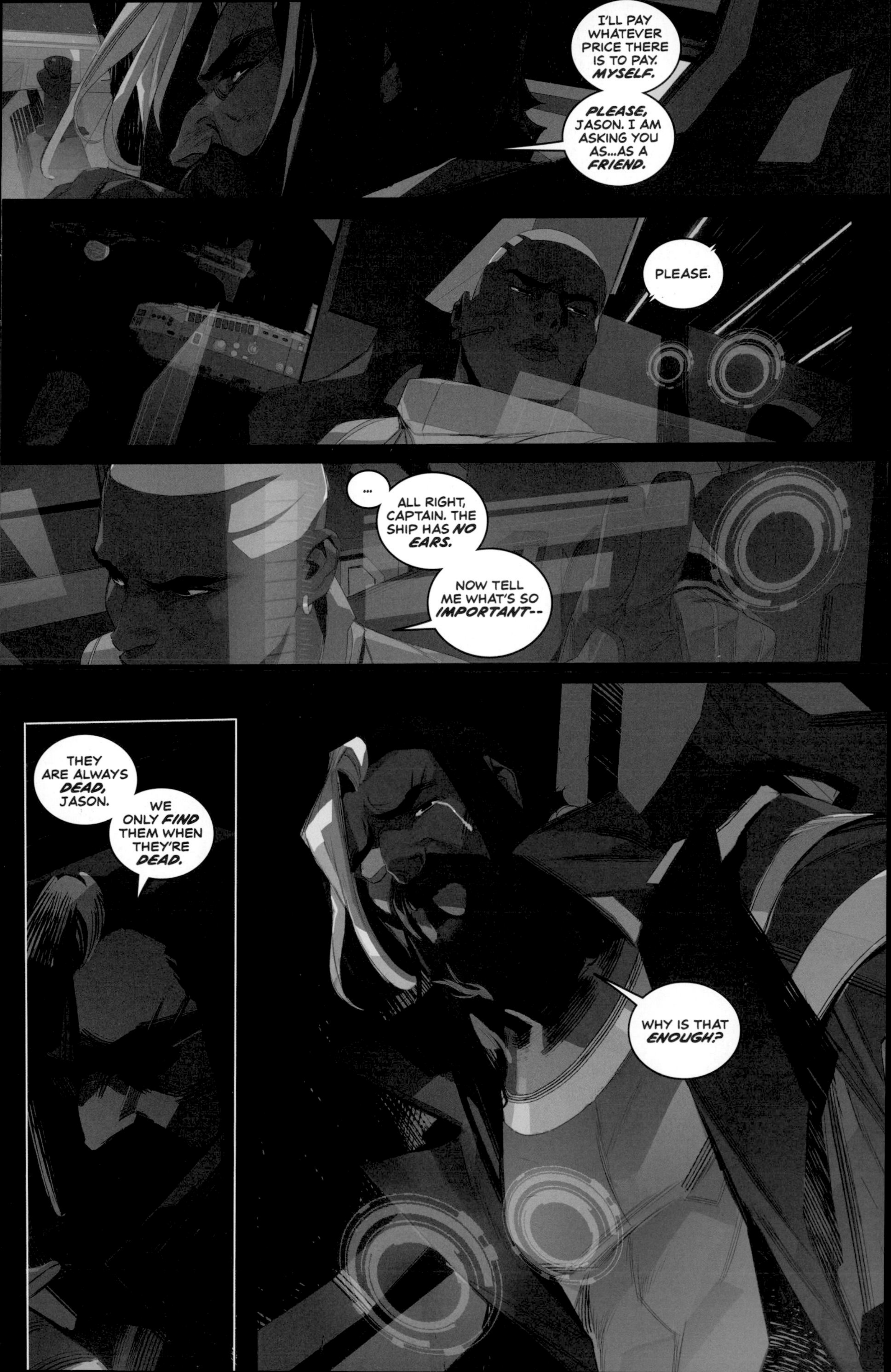
I'LL PAY WHATEVER PRICE THERE IS TO PAY. MYSELF.
PLEASE, JASON. I AM ASKING YOU AS...AS A FRIEND.
PLEASE.
...
ALL RIGHT, CAPTAIN. THE SHIP HAS NO EARS.
NOW TELL ME WHAT'S SO IMPORTANT--
THEY ARE ALWAYS DEAD, JASON.
WE ONLY FIND THEM WHEN THEY'RE DEAD.
WHY IS THAT ENOUGH?

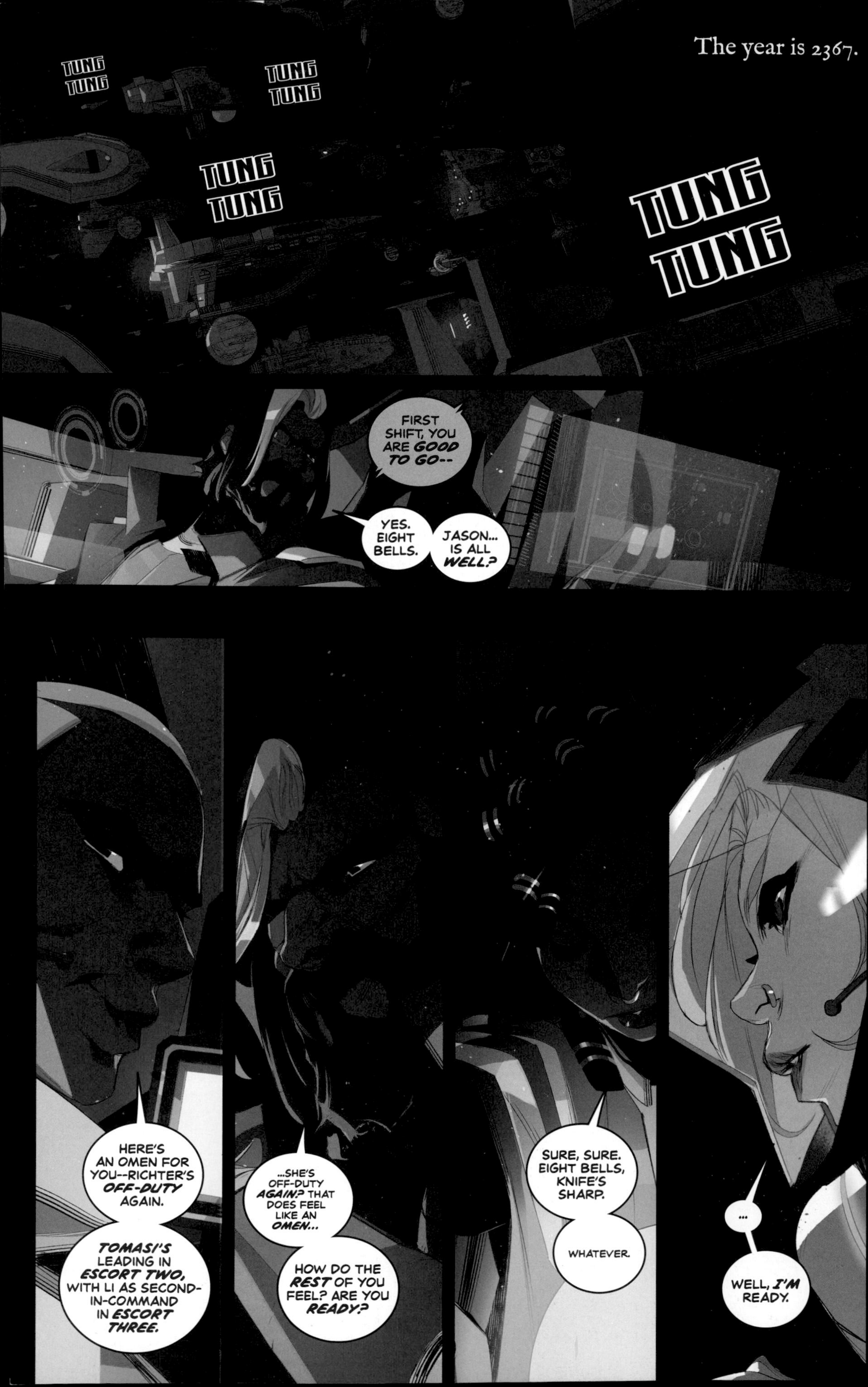
The year is 2367.
TUNG TUNG
TUNG TUNG
TUNG TUNG
TUNG TUNG
FIRST SHIFT, YOU ARE GOOD TO GO--
YES. EIGHT BELLS.
JASON... IS ALL WELL?
HERE'S AN OMEN FOR YOU--RICHTER'S OFF-DUTY AGAIN.
TOMASI'S LEADING IN ESCORT TWO, WITH LI AS SECOND-IN-COMMAND IN ESCORT THREE.
...SHE'S OFF-DUTY AGAIN!? THAT DOES FEEL LIKE AN OMEN...
HOW DO THE REST OF YOU FEEL? ARE YOU READY?
SURE, SURE. EIGHT BELLS, KNIFE'S SHARP.
WHATEVER.
...
WELL, I'M READY.

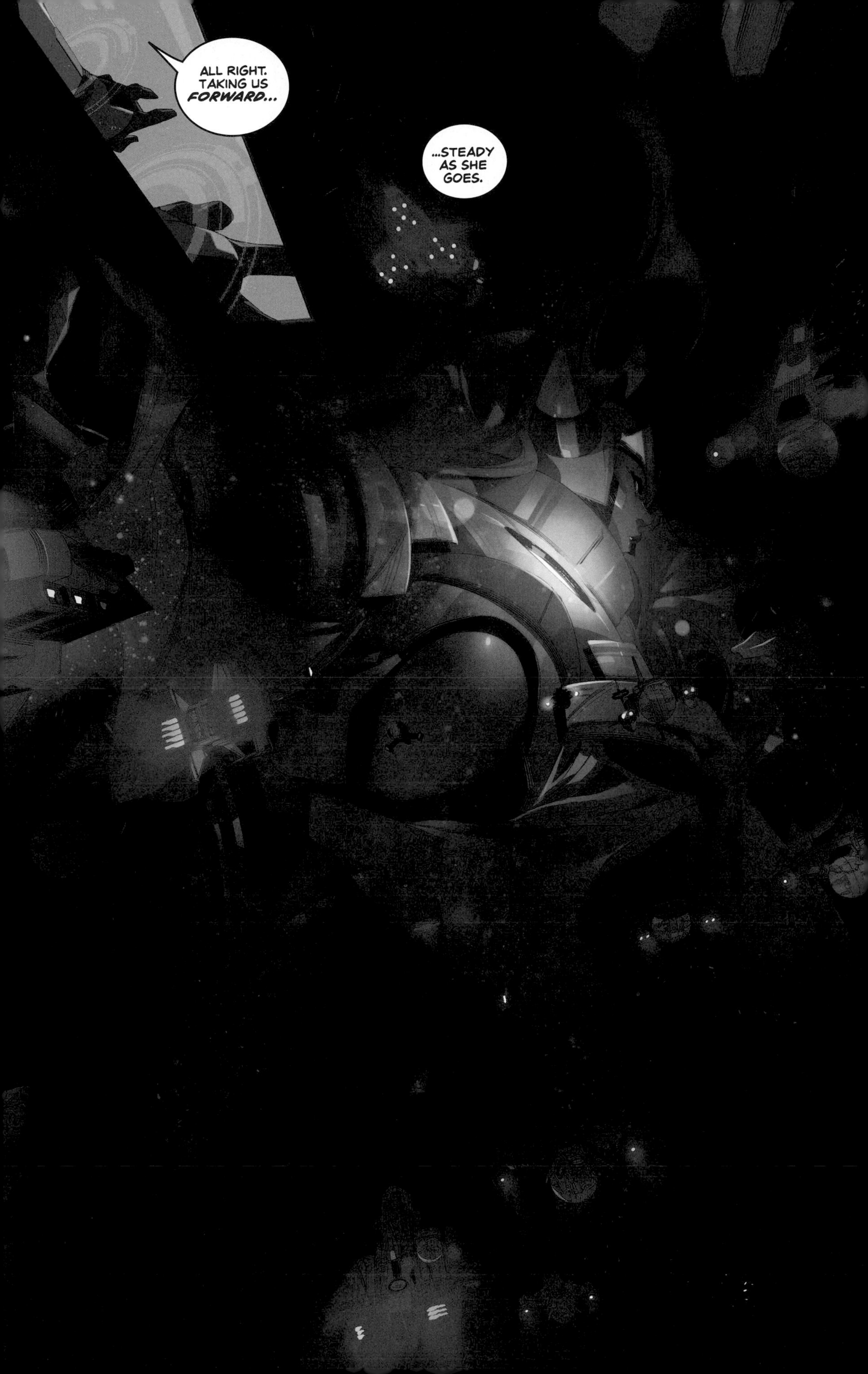
ALL RIGHT. TAKING US FORWARD...
...STEADY AS SHE GOES.

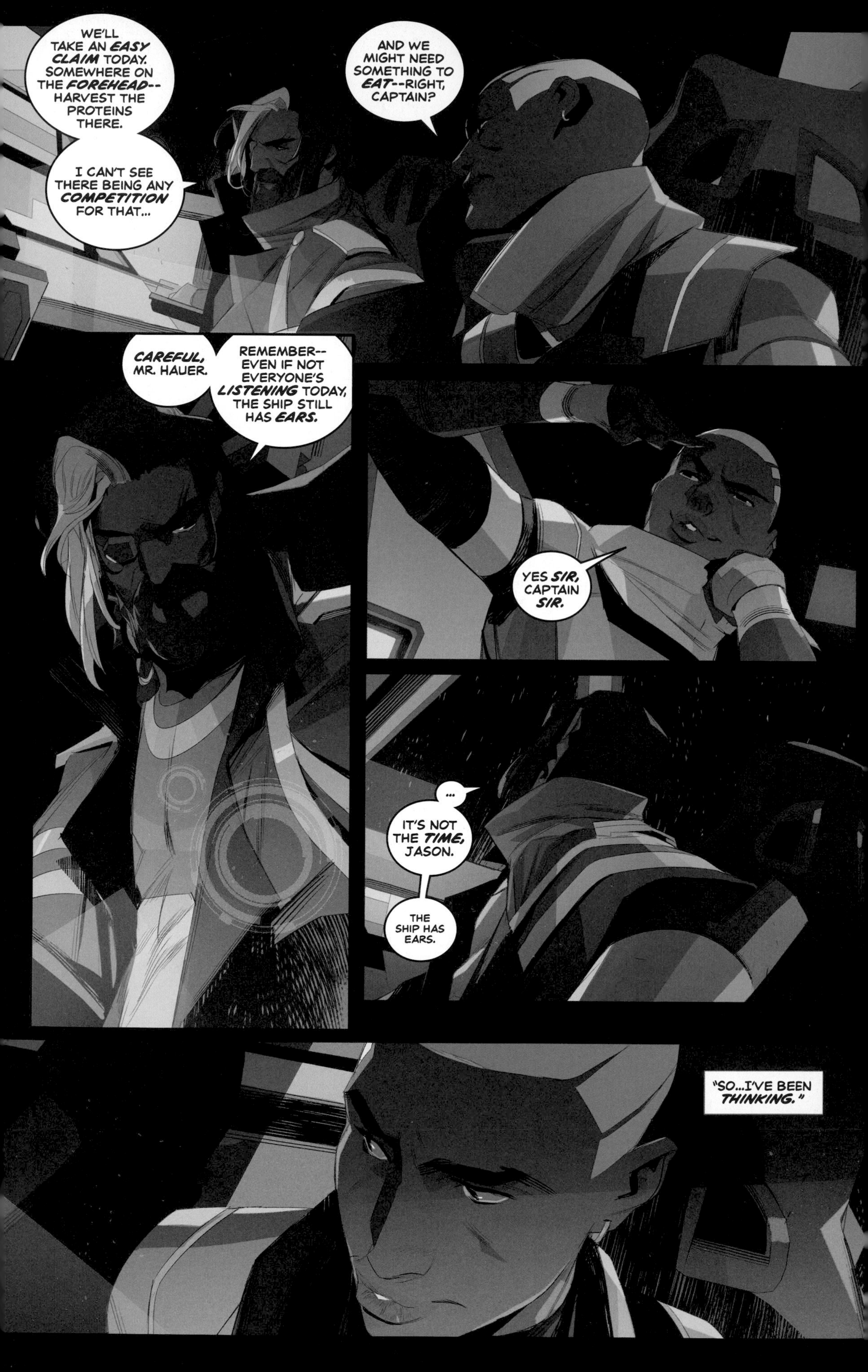
WE'LL TAKE AN EASY CLAIM TODAY. SOMEWHERE ON THE FOREHEAD--HARVEST THE PROTEINS THERE.
I CAN'T SEE THERE BEING ANY COMPETITION FOR THAT...
AND WE MIGHT NEED SOMETHING TO EAT--RIGHT, CAPTAIN?
CAREFUL, MR. HAUER.
REMEMBER--EVEN IF NOT EVERYONE'S LISTENING TODAY, THE SHIP STILL HAS EARS.
YES SIR, CAPTAIN SIR.
...
IT'S NOT THE TIME, JASON.
THE SHIP HAS EARS.
"SO...I'VE BEEN THINKING."

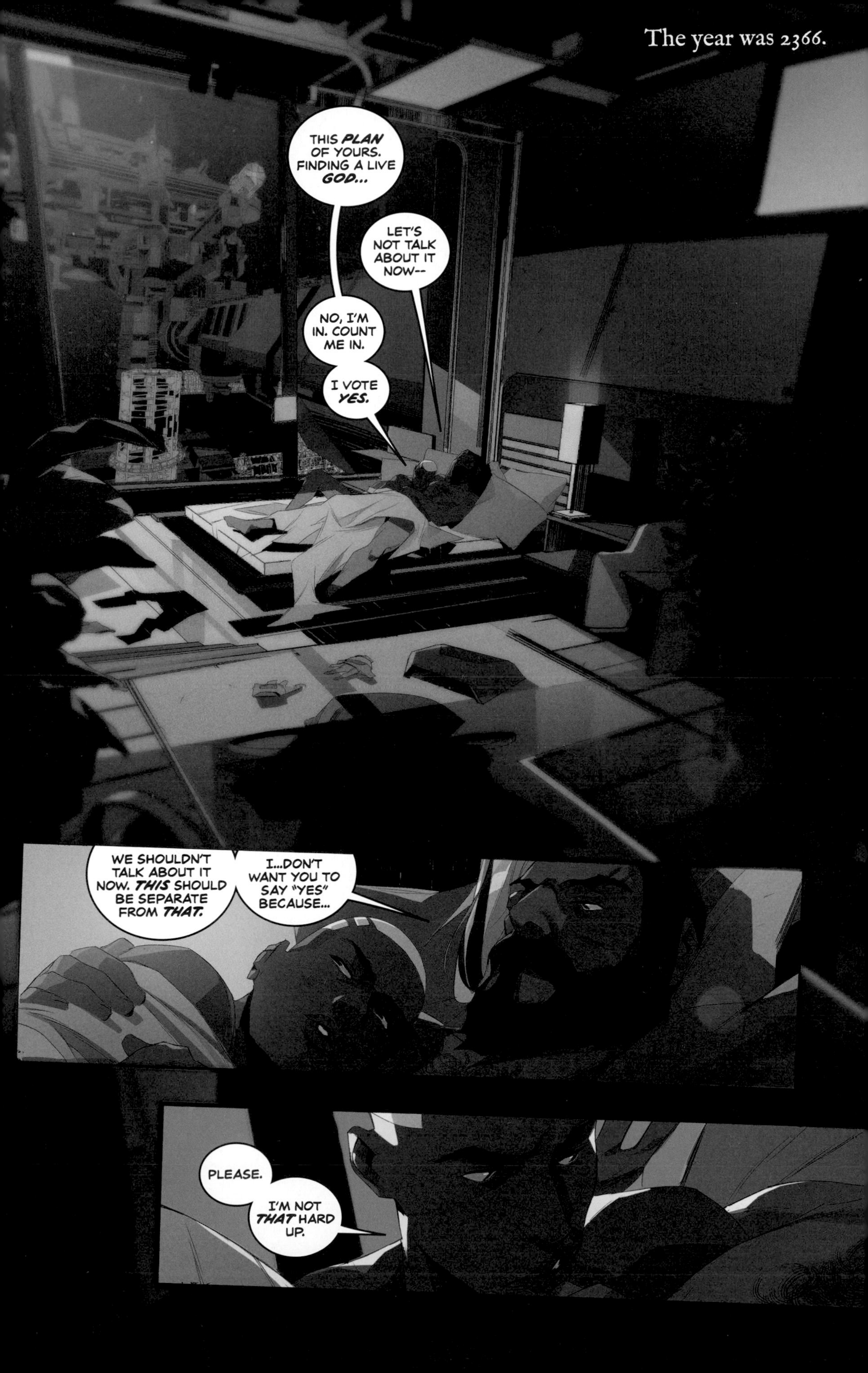

The year was 2366.
THIS *PLAN* OF YOURS. FINDING A LIVE *GOD...*
LET'S NOT TALK ABOUT IT NOW--
NO, I'M IN. COUNT ME IN.
I VOTE *YES.*
WE SHOULDN'T TALK ABOUT IT NOW. *THIS* SHOULD BE SEPARATE FROM *THAT.*
I...DON'T WANT YOU TO SAY "YES" BECAUSE...
PLEASE.
I'M NOT *THAT* HARD UP.

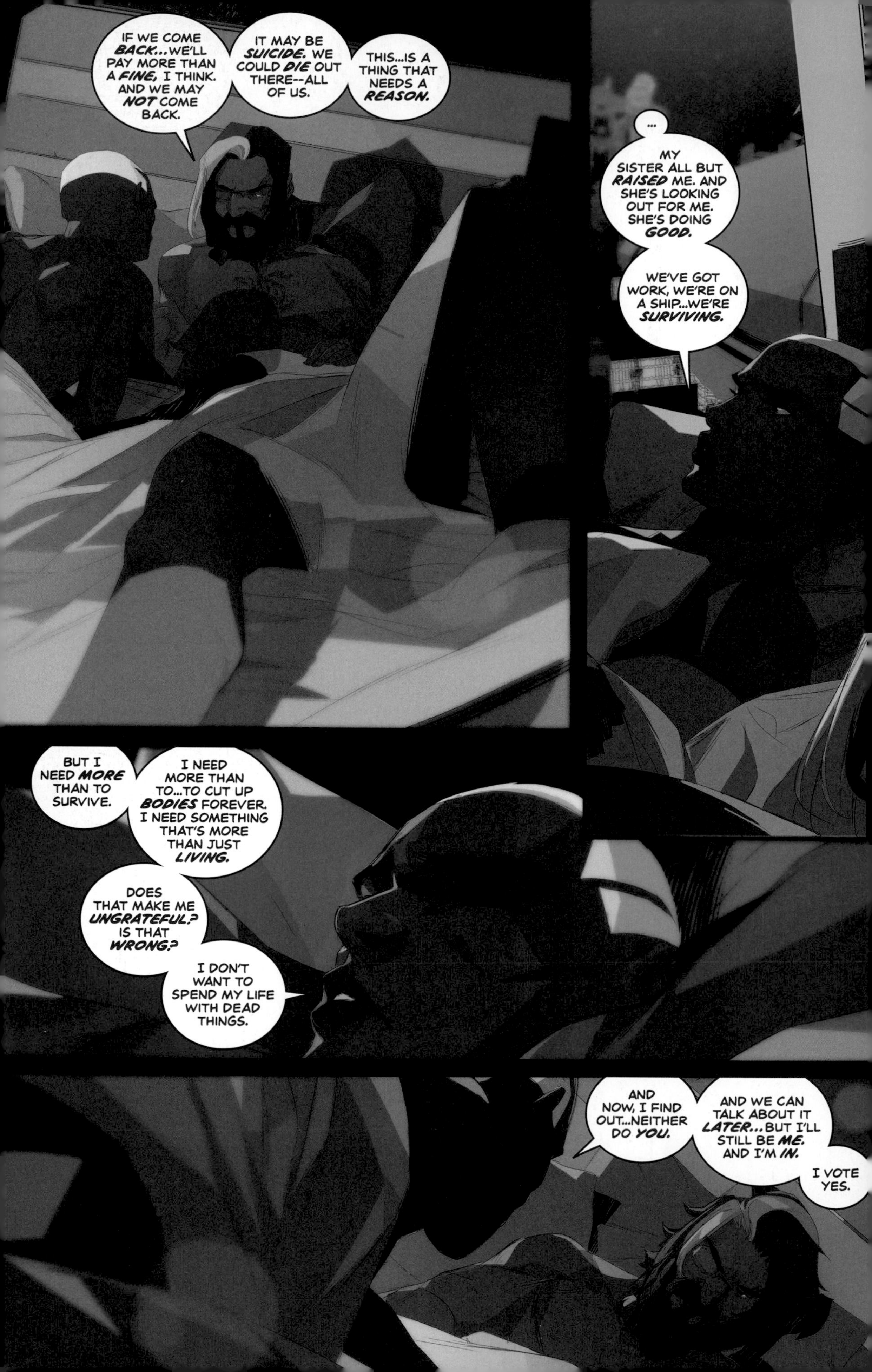

IF WE COME BACK... WE'LL PAY MORE THAN A FINE, I THINK. AND WE MAY NOT COME BACK.
IT MAY BE SUICIDE. WE COULD DIE OUT THERE--ALL OF US.
THIS...IS A THING THAT NEEDS A REASON.
...
MY SISTER ALL BUT RAISED ME. AND SHE'S LOOKING OUT FOR ME. SHE'S DOING GOOD.
WE'VE GOT WORK, WE'RE ON A SHIP...WE'RE SURVIVING.
BUT I NEED MORE THAN TO SURVIVE.
I NEED MORE THAN TO...TO CUT UP BODIES FOREVER. I NEED SOMETHING THAT'S MORE THAN JUST LIVING.
DOES THAT MAKE ME UNGRATEFUL? IS THAT WRONG?
I DON'T WANT TO SPEND MY LIFE WITH DEAD THINGS.
AND NOW, I FIND OUT...NEITHER DO YOU.
AND WE CAN TALK ABOUT IT LATER... BUT I'LL STILL BE ME. AND I'M IN.
I VOTE YES.

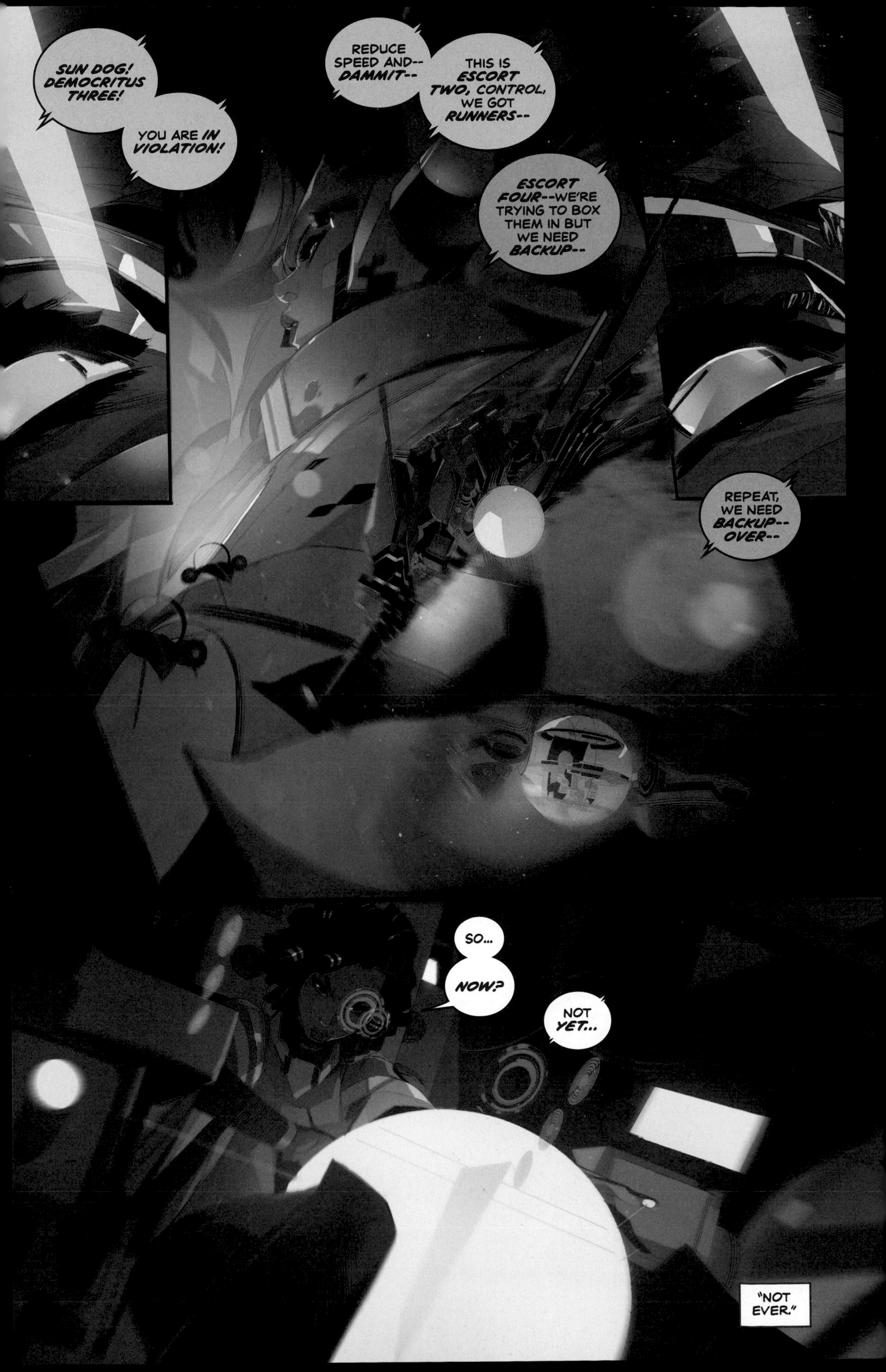
SUN DOG! DEMOCRITUS THREE!
YOU ARE IN VIOLATION!
REDUCE SPEED AND-- DAMMIT--
THIS IS ESCORT TWO, CONTROL, WE GOT RUNNERS--
ESCORT FOUR--WE'RE TRYING TO BOX THEM IN BUT WE NEED BACKUP--
REPEAT, WE NEED BACKUP-- OVER--
SO...
NOW?
NOT YET...
"NOT EVER."

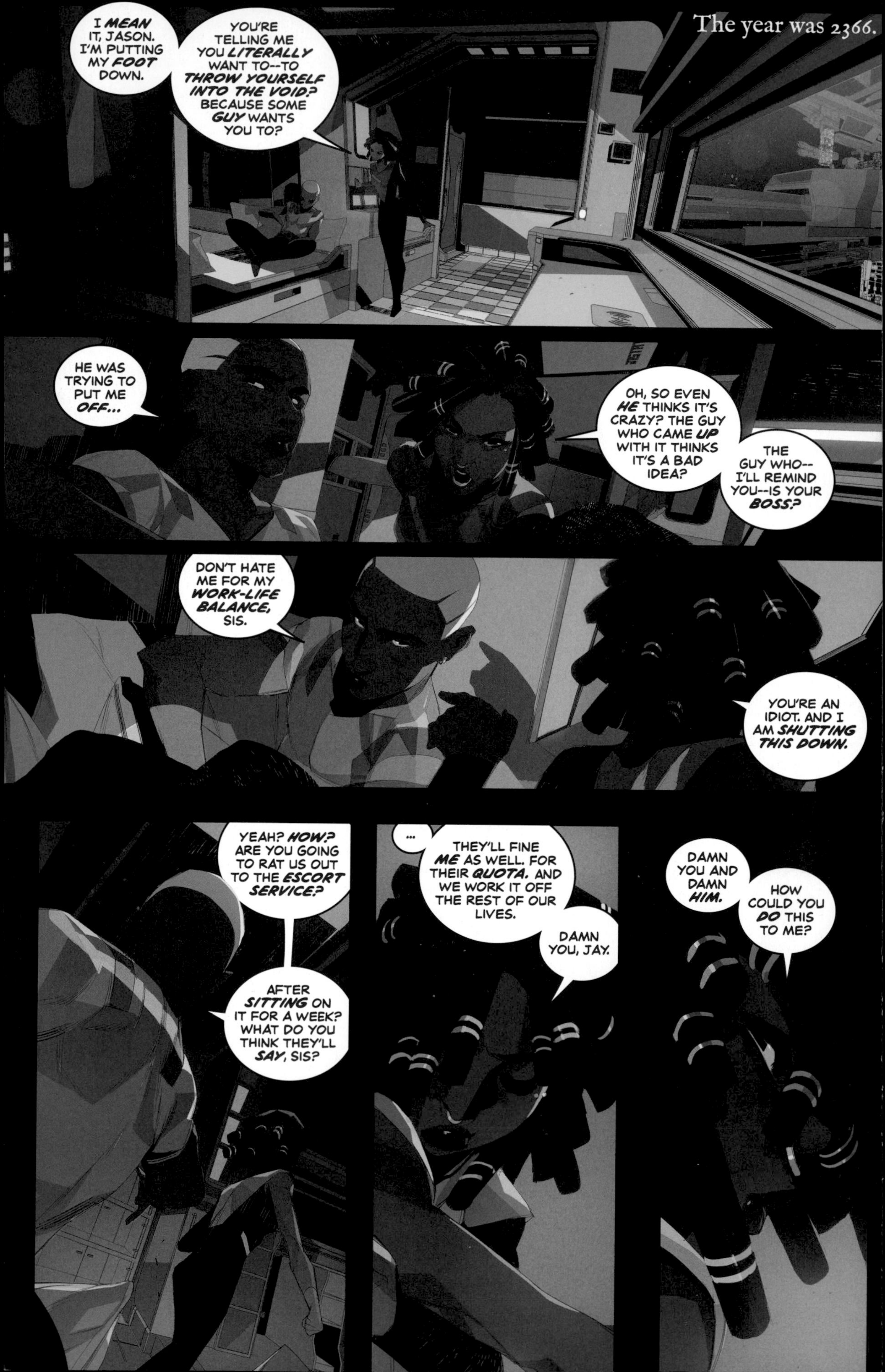
The year was 2366.
I MEAN IT, JASON. I'M PUTTING MY FOOT DOWN.
YOU'RE TELLING ME YOU LITERALLY WANT TO--TO THROW YOURSELF INTO THE VOID? BECAUSE SOME GUY WANTS YOU TO?
HE WAS TRYING TO PUT ME OFF...
OH, SO EVEN HE THINKS IT'S CRAZY? THE GUY WHO CAME UP WITH IT THINKS IT'S A BAD IDEA?
THE GUY WHO--I'LL REMIND YOU--IS YOUR BOSS?
DON'T HATE ME FOR MY WORK-LIFE BALANCE, SIS.
YOU'RE AN IDIOT. AND I AM SHUTTING THIS DOWN.
YEAH? HOW? ARE YOU GOING TO RAT US OUT TO THE ESCORT SERVICE?
AFTER SITTING ON IT FOR A WEEK? WHAT DO YOU THINK THEY'LL SAY, SIS?
...
THEY'LL FINE ME AS WELL. FOR THEIR QUOTA. AND WE WORK IT OFF THE REST OF OUR LIVES.
DAMN YOU, JAY.
DAMN YOU AND DAMN HIM.
HOW COULD YOU DO THIS TO ME?

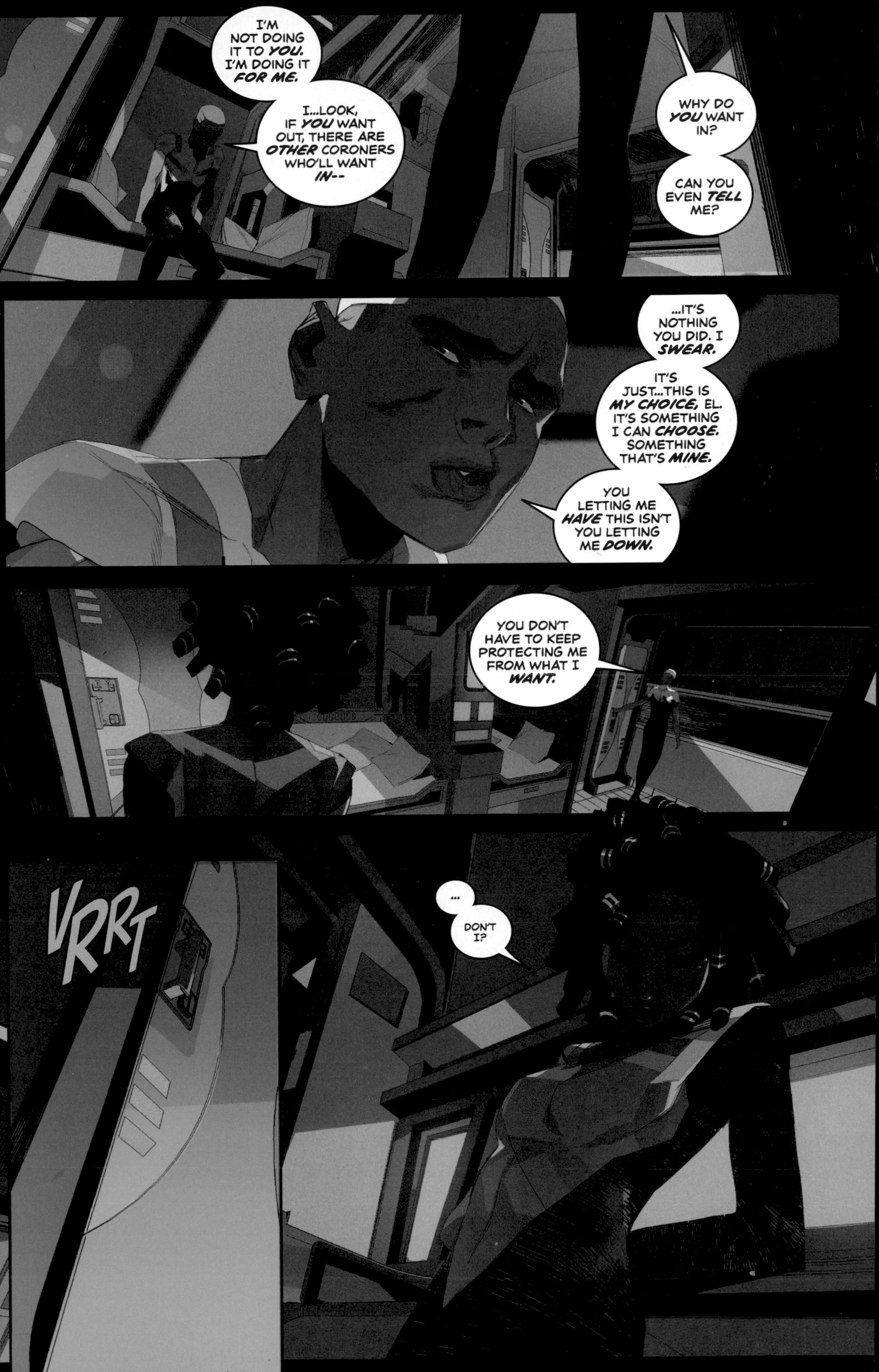
I'M NOT DOING IT TO YOU. I'M DOING IT FOR ME.
I...LOOK, IF YOU WANT OUT, THERE ARE OTHER CORONERS WHO'LL WANT IN--
WHY DO YOU WANT IN?
CAN YOU EVEN TELL ME?
...IT'S NOTHING YOU DID. I SWEAR.
IT'S JUST...THIS IS MY CHOICE, EL. IT'S SOMETHING I CAN CHOOSE. SOMETHING THAT'S MINE.
YOU LETTING ME HAVE THIS ISN'T YOU LETTING ME DOWN.
YOU DON'T HAVE TO KEEP PROTECTING ME FROM WHAT I WANT.
VRRT
...
DON'T I?

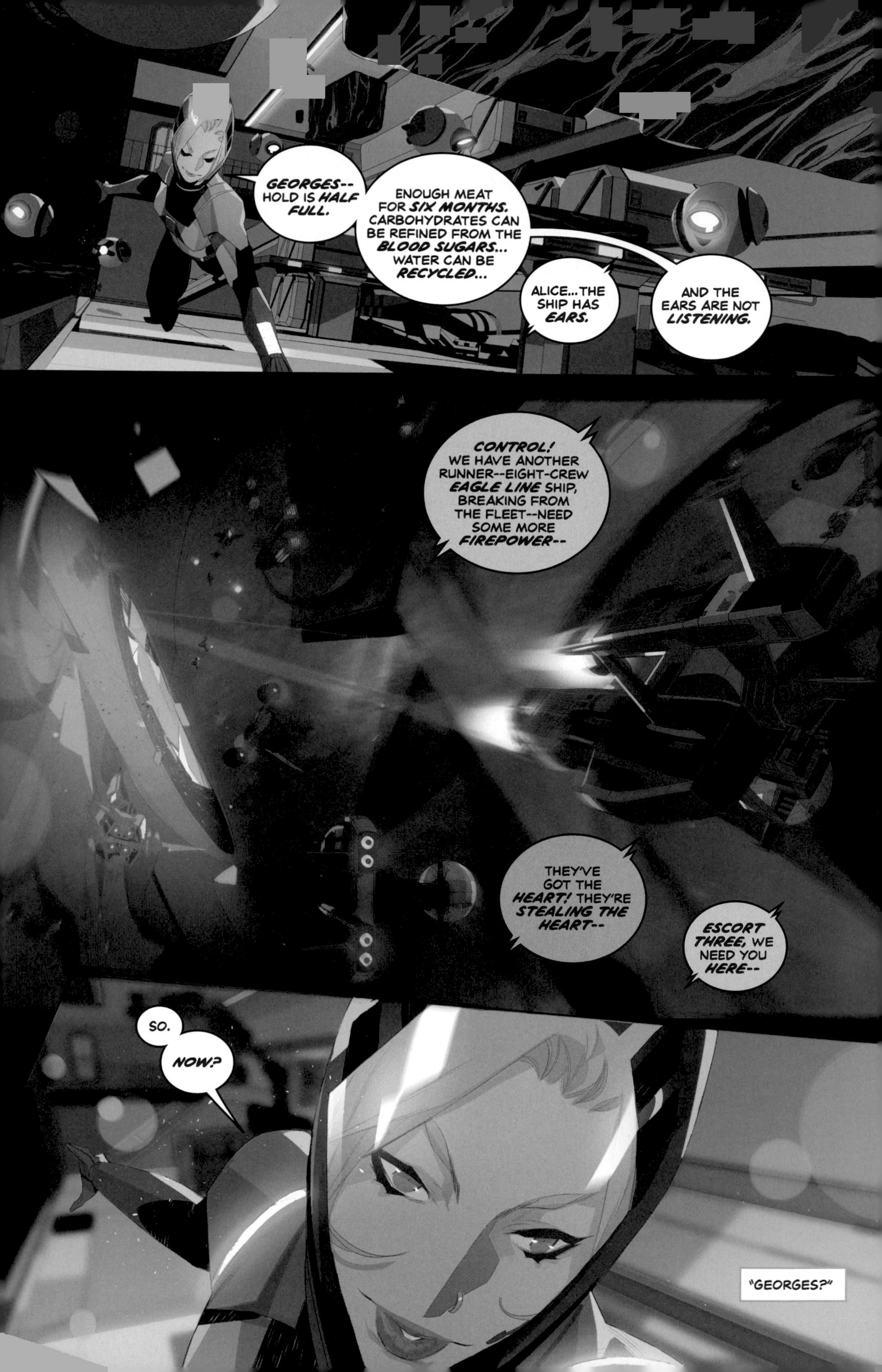
GEORGES--
HOLD IS HALF FULL.
ENOUGH MEAT FOR SIX MONTHS. CARBOHYDRATES CAN BE REFINED FROM THE BLOOD SUGARS... WATER CAN BE RECYCLED...
ALICE...THE SHIP HAS EARS.
AND THE EARS ARE NOT LISTENING.
CONTROL! WE HAVE ANOTHER RUNNER--EIGHT-CREW EAGLE LINE SHIP, BREAKING FROM THE FLEET--NEED SOME MORE FIREPOWER--
THEY'VE GOT THE HEART! THEY'RE STEALING THE HEART--
ESCORT THREE, WE NEED YOU HERE--
SO.
NOW?
"GEORGES?"

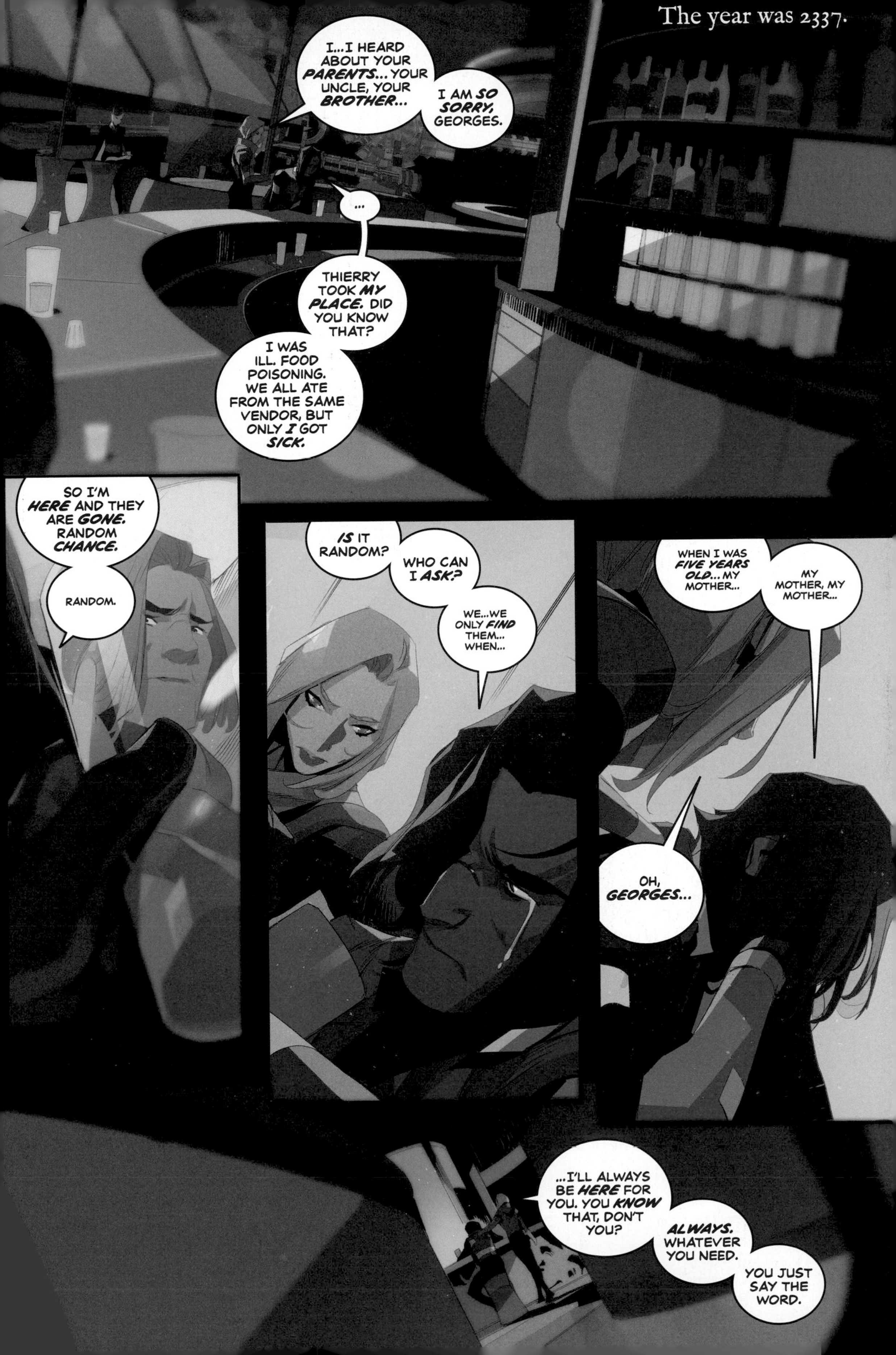
The year was 2337.
I...I HEARD ABOUT YOUR PARENTS... YOUR UNCLE, YOUR BROTHER...
I AM SO SORRY, GEORGES.
...
THIERRY TOOK MY PLACE. DID YOU KNOW THAT?
I WAS ILL. FOOD POISONING. WE ALL ATE FROM THE SAME VENDOR, BUT ONLY I GOT SICK.
SO I'M HERE AND THEY ARE GONE. RANDOM CHANCE.
RANDOM.
IS IT RANDOM?
WHO CAN I ASK?
WE...WE ONLY FIND THEM... WHEN...
WHEN I WAS FIVE YEARS OLD... MY MOTHER...
MY MOTHER, MY MOTHER...
OH, GEORGES...
...I'LL ALWAYS BE HERE FOR YOU. YOU KNOW THAT, DON'T YOU?
ALWAYS. WHATEVER YOU NEED.
YOU JUST SAY THE WORD.

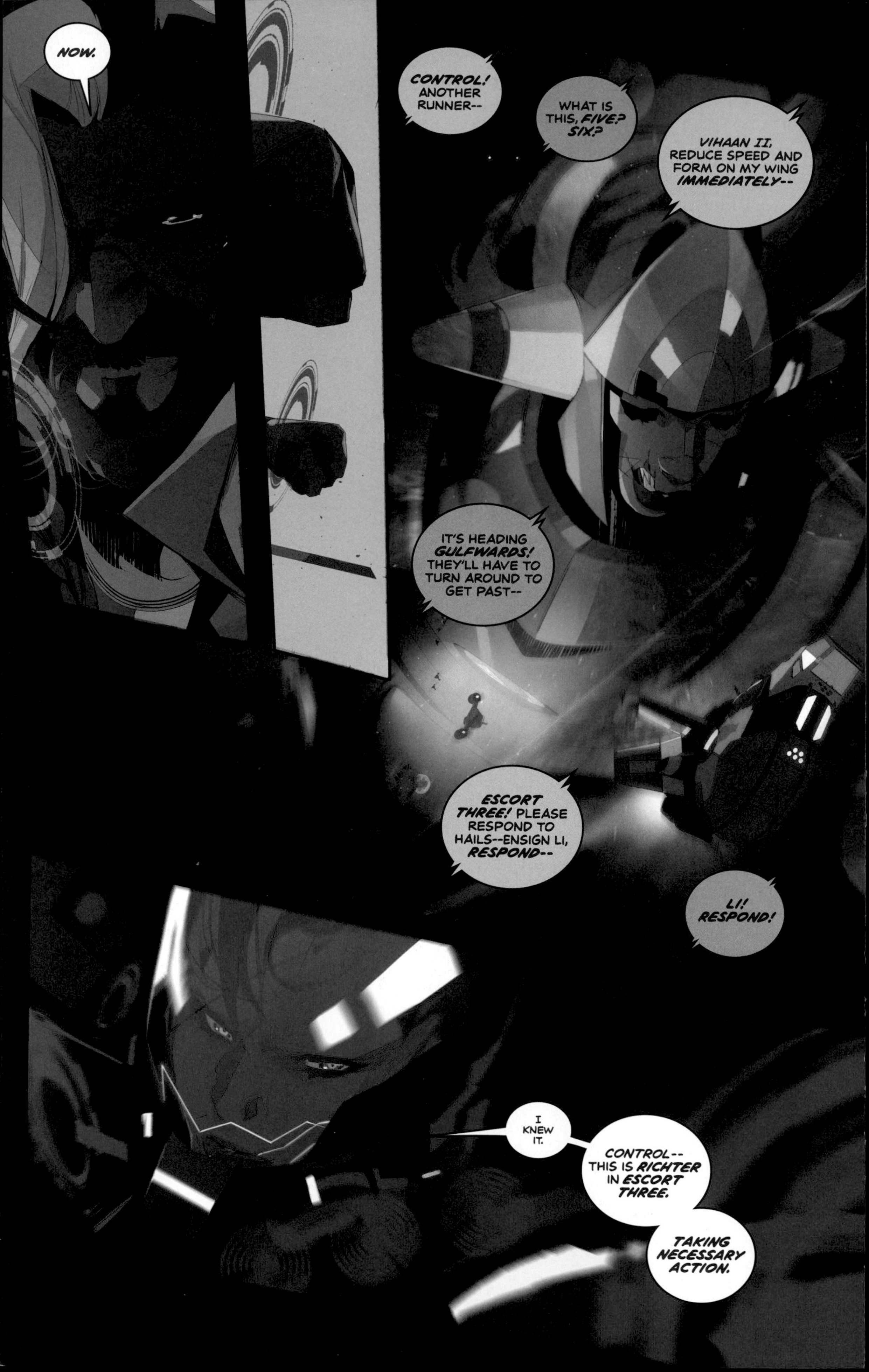
NOW.
CONTROL! ANOTHER RUNNER--
WHAT IS THIS, FIVE? SIX?
VIHAAN II, REDUCE SPEED AND FORM ON MY WING IMMEDIATELY--
IT'S HEADING GULFWARDS! THEY'LL HAVE TO TURN AROUND TO GET PAST--
ESCORT THREE! PLEASE RESPOND TO HAILS--ENSIGN LI, RESPOND--
LI! RESPOND!
I KNEW IT.
CONTROL-- THIS IS RICHTER IN ESCORT THREE.
TAKING NECESSARY ACTION.

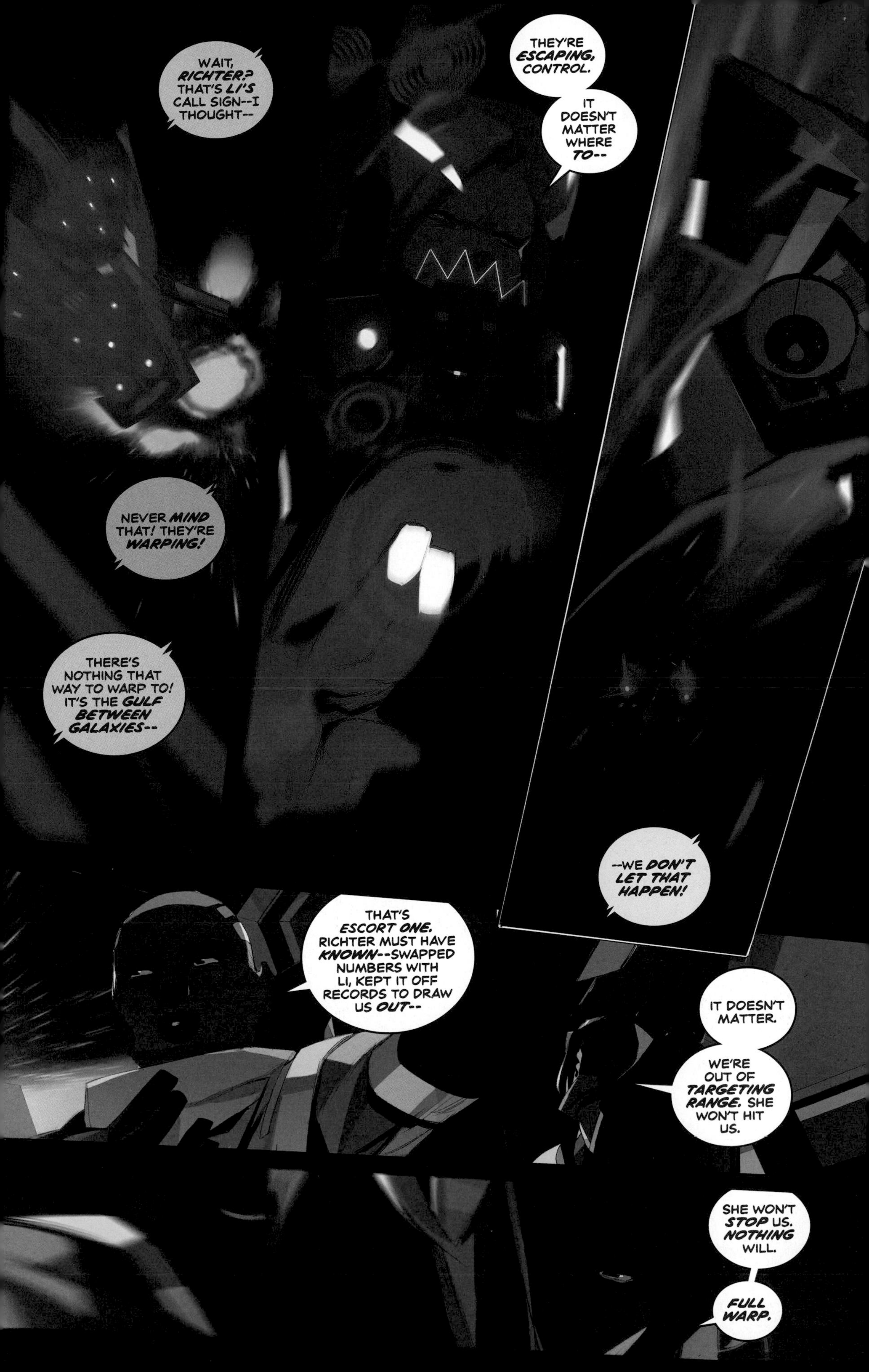
WAIT, RICHTER? THAT'S LI'S CALL SIGN--I THOUGHT--
THEY'RE ESCAPING, CONTROL.
IT DOESN'T MATTER WHERE TO--
NEVER MIND THAT! THEY'RE WARPING!
THERE'S NOTHING THAT WAY TO WARP TO! IT'S THE GULF BETWEEN GALAXIES--
--WE DON'T LET THAT HAPPEN!
THAT'S ESCORT ONE. RICHTER MUST HAVE KNOWN--SWAPPED NUMBERS WITH LI, KEPT IT OFF RECORDS TO DRAW US OUT--
IT DOESN'T MATTER.
WE'RE OUT OF TARGETING RANGE. SHE WON'T HIT US.
SHE WON'T STOP US. NOTHING WILL.
FULL WARP.

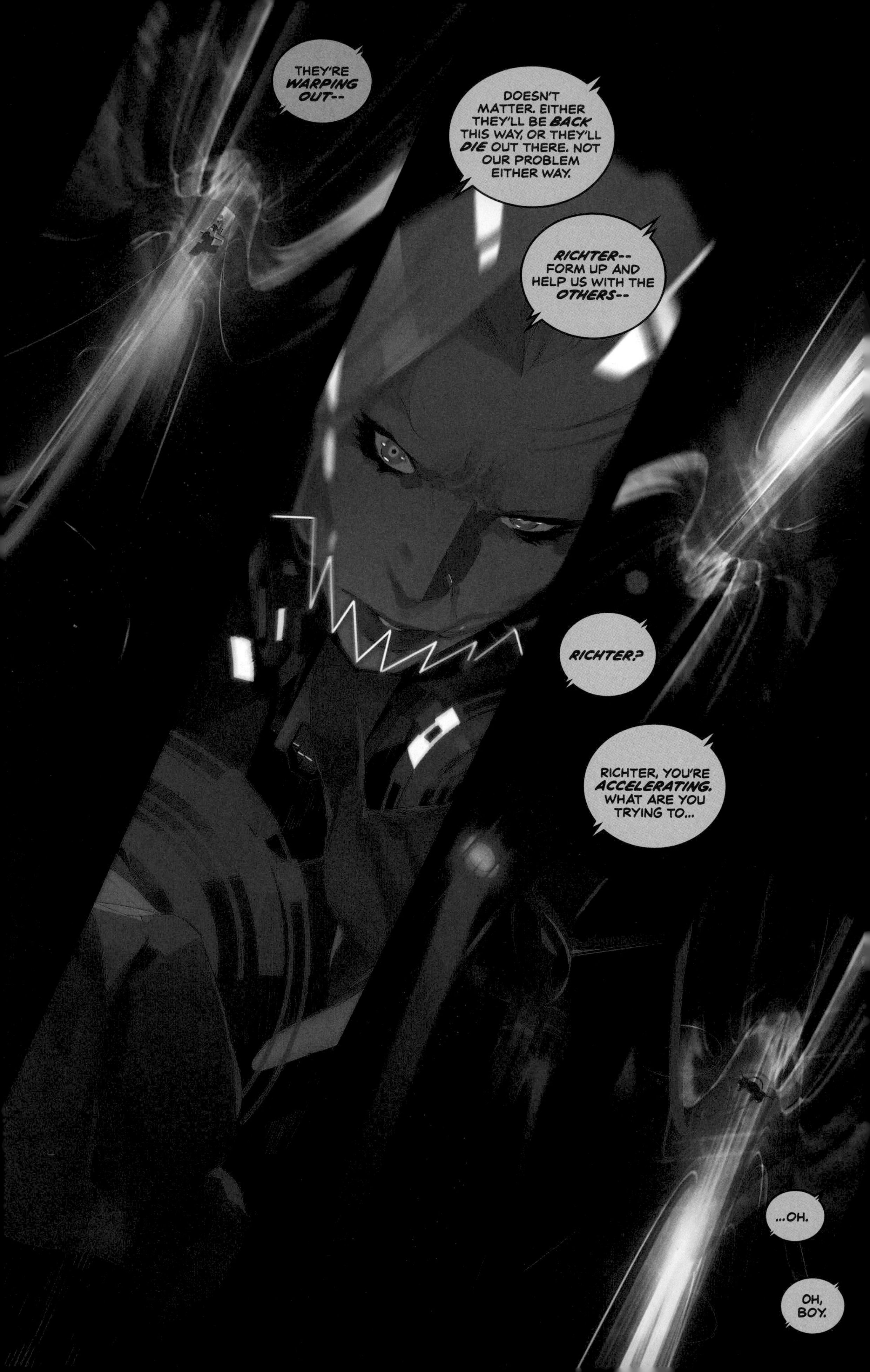
THEY'RE *WARPING OUT*--
DOESN'T MATTER. EITHER THEY'LL BE *BACK* THIS WAY, OR THEY'LL *DIE* OUT THERE. NOT OUR PROBLEM EITHER WAY.
RICHTER-- FORM UP AND HELP US WITH THE *OTHERS*--
RICHTER?
RICHTER, YOU'RE *ACCELERATING.* WHAT ARE YOU TRYING TO...
...OH.
OH, BOY.

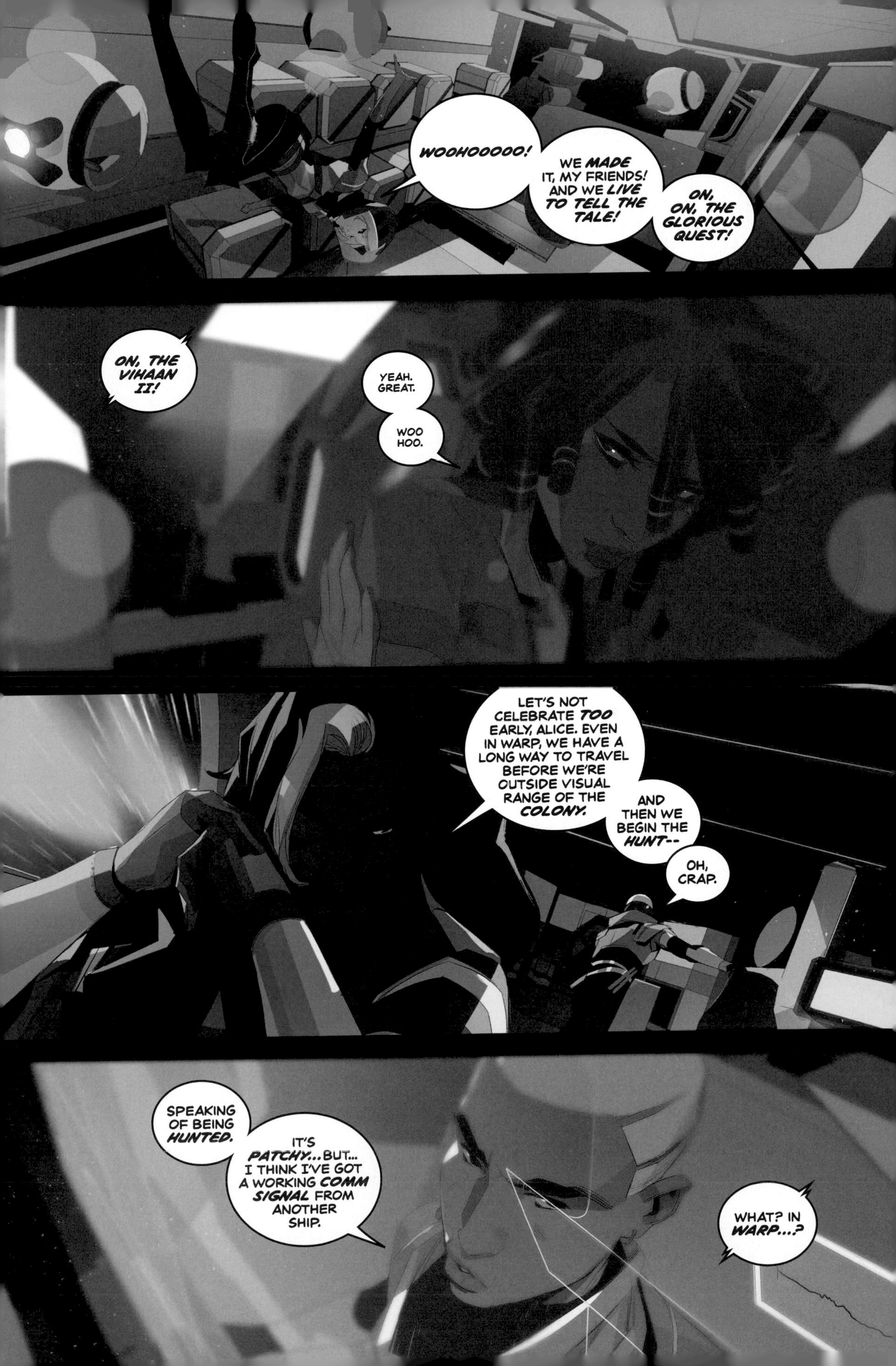
WOOHOOOOO!
WE MADE IT, MY FRIENDS! AND WE LIVE TO TELL THE TALE!
ON, ON, THE GLORIOUS QUEST!
ON, THE VIHAAN II!
YEAH. GREAT.
WOO HOO.
LET'S NOT CELEBRATE TOO EARLY, ALICE. EVEN IN WARP, WE HAVE A LONG WAY TO TRAVEL BEFORE WE'RE OUTSIDE VISUAL RANGE OF THE COLONY.
AND THEN WE BEGIN THE HUNT--
OH, CRAP.
SPEAKING OF BEING HUNTED.
IT'S PATCHY... BUT... I THINK I'VE GOT A WORKING COMM SIGNAL FROM ANOTHER SHIP.
WHAT? IN WARP...?

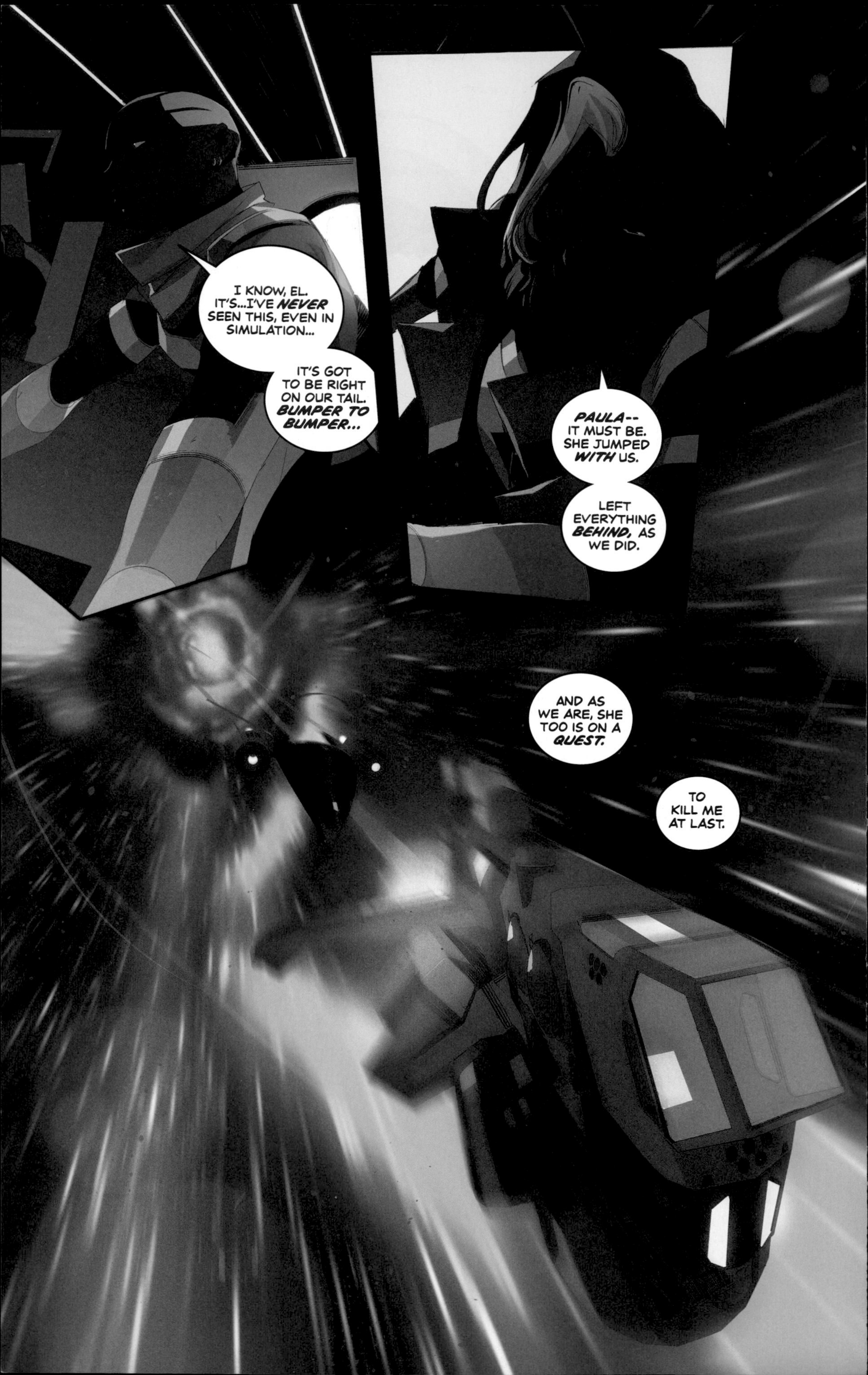
I KNOW, EL. IT'S...I'VE NEVER SEEN THIS, EVEN IN SIMULATION...
IT'S GOT TO BE RIGHT ON OUR TAIL. BUMPER TO BUMPER...
PAULA-- IT MUST BE. SHE JUMPED WITH US.
LEFT EVERYTHING BEHIND, AS WE DID.
AND AS WE ARE, SHE TOO IS ON A QUEST.
TO KILL ME AT LAST.

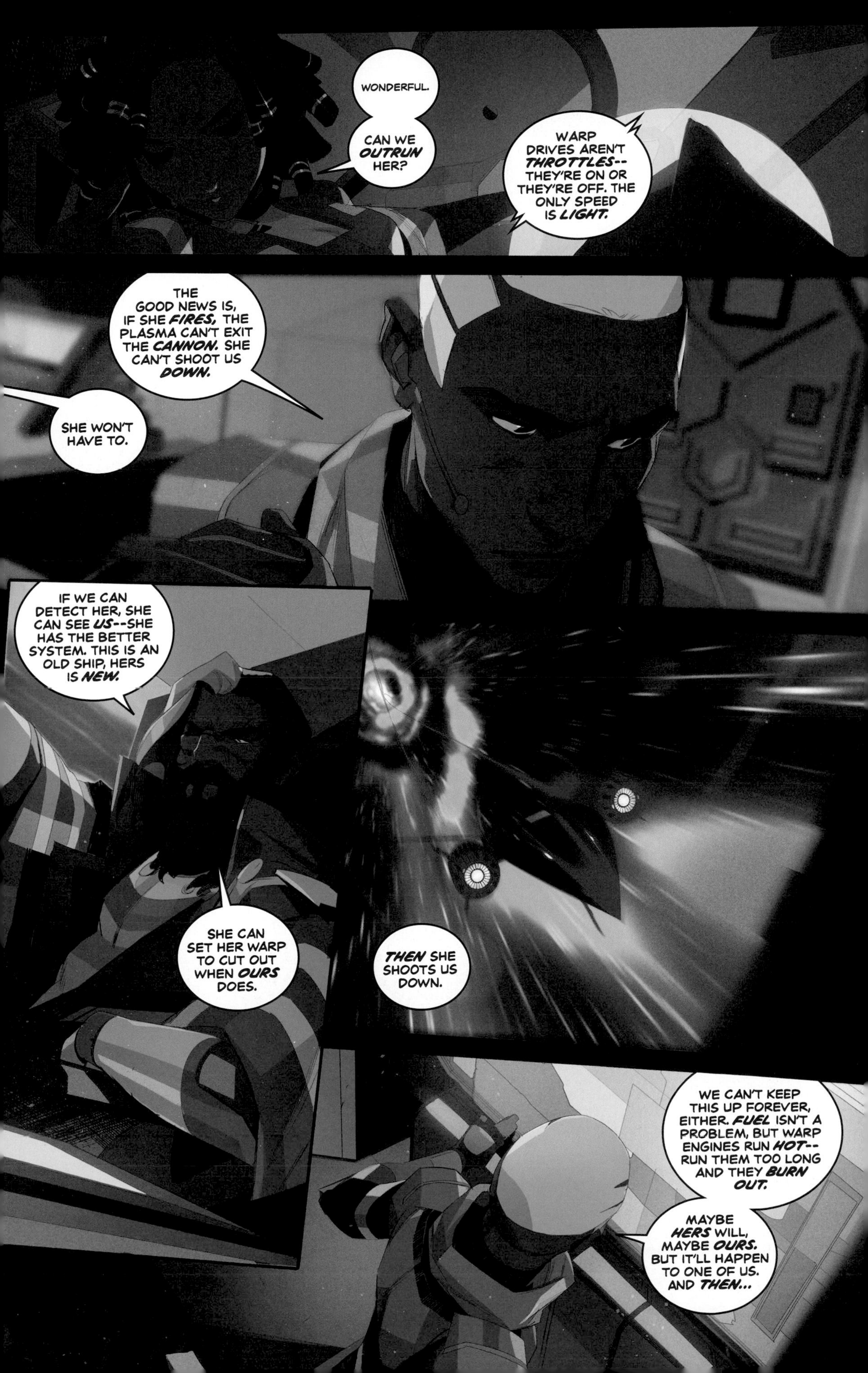
WONDERFUL.
CAN WE OUTRUN HER?
WARP DRIVES AREN'T THROTTLES--THEY'RE ON OR THEY'RE OFF. THE ONLY SPEED IS LIGHT.
THE GOOD NEWS IS, IF SHE FIRES, THE PLASMA CAN'T EXIT THE CANNON. SHE CAN'T SHOOT US DOWN.
SHE WON'T HAVE TO.
IF WE CAN DETECT HER, SHE CAN SEE US--SHE HAS THE BETTER SYSTEM. THIS IS AN OLD SHIP, HERS IS NEW.
SHE CAN SET HER WARP TO CUT OUT WHEN OURS DOES.
THEN SHE SHOOTS US DOWN.
WE CAN'T KEEP THIS UP FOREVER, EITHER. FUEL ISN'T A PROBLEM, BUT WARP ENGINES RUN HOT--RUN THEM TOO LONG AND THEY BURN OUT.
MAYBE HERS WILL, MAYBE OURS. BUT IT'LL HAPPEN TO ONE OF US. AND THEN...

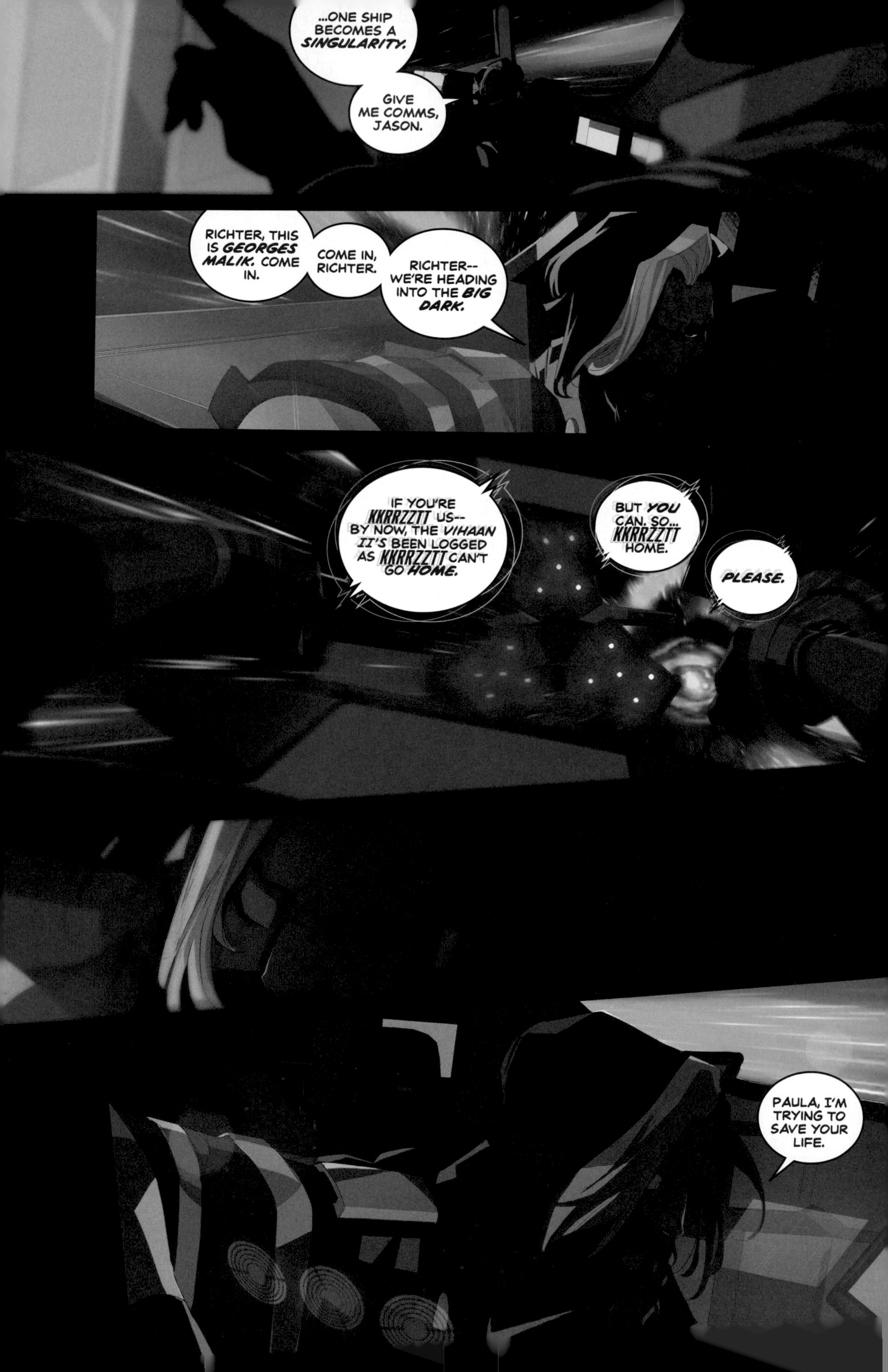
...ONE SHIP BECOMES A SINGULARITY.
GIVE ME COMMS, JASON.
RICHTER, THIS IS GEORGES MALIK. COME IN.
COME IN, RICHTER.
RICHTER-- WE'RE HEADING INTO THE BIG DARK.
IF YOU'RE KKRRZZTT US-- BY NOW, THE VIHAAN II'S BEEN LOGGED AS KKRRZZTT CAN'T GO HOME.
BUT YOU CAN. SO... KKRRZZTT HOME.
PLEASE.
PAULA, I'M TRYING TO SAVE YOUR LIFE.

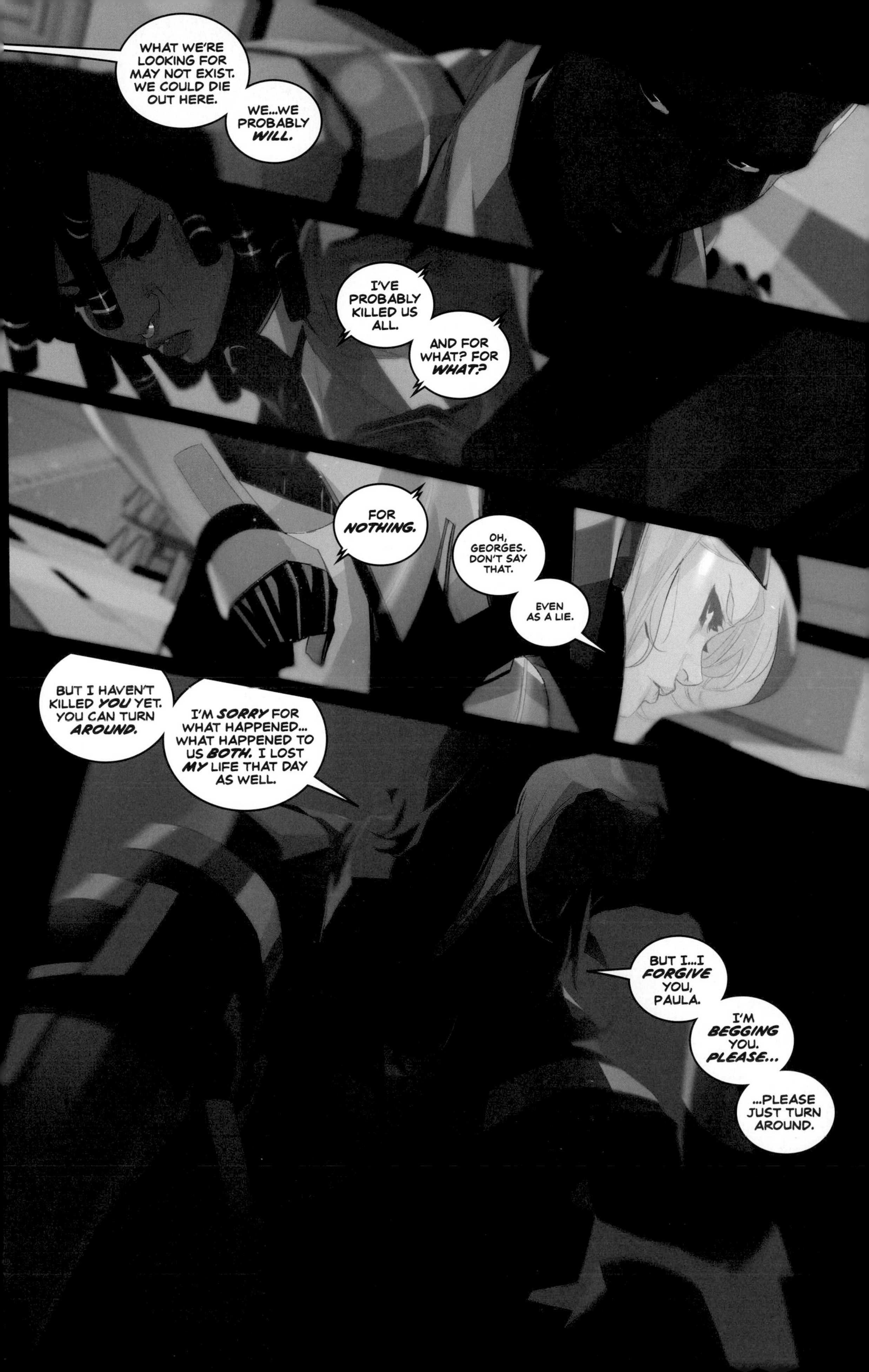
WHAT WE'RE LOOKING FOR MAY NOT EXIST. WE COULD DIE OUT HERE.
WE...WE PROBABLY WILL.
I'VE PROBABLY KILLED US ALL.
AND FOR WHAT? FOR WHAT?
FOR NOTHING.
OH, GEORGES. DON'T SAY THAT.
EVEN AS A LIE.
BUT I HAVEN'T KILLED YOU YET. YOU CAN TURN AROUND.
I'M SORRY FOR WHAT HAPPENED... WHAT HAPPENED TO US BOTH. I LOST MY LIFE THAT DAY AS WELL.
BUT I...I FORGIVE YOU, PAULA.
I'M BEGGING YOU. PLEASE...
...PLEASE JUST TURN AROUND.

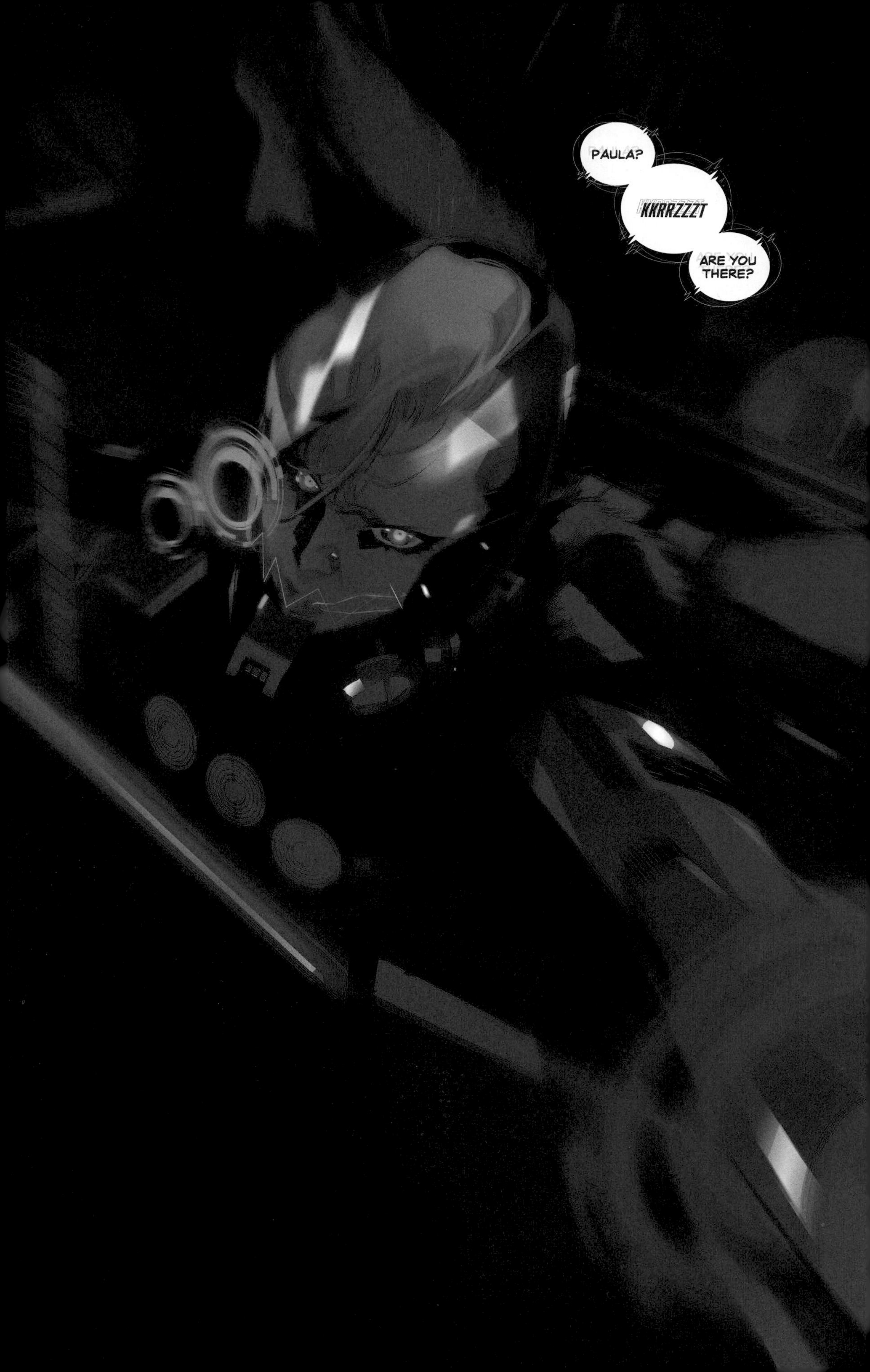
PAULA?
KKRRZZZT
ARE YOU THERE?

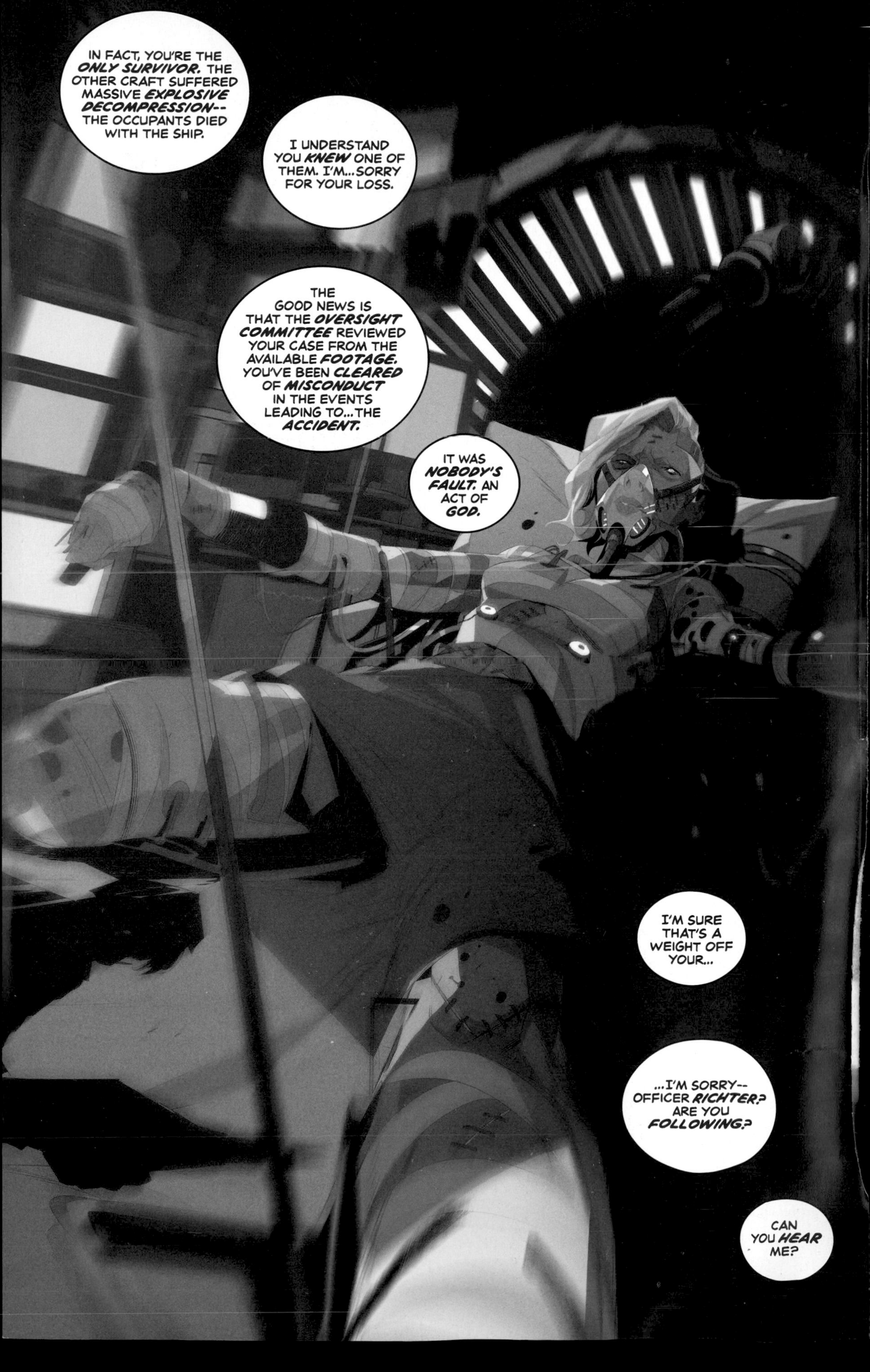
IN FACT, YOU'RE THE ONLY SURVIVOR. THE OTHER CRAFT SUFFERED MASSIVE EXPLOSIVE DECOMPRESSION-- THE OCCUPANTS DIED WITH THE SHIP.
I UNDERSTAND YOU KNEW ONE OF THEM. I'M...SORRY FOR YOUR LOSS.
THE GOOD NEWS IS THAT THE OVERSIGHT COMMITTEE REVIEWED YOUR CASE FROM THE AVAILABLE FOOTAGE. YOU'VE BEEN CLEARED OF MISCONDUCT IN THE EVENTS LEADING TO...THE ACCIDENT.
IT WAS NOBODY'S FAULT. AN ACT OF GOD.
I'M SURE THAT'S A WEIGHT OFF YOUR...
...I'M SORRY-- OFFICER RICHTER? ARE YOU FOLLOWING?
CAN YOU HEAR ME?

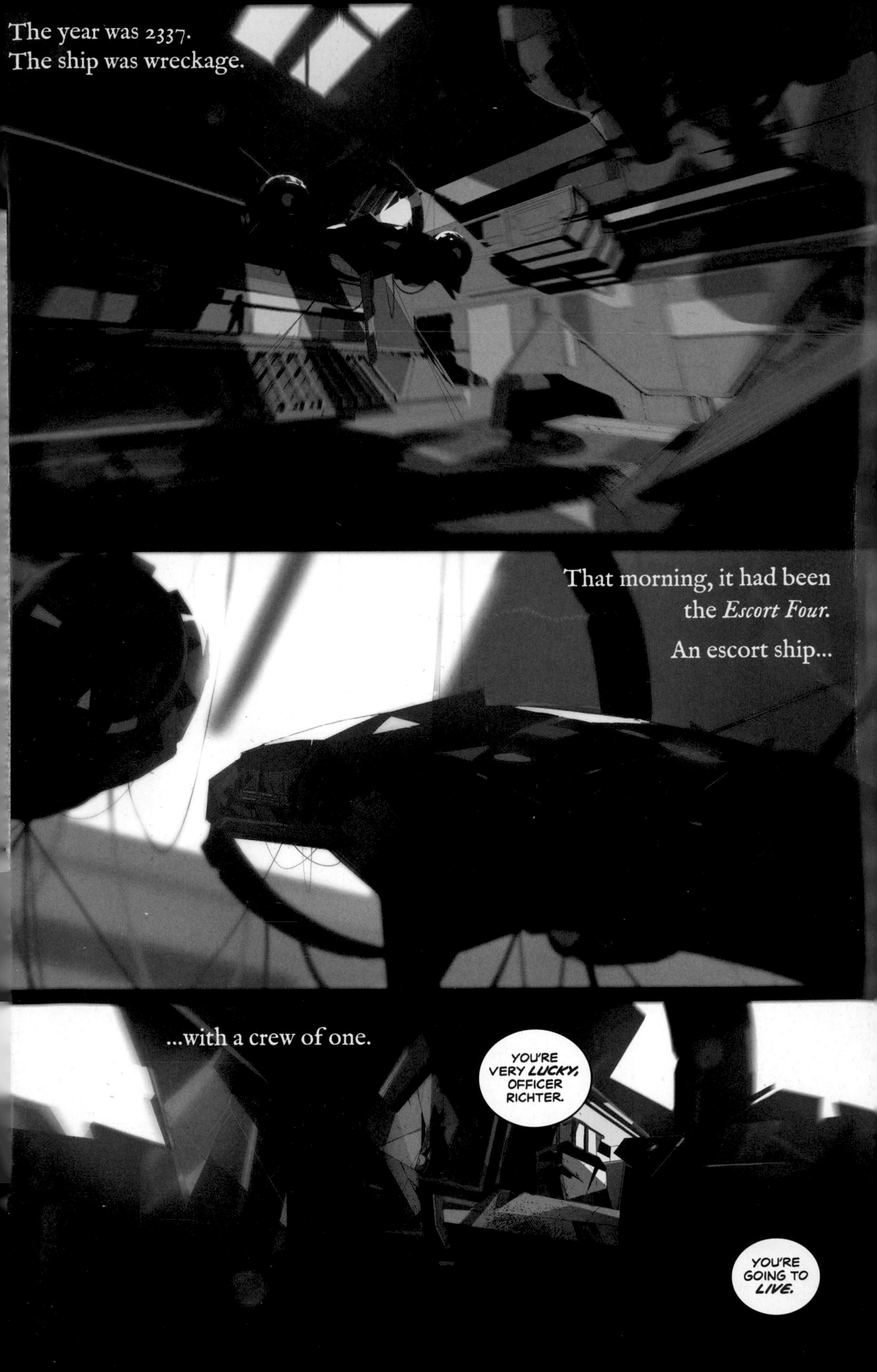

The year was 2337.
The ship was wreckage.
That morning, it had been the *Escort Four*.
An escort ship...
...with a crew of one.
YOU'RE VERY LUCKY, OFFICER RICHTER.
YOU'RE GOING TO LIVE.

Chapter Three

All of Us Together

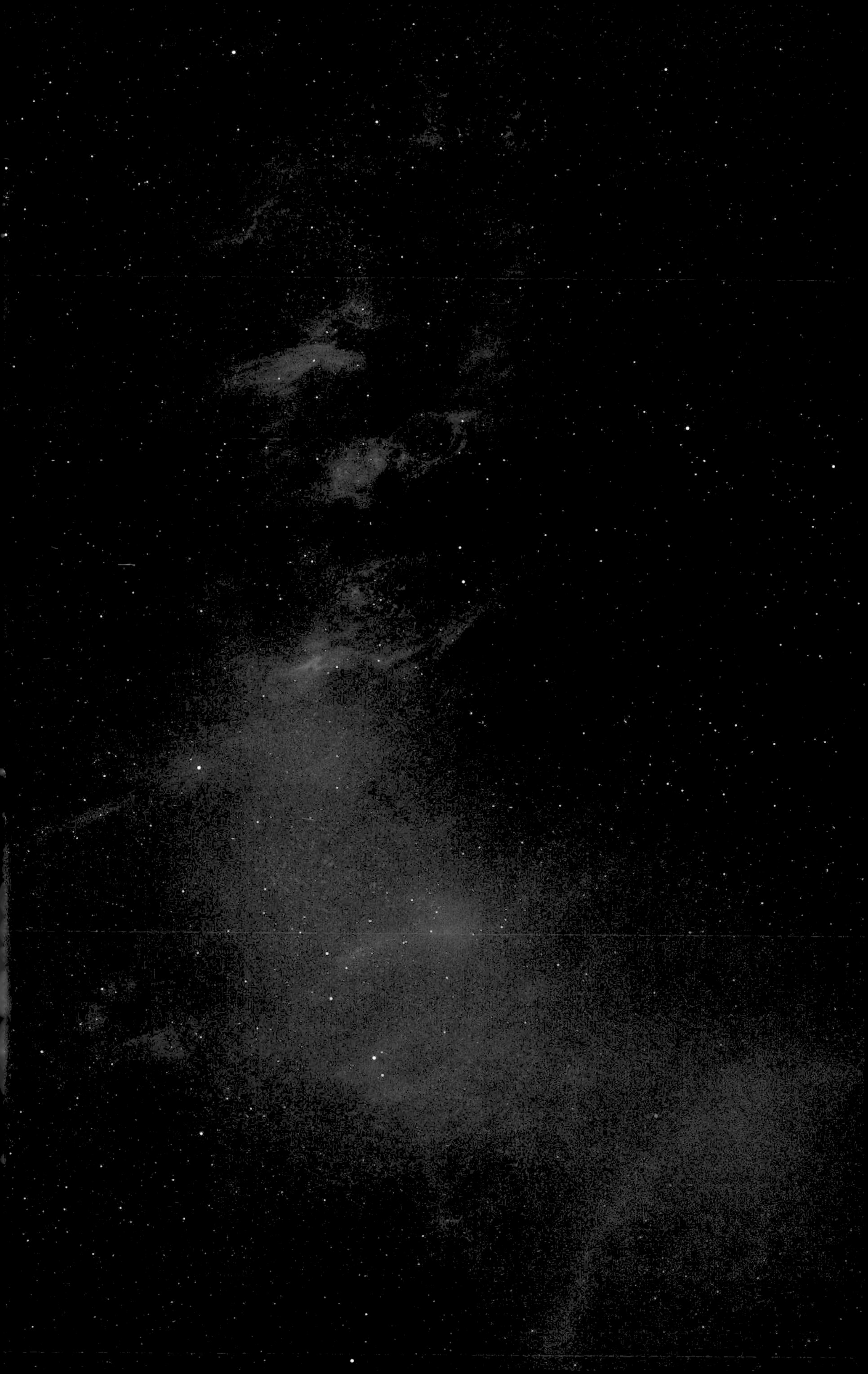

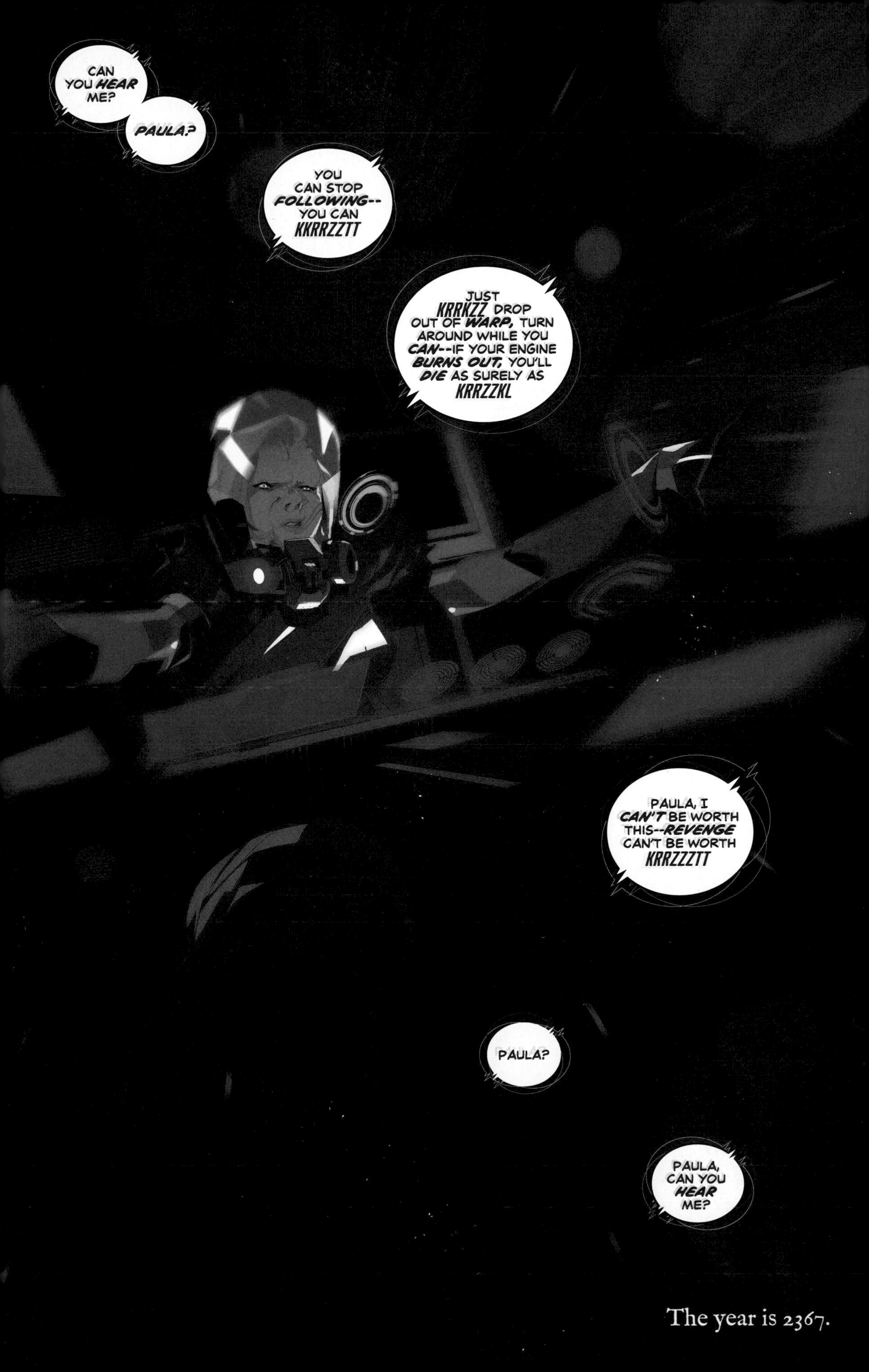
CAN YOU HEAR ME?
PAULA?
YOU CAN STOP FOLLOWING-- YOU CAN KKRRZZZTT
JUST KRRKZZ DROP OUT OF WARP, TURN AROUND WHILE YOU CAN--IF YOUR ENGINE BURNS OUT, YOU'LL DIE AS SURELY AS KRRZZKL
PAULA, I CAN'T BE WORTH THIS--REVENGE CAN'T BE WORTH KRRZZZZTT
PAULA?
PAULA, CAN YOU HEAR ME?
The year is 2367.

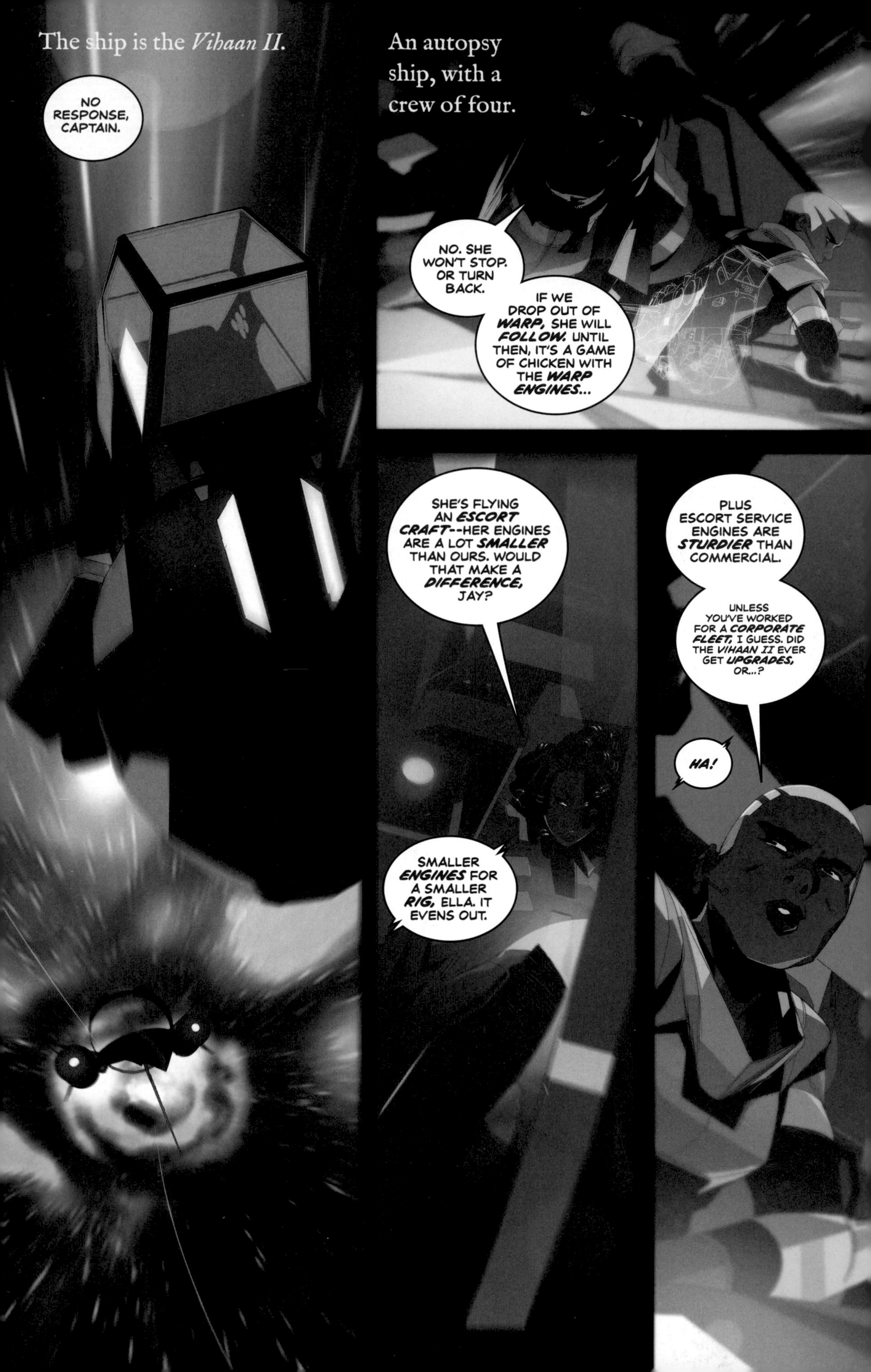
The ship is the *Vihaan II*.
NO RESPONSE, CAPTAIN.
An autopsy ship, with a crew of four.
NO. SHE WON'T STOP. OR TURN BACK.
IF WE DROP OUT OF WARP, SHE WILL FOLLOW. UNTIL THEN, IT'S A GAME OF CHICKEN WITH THE WARP ENGINES...
SHE'S FLYING AN ESCORT CRAFT--HER ENGINES ARE A LOT SMALLER THAN OURS. WOULD THAT MAKE A DIFFERENCE, JAY?
SMALLER ENGINES FOR A SMALLER RIG, ELLA. IT EVENS OUT.
PLUS ESCORT SERVICE ENGINES ARE STURDIER THAN COMMERCIAL.
UNLESS YOU'VE WORKED FOR A CORPORATE FLEET, I GUESS. DID THE VIHAAN II EVER GET UPGRADES, OR...?
HA!

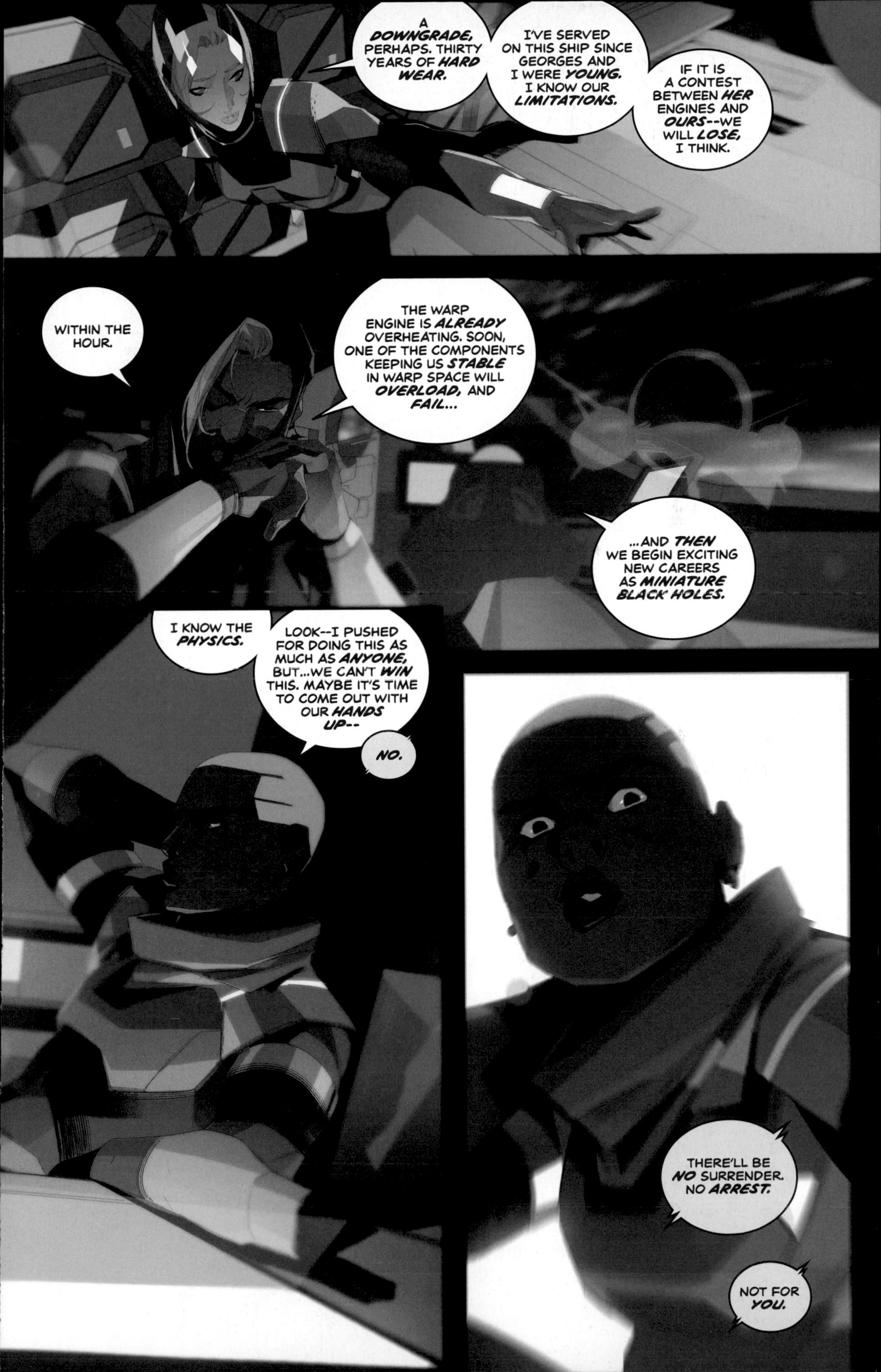
A DOWNGRADE, PERHAPS. THIRTY YEARS OF HARD WEAR.
I'VE SERVED ON THIS SHIP SINCE GEORGES AND I WERE YOUNG. I KNOW OUR LIMITATIONS.
IF IT IS A CONTEST BETWEEN HER ENGINES AND OURS--WE WILL LOSE, I THINK.
WITHIN THE HOUR.
THE WARP ENGINE IS ALREADY OVERHEATING. SOON, ONE OF THE COMPONENTS KEEPING US STABLE IN WARP SPACE WILL OVERLOAD, AND FAIL...
...AND THEN WE BEGIN EXCITING NEW CAREERS AS MINIATURE BLACK HOLES.
I KNOW THE PHYSICS.
LOOK--I PUSHED FOR DOING THIS AS MUCH AS ANYONE, BUT...WE CAN'T WIN THIS. MAYBE IT'S TIME TO COME OUT WITH OUR HANDS UP--
NO.
THERE'LL BE NO SURRENDER. NO ARREST.
NOT FOR YOU.

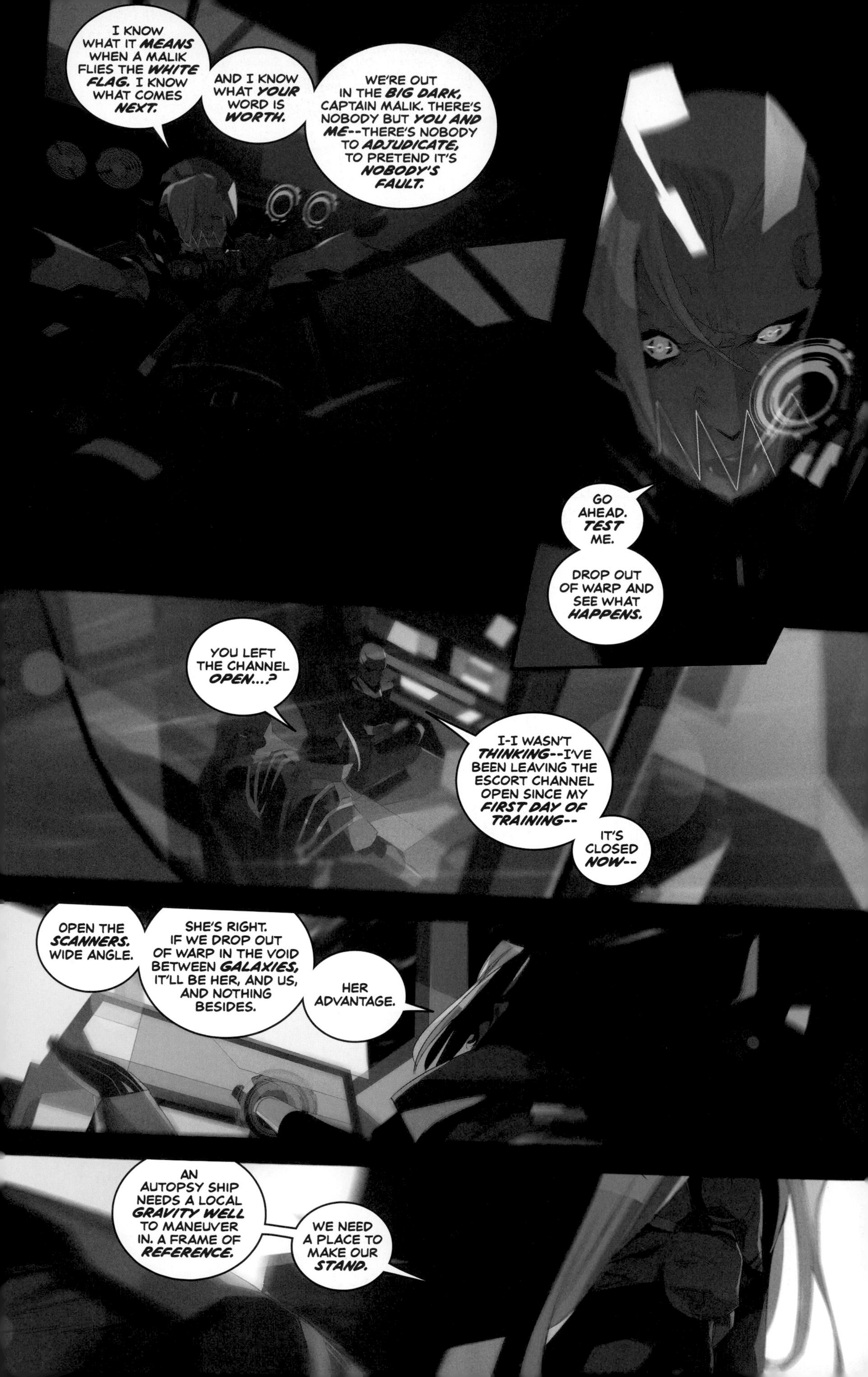
I KNOW WHAT IT MEANS WHEN A MALIK FLIES THE WHITE FLAG. I KNOW WHAT COMES NEXT.
AND I KNOW WHAT YOUR WORD IS WORTH.
WE'RE OUT IN THE BIG DARK, CAPTAIN MALIK. THERE'S NOBODY BUT YOU AND ME--THERE'S NOBODY TO ADJUDICATE, TO PRETEND IT'S NOBODY'S FAULT.
GO AHEAD. TEST ME.
DROP OUT OF WARP AND SEE WHAT HAPPENS.
YOU LEFT THE CHANNEL OPEN...?
I-I WASN'T THINKING--I'VE BEEN LEAVING THE ESCORT CHANNEL OPEN SINCE MY FIRST DAY OF TRAINING--
IT'S CLOSED NOW--
OPEN THE SCANNERS. WIDE ANGLE.
SHE'S RIGHT. IF WE DROP OUT OF WARP IN THE VOID BETWEEN GALAXIES, IT'LL BE HER, AND US, AND NOTHING BESIDES.
HER ADVANTAGE.
AN AUTOPSY SHIP NEEDS A LOCAL GRAVITY WELL TO MANEUVER IN. A FRAME OF REFERENCE.
WE NEED A PLACE TO MAKE OUR STAND.

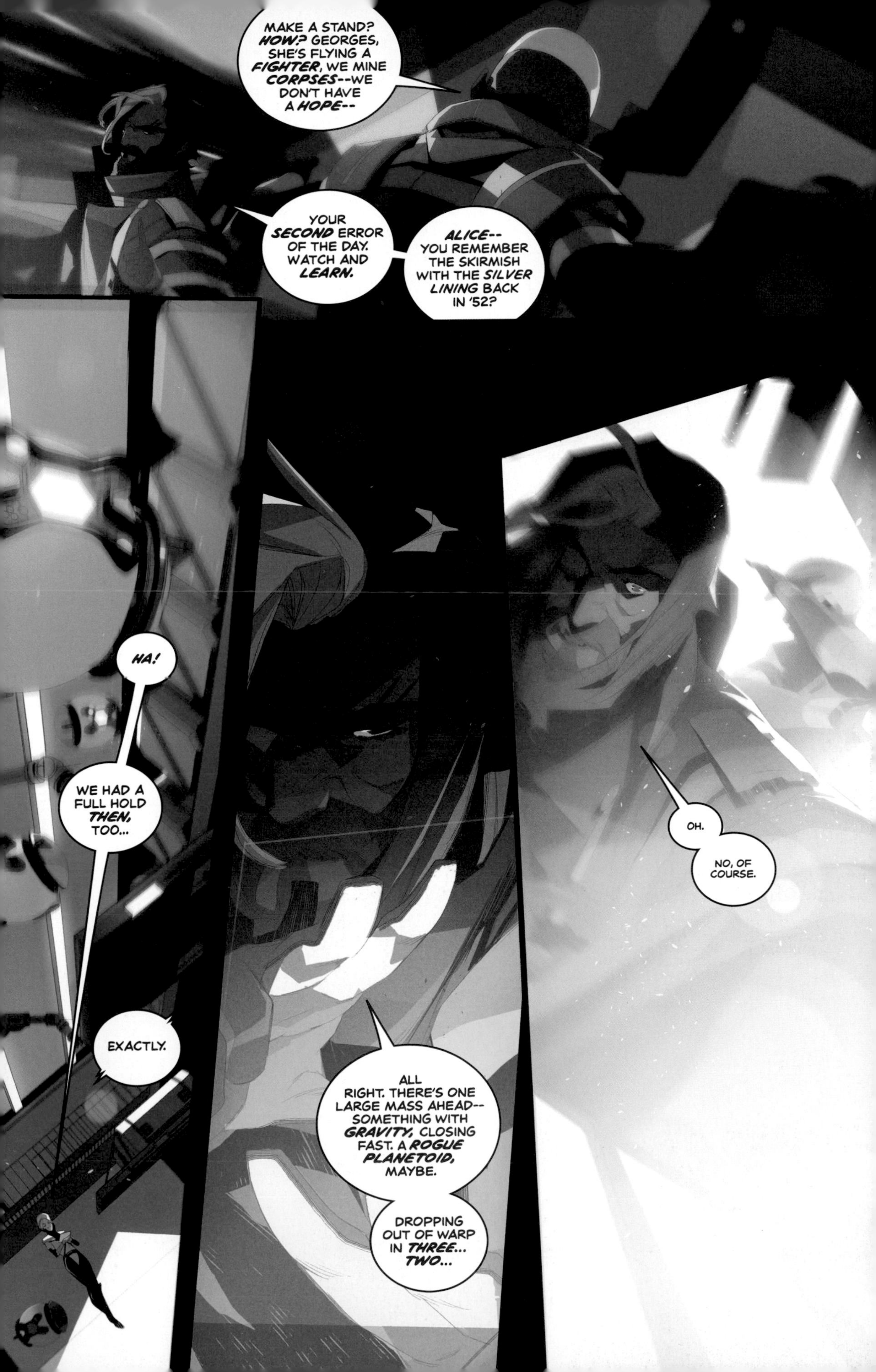
MAKE A STAND? HOW? GEORGES, SHE'S FLYING A FIGHTER, WE MINE CORPSES--WE DON'T HAVE A HOPE--
YOUR SECOND ERROR OF THE DAY. WATCH AND LEARN.
ALICE-- YOU REMEMBER THE SKIRMISH WITH THE SILVER LINING BACK IN '52?
HA!
WE HAD A FULL HOLD THEN, TOO...
OH.
NO, OF COURSE.
EXACTLY.
ALL RIGHT. THERE'S ONE LARGE MASS AHEAD-- SOMETHING WITH GRAVITY, CLOSING FAST. A ROGUE PLANETOID, MAYBE.
DROPPING OUT OF WARP IN THREE... TWO...

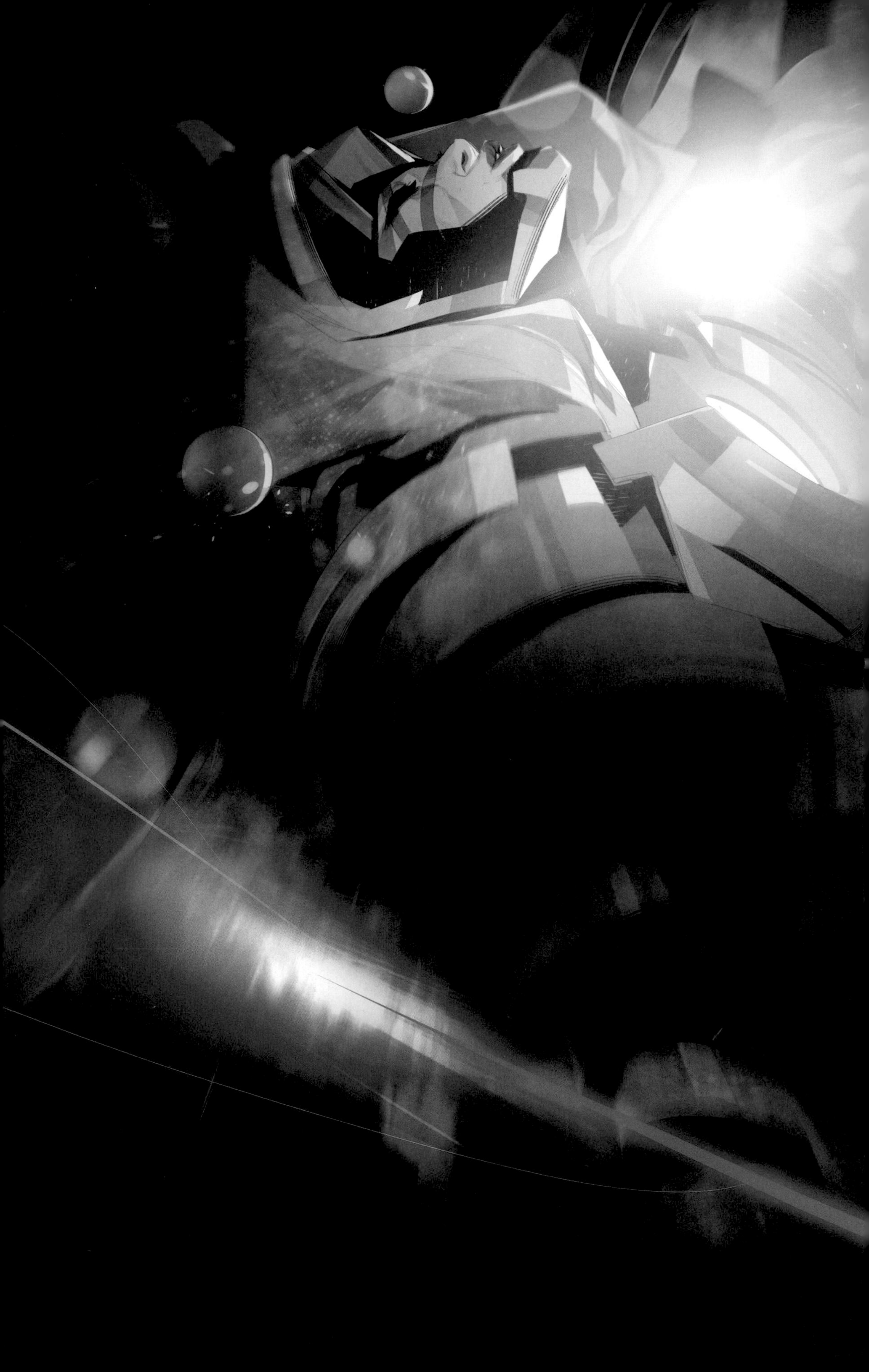

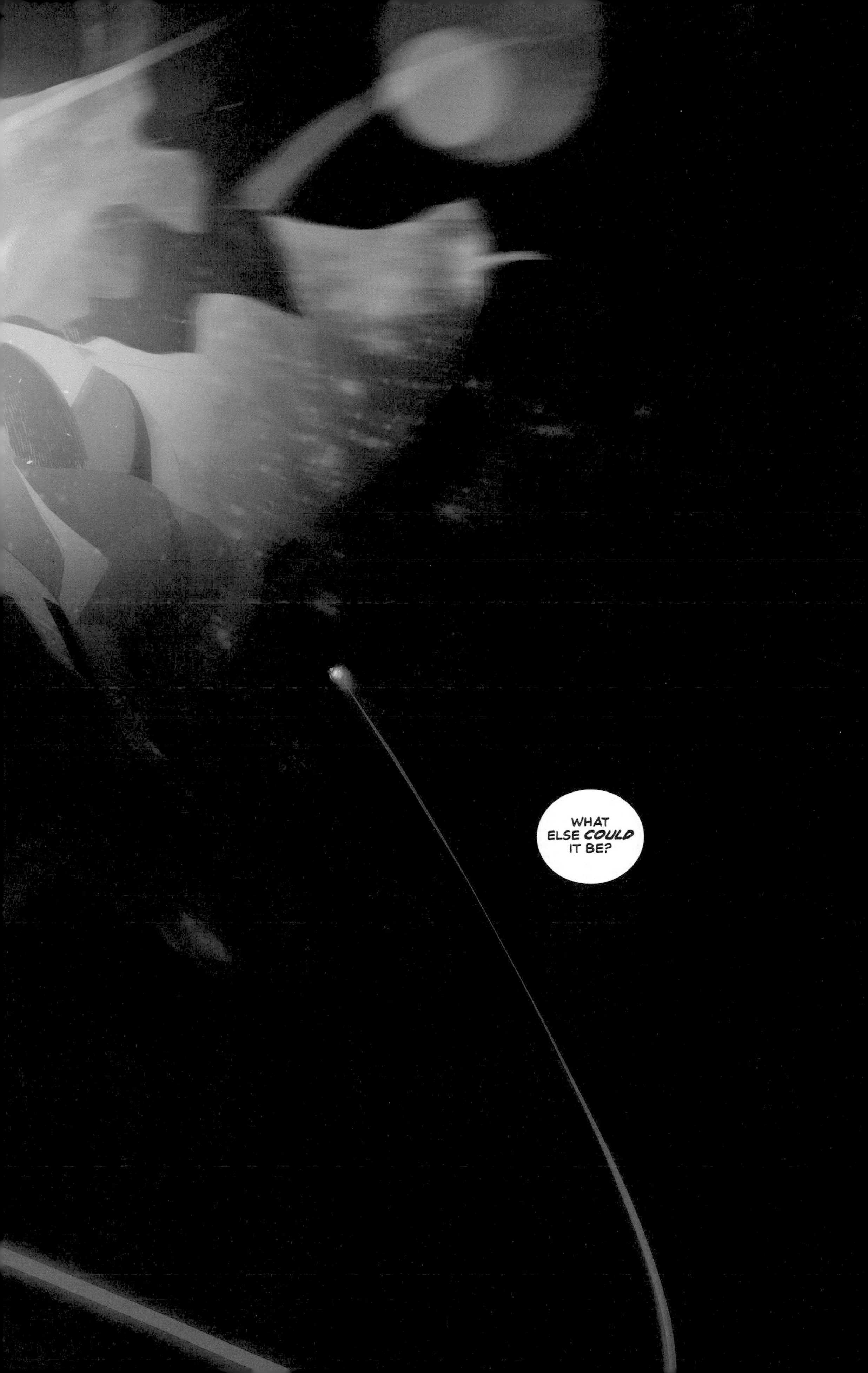
WHAT ELSE ***COULD*** IT BE?

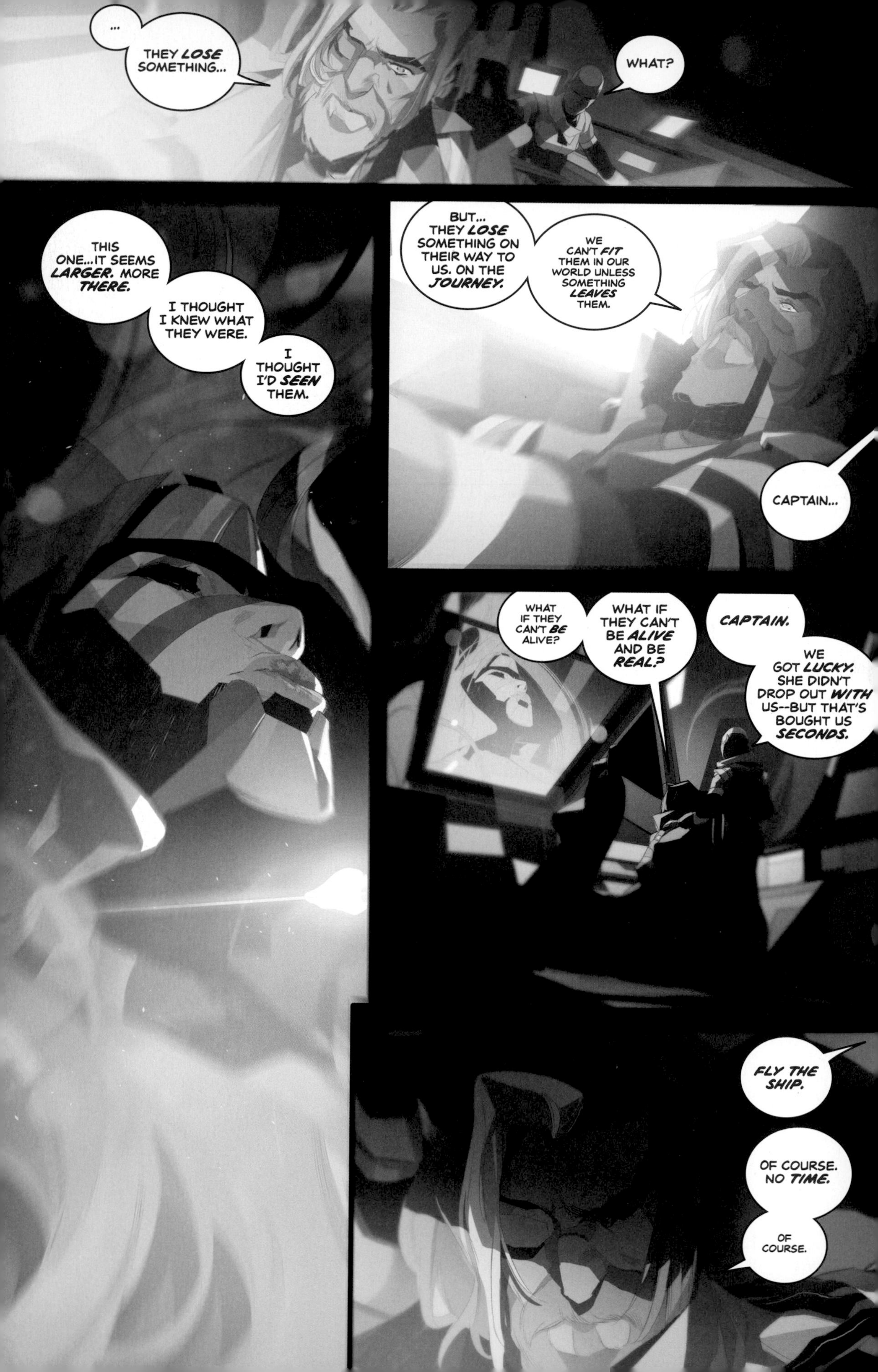
...
THEY LOSE SOMETHING...
WHAT?
THIS ONE...IT SEEMS LARGER. MORE THERE.
I THOUGHT I KNEW WHAT THEY WERE.
I THOUGHT I'D SEEN THEM.
BUT... THEY LOSE SOMETHING ON THEIR WAY TO US. ON THE JOURNEY.
WE CAN'T FIT THEM IN OUR WORLD UNLESS SOMETHING LEAVES THEM.
CAPTAIN...
WHAT IF THEY CAN'T BE ALIVE?
WHAT IF THEY CAN'T BE ALIVE AND BE REAL?
CAPTAIN.
WE GOT LUCKY. SHE DIDN'T DROP OUT WITH US--BUT THAT'S BOUGHT US SECONDS.
FLY THE SHIP.
OF COURSE. NO TIME.
OF COURSE.

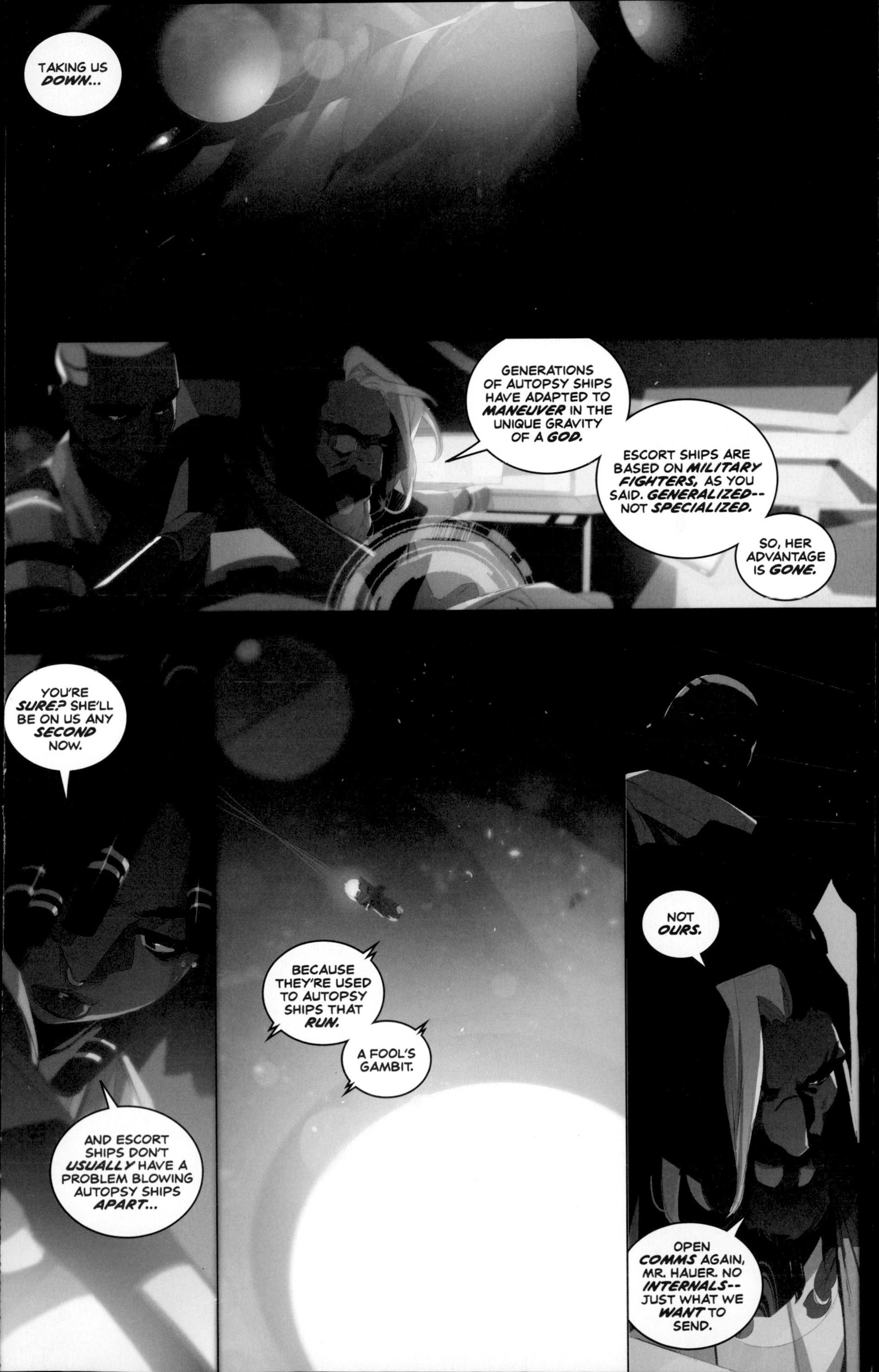
TAKING US DOWN...
GENERATIONS OF AUTOPSY SHIPS HAVE ADAPTED TO MANEUVER IN THE UNIQUE GRAVITY OF A GOD.
ESCORT SHIPS ARE BASED ON MILITARY FIGHTERS, AS YOU SAID. GENERALIZED-- NOT SPECIALIZED.
SO, HER ADVANTAGE IS GONE.
YOU'RE SURE? SHE'LL BE ON US ANY SECOND NOW.
AND ESCORT SHIPS DON'T USUALLY HAVE A PROBLEM BLOWING AUTOPSY SHIPS APART...
BECAUSE THEY'RE USED TO AUTOPSY SHIPS THAT RUN.
A FOOL'S GAMBIT.
NOT OURS.
OPEN COMMS AGAIN, MR. HAUER. NO INTERNALS-- JUST WHAT WE WANT TO SEND.

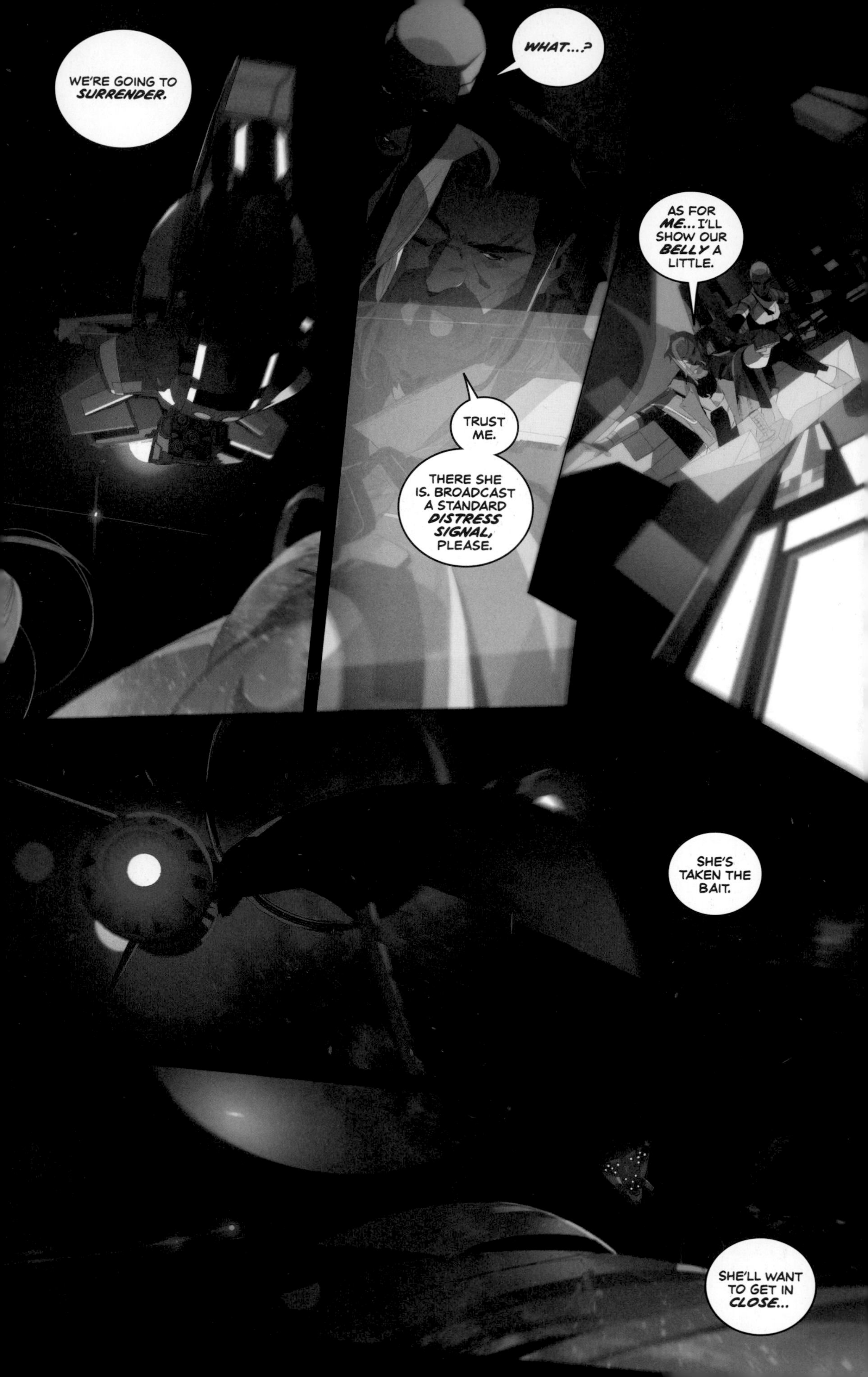
WE'RE GOING TO SURRENDER.
WHAT...?
AS FOR ME... I'LL SHOW OUR BELLY A LITTLE.
TRUST ME.
THERE SHE IS. BROADCAST A STANDARD DISTRESS SIGNAL, PLEASE.
SHE'S TAKEN THE BAIT.
SHE'LL WANT TO GET IN CLOSE...

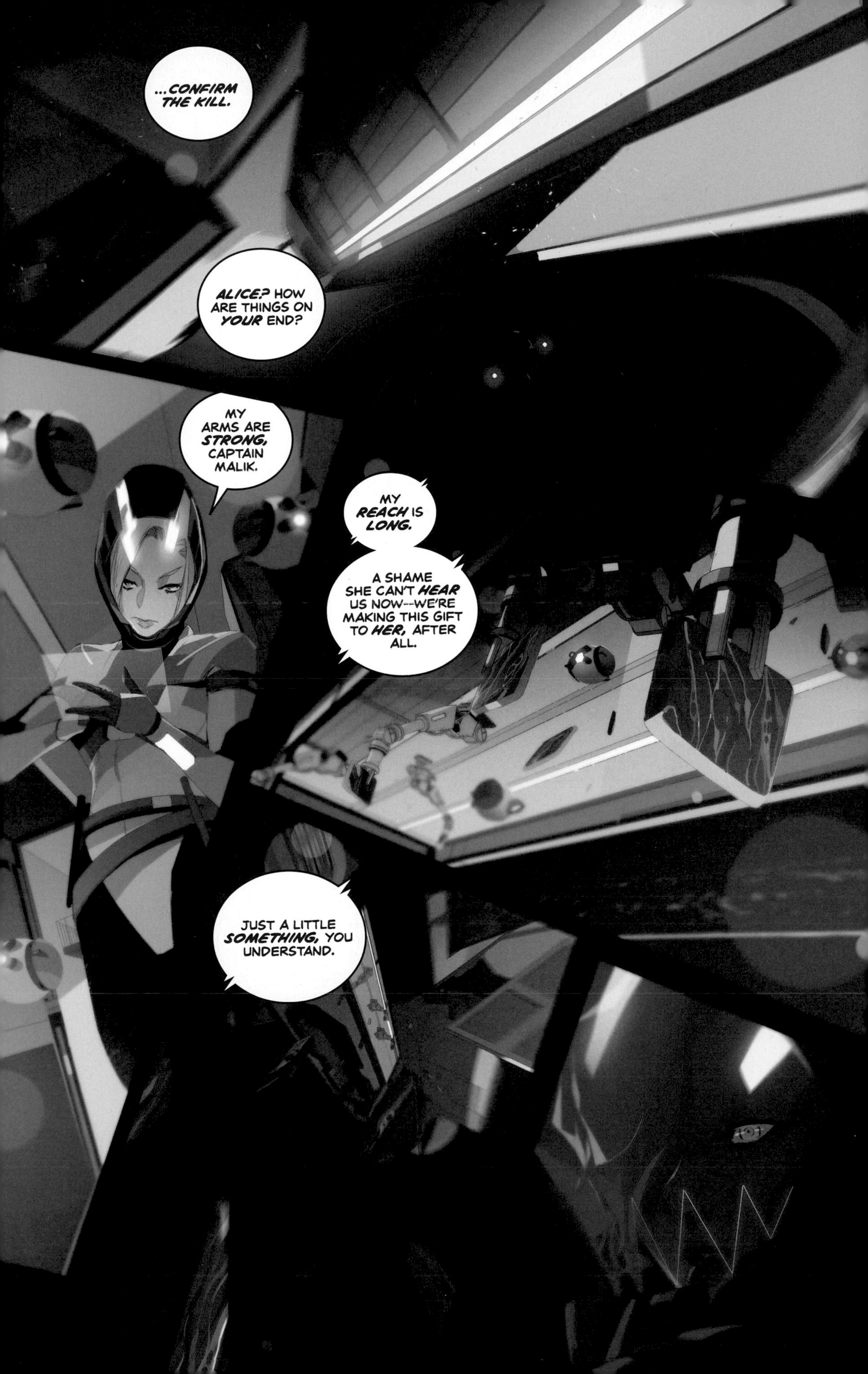
...CONFIRM THE KILL.
ALICE? HOW ARE THINGS ON YOUR END?
MY ARMS ARE STRONG, CAPTAIN MALIK.
MY REACH IS LONG.
A SHAME SHE CAN'T HEAR US NOW--WE'RE MAKING THIS GIFT TO HER, AFTER ALL.
JUST A LITTLE SOMETHING, YOU UNDERSTAND.

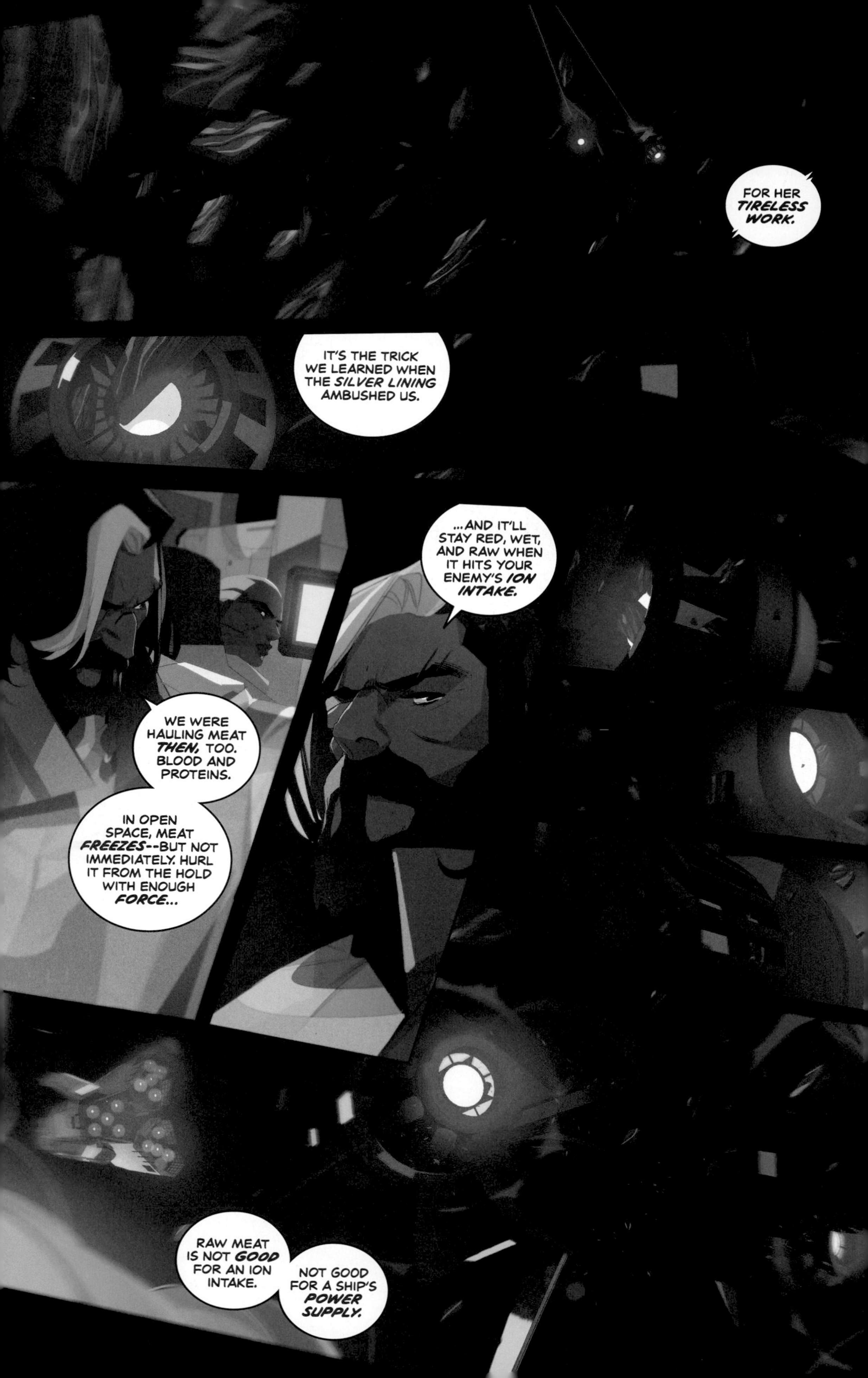

FOR HER TIRELESS WORK.
IT'S THE TRICK WE LEARNED WHEN THE SILVER LINING AMBUSHED US.
WE WERE HAULING MEAT THEN, TOO. BLOOD AND PROTEINS.
IN OPEN SPACE, MEAT FREEZES--BUT NOT IMMEDIATELY. HURL IT FROM THE HOLD WITH ENOUGH FORCE...
...AND IT'LL STAY RED, WET, AND RAW WHEN IT HITS YOUR ENEMY'S ION INTAKE.
RAW MEAT IS NOT GOOD FOR AN ION INTAKE.
NOT GOOD FOR A SHIP'S POWER SUPPLY.

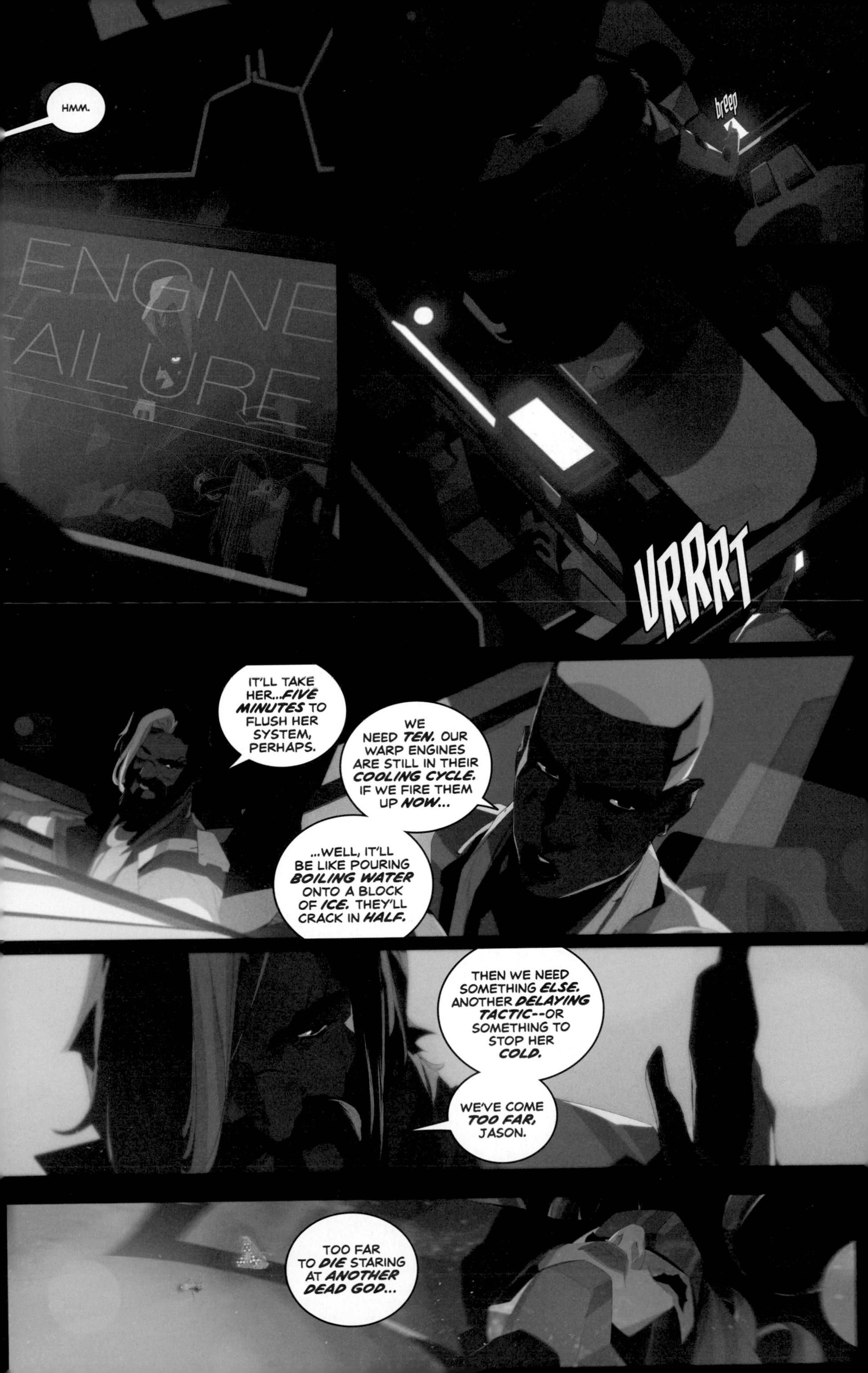
HMM.
breep
ENGINE FAILURE
VRRRT
IT'LL TAKE HER...FIVE MINUTES TO FLUSH HER SYSTEM, PERHAPS.
WE NEED TEN. OUR WARP ENGINES ARE STILL IN THEIR COOLING CYCLE. IF WE FIRE THEM UP NOW...
...WELL, IT'LL BE LIKE POURING BOILING WATER ONTO A BLOCK OF ICE. THEY'LL CRACK IN HALF.
THEN WE NEED SOMETHING ELSE. ANOTHER DELAYING TACTIC--OR SOMETHING TO STOP HER COLD.
WE'VE COME TOO FAR, JASON.
TOO FAR TO DIE STARING AT ANOTHER DEAD GOD...

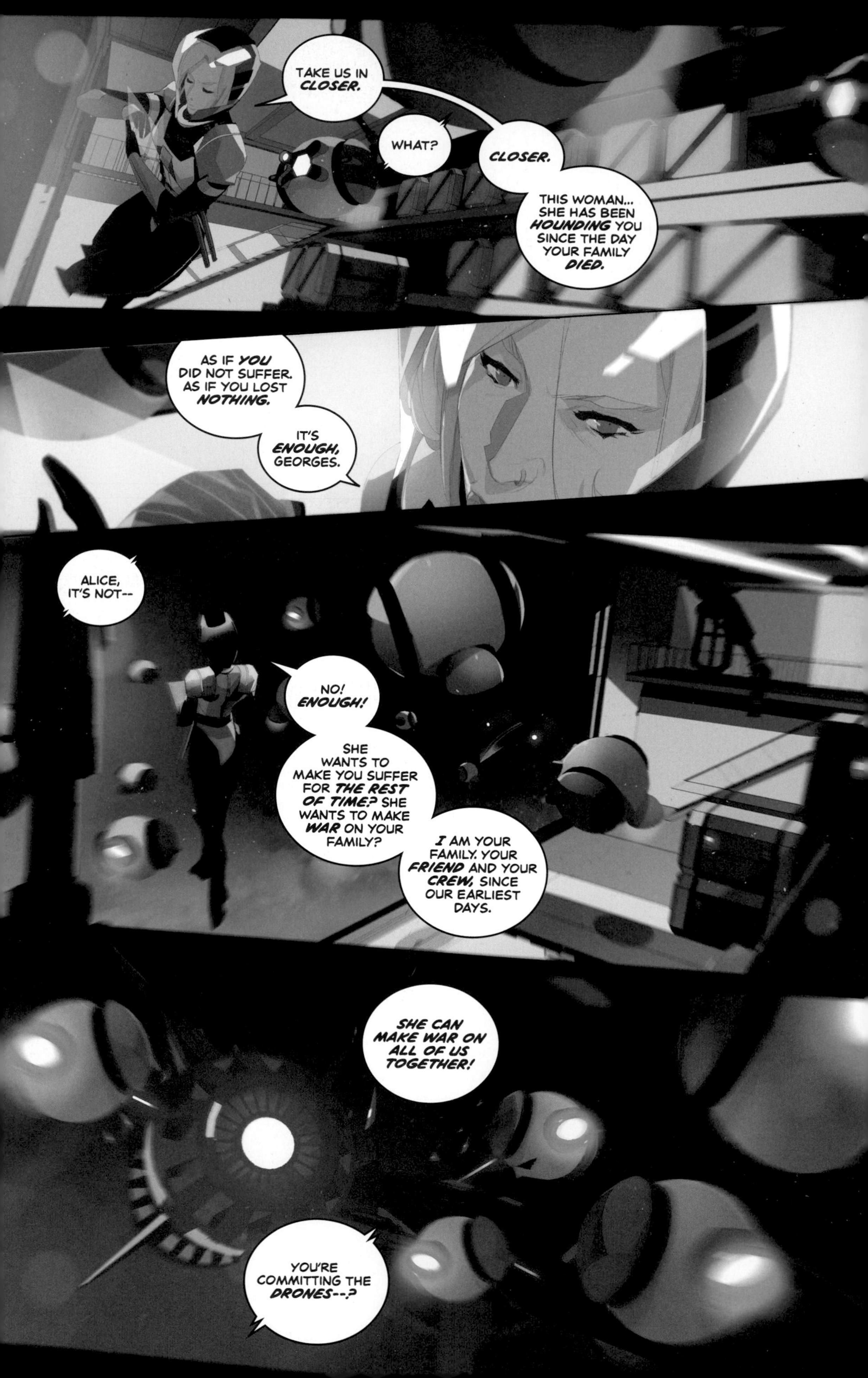
TAKE US IN CLOSER.
WHAT?
CLOSER.
THIS WOMAN... SHE HAS BEEN HOUNDING YOU SINCE THE DAY YOUR FAMILY DIED.
AS IF YOU DID NOT SUFFER. AS IF YOU LOST NOTHING.
IT'S ENOUGH, GEORGES.
ALICE, IT'S NOT--
NO! ENOUGH!
SHE WANTS TO MAKE YOU SUFFER FOR THE REST OF TIME? SHE WANTS TO MAKE WAR ON YOUR FAMILY?
I AM YOUR FAMILY. YOUR FRIEND AND YOUR CREW, SINCE OUR EARLIEST DAYS.
SHE CAN MAKE WAR ON ALL OF US TOGETHER!
YOU'RE COMMITTING THE DRONES--?

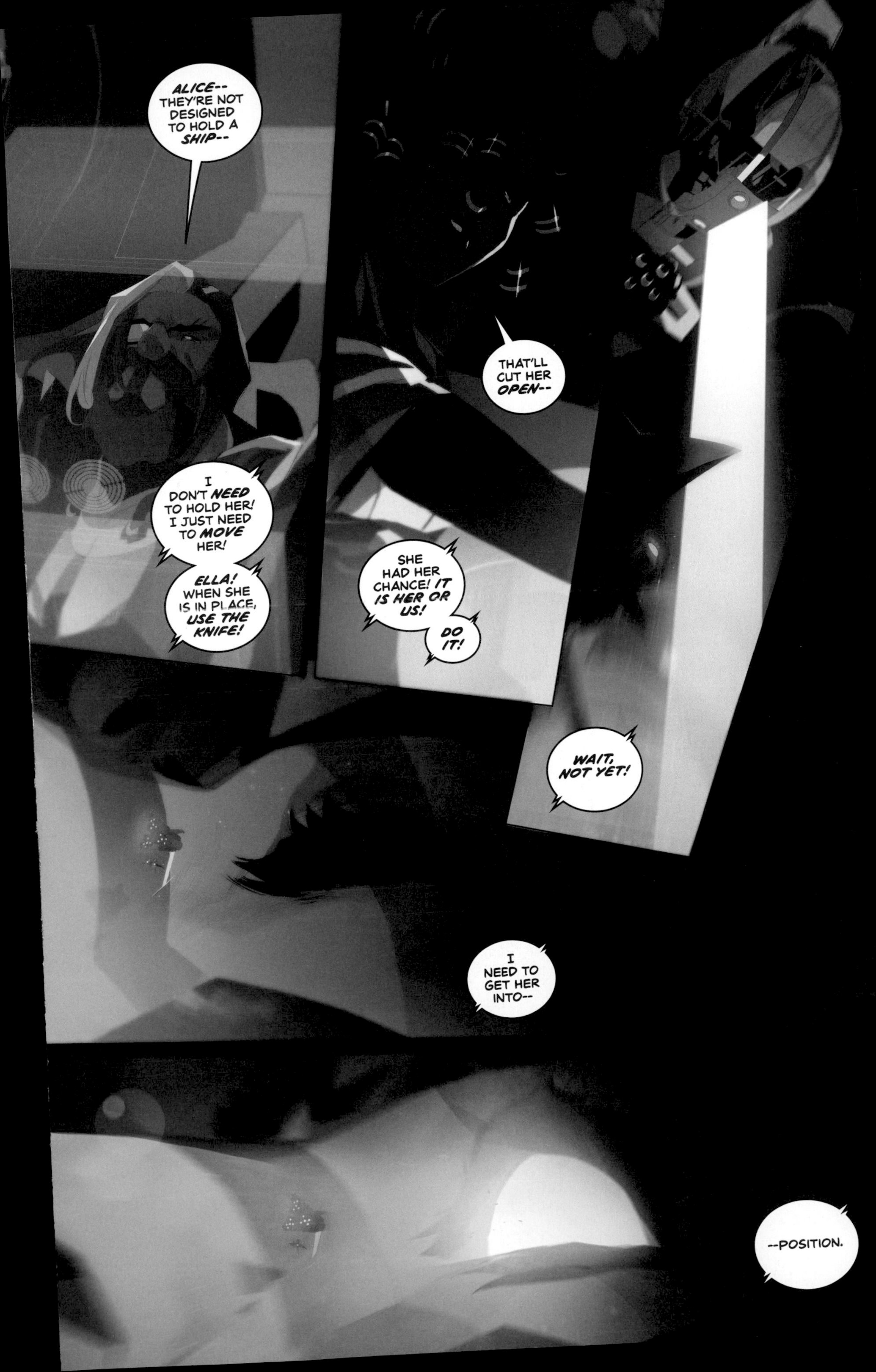
ALICE-- THEY'RE NOT DESIGNED TO HOLD A SHIP--
THAT'LL CUT HER OPEN--
I DON'T NEED TO HOLD HER! I JUST NEED TO MOVE HER!
ELLA! WHEN SHE IS IN PLACE, USE THE KNIFE!
SHE HAD HER CHANCE! IT IS HER OR US!
DO IT!
WAIT, NOT YET!
I NEED TO GET HER INTO--
--POSITION.

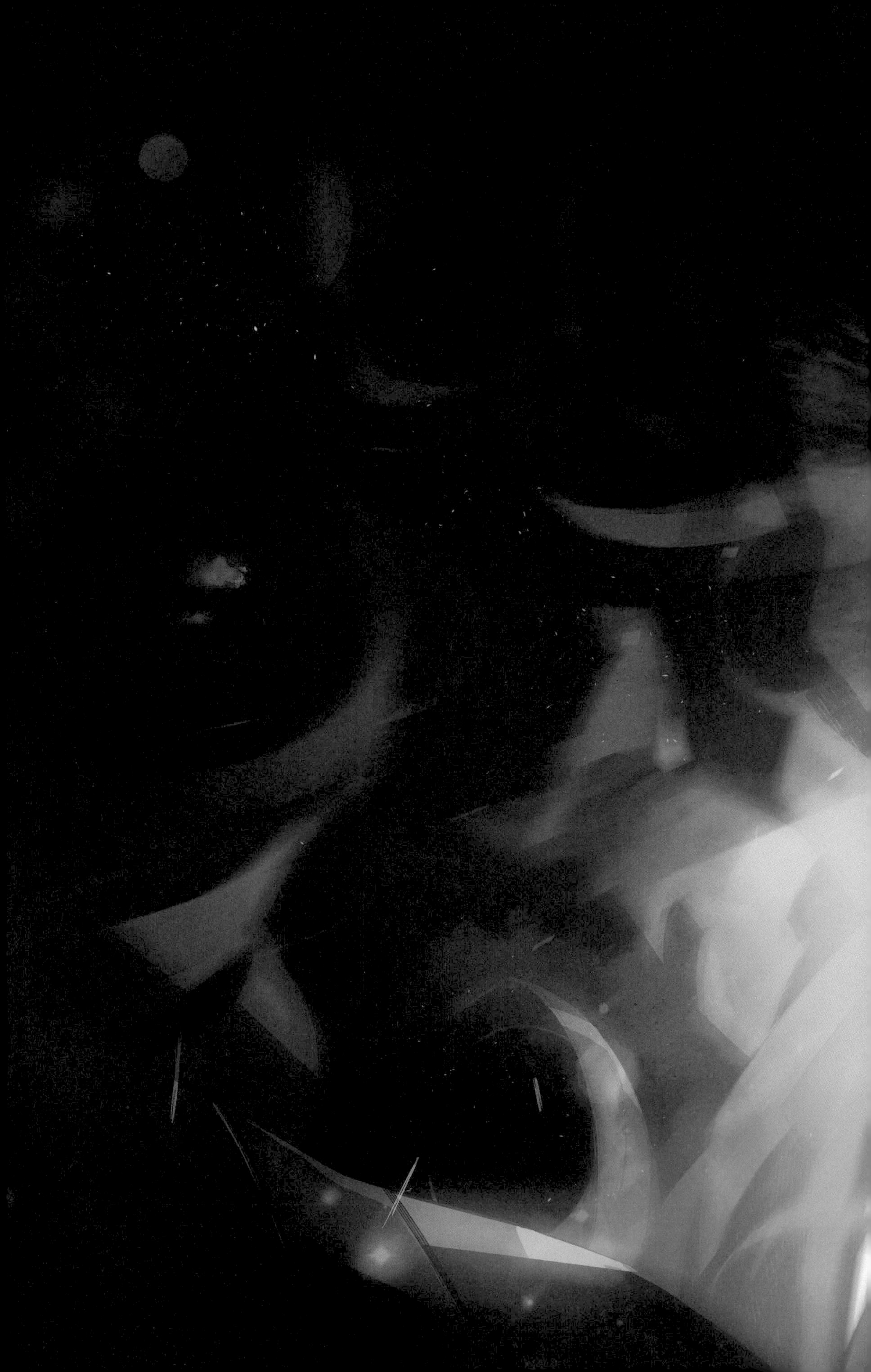

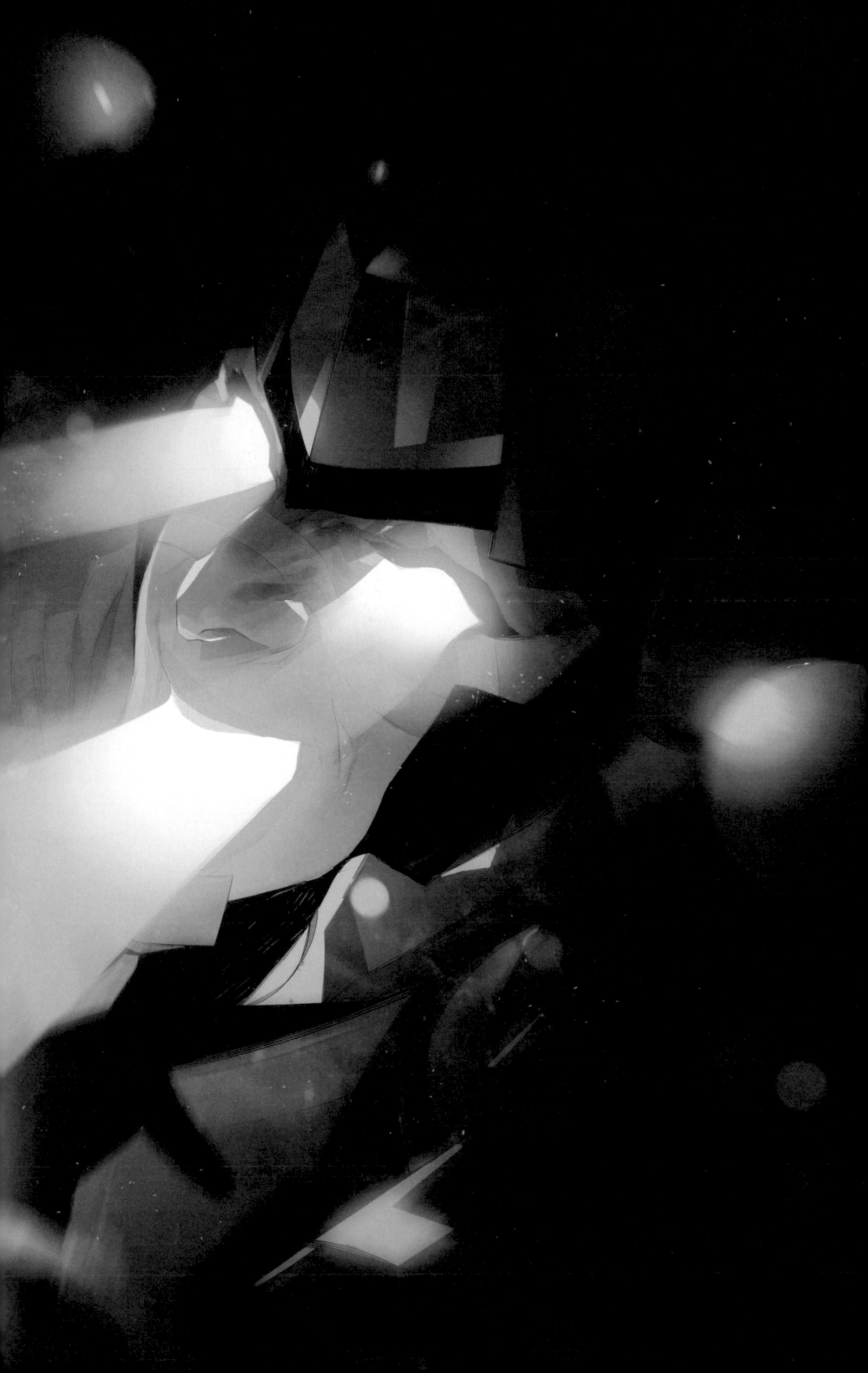

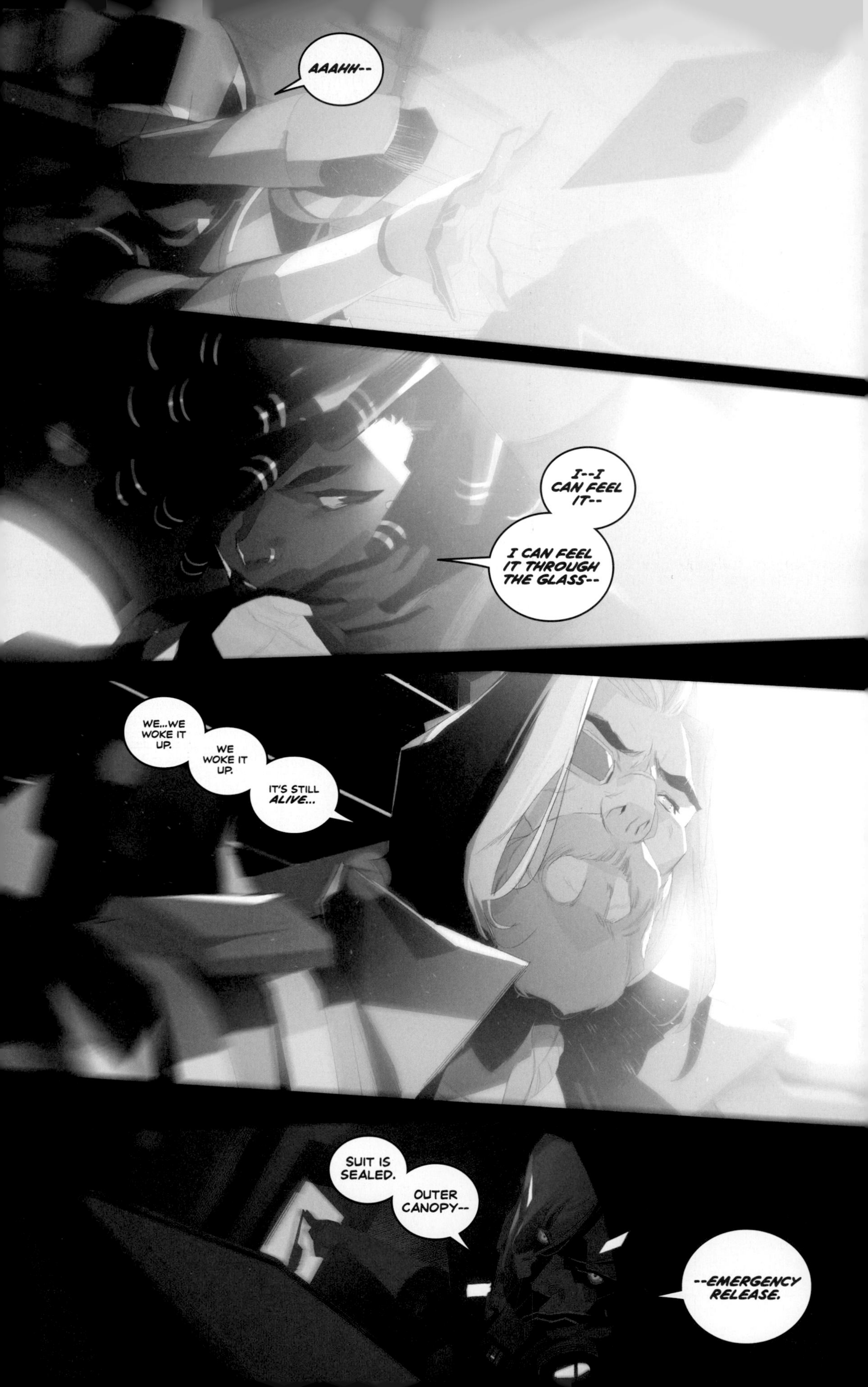
AAAHH--
I--I CAN FEEL IT--
I CAN FEEL IT THROUGH THE GLASS--
WE...WE WOKE IT UP.
WE WOKE IT UP.
IT'S STILL ALIVE...
SUIT IS SEALED.
OUTER CANOPY--
--EMERGENCY RELEASE.

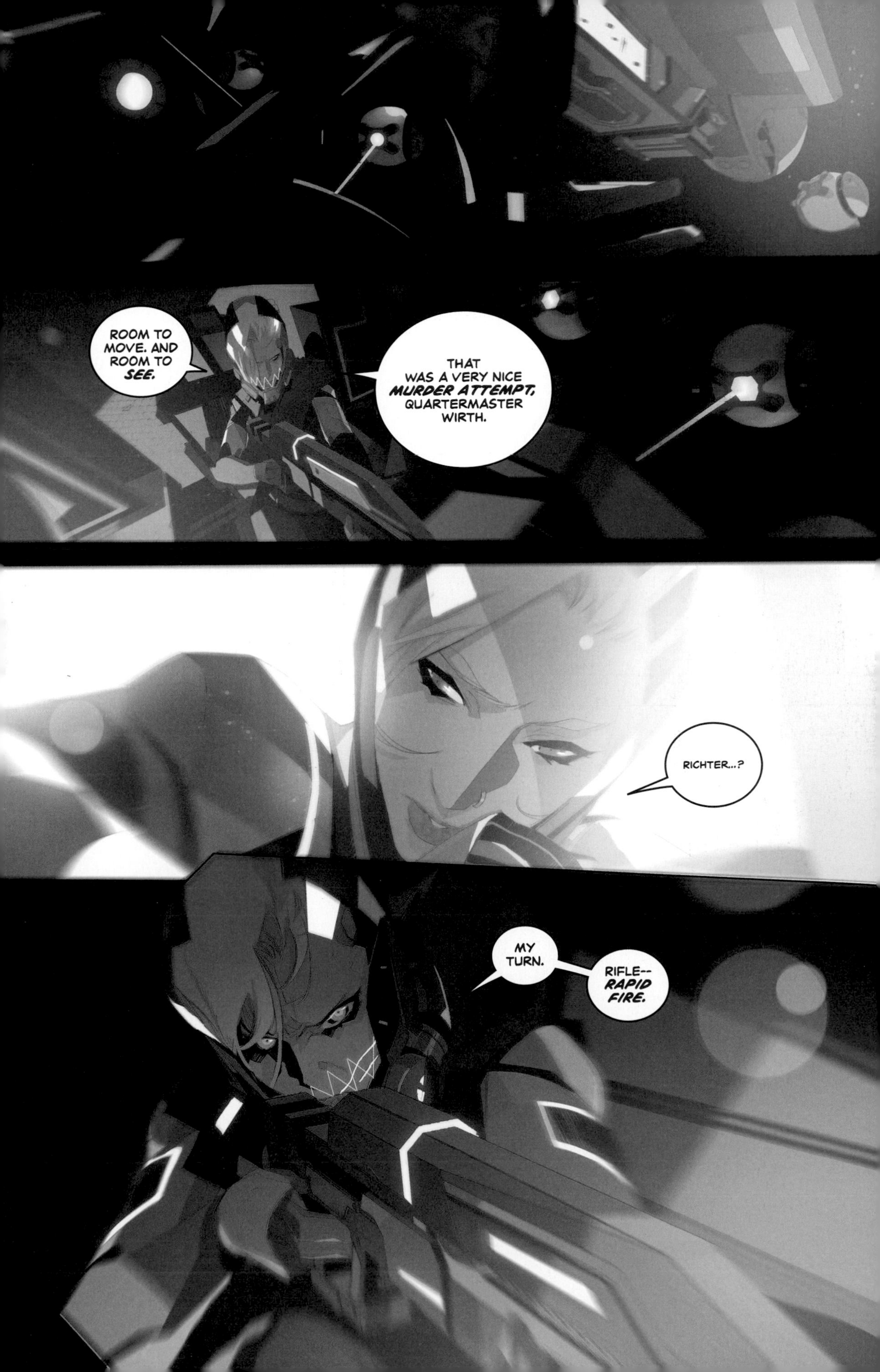
ROOM TO MOVE. AND ROOM TO SEE.
THAT WAS A VERY NICE MURDER ATTEMPT, QUARTERMASTER WIRTH.
RICHTER...?
MY TURN.
RIFLE-- RAPID FIRE.

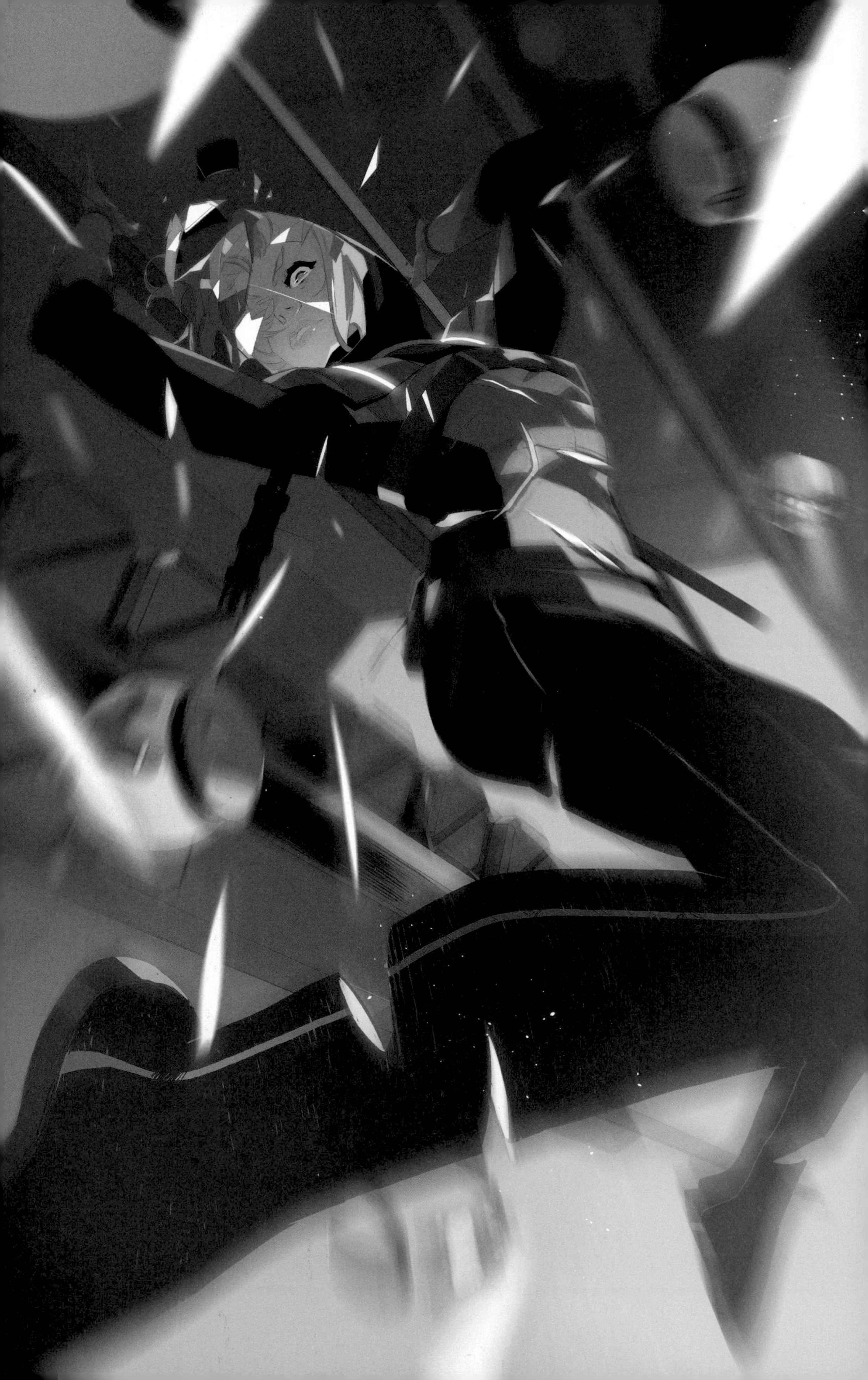

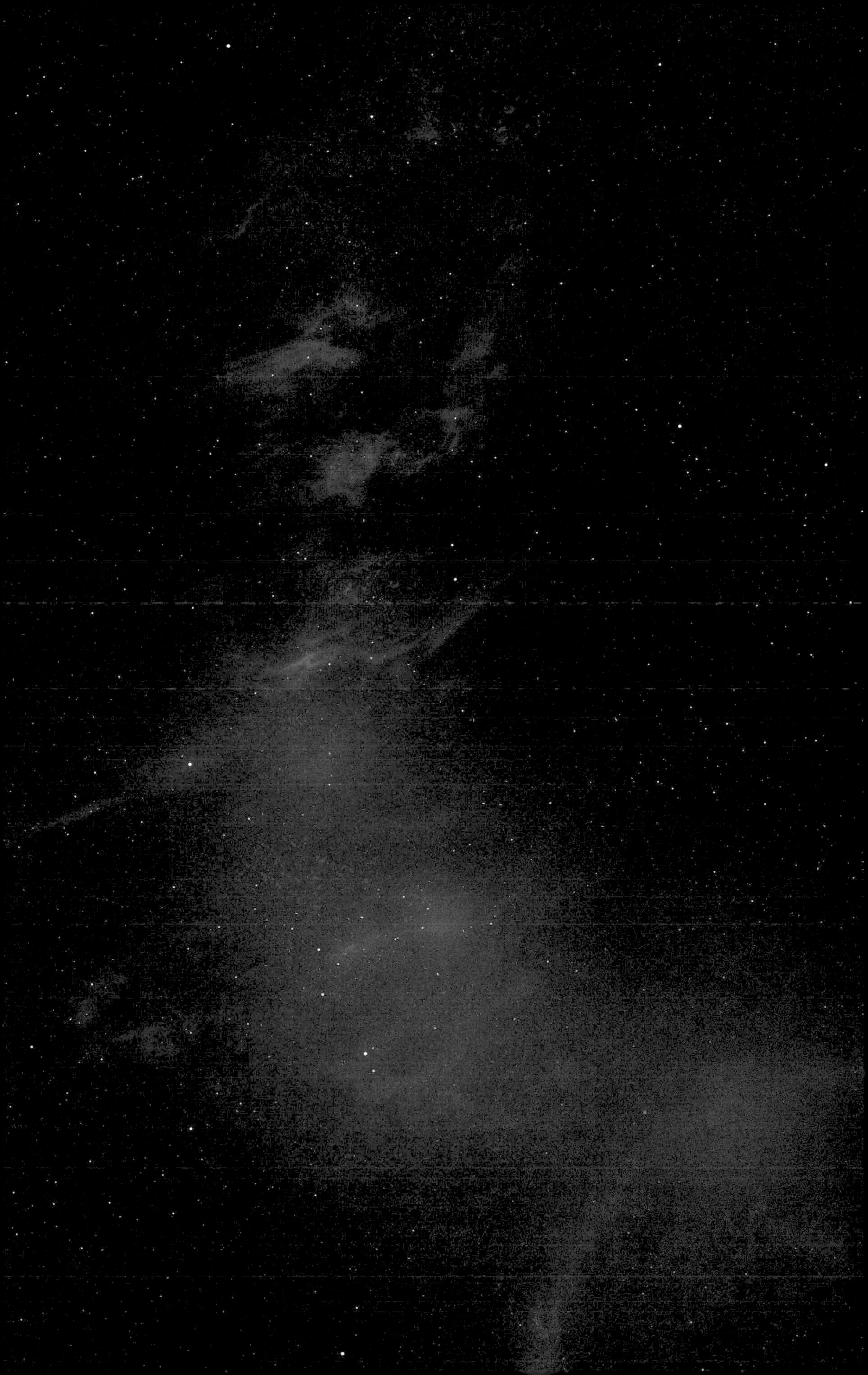

Chapter Four

The Glorious Quest

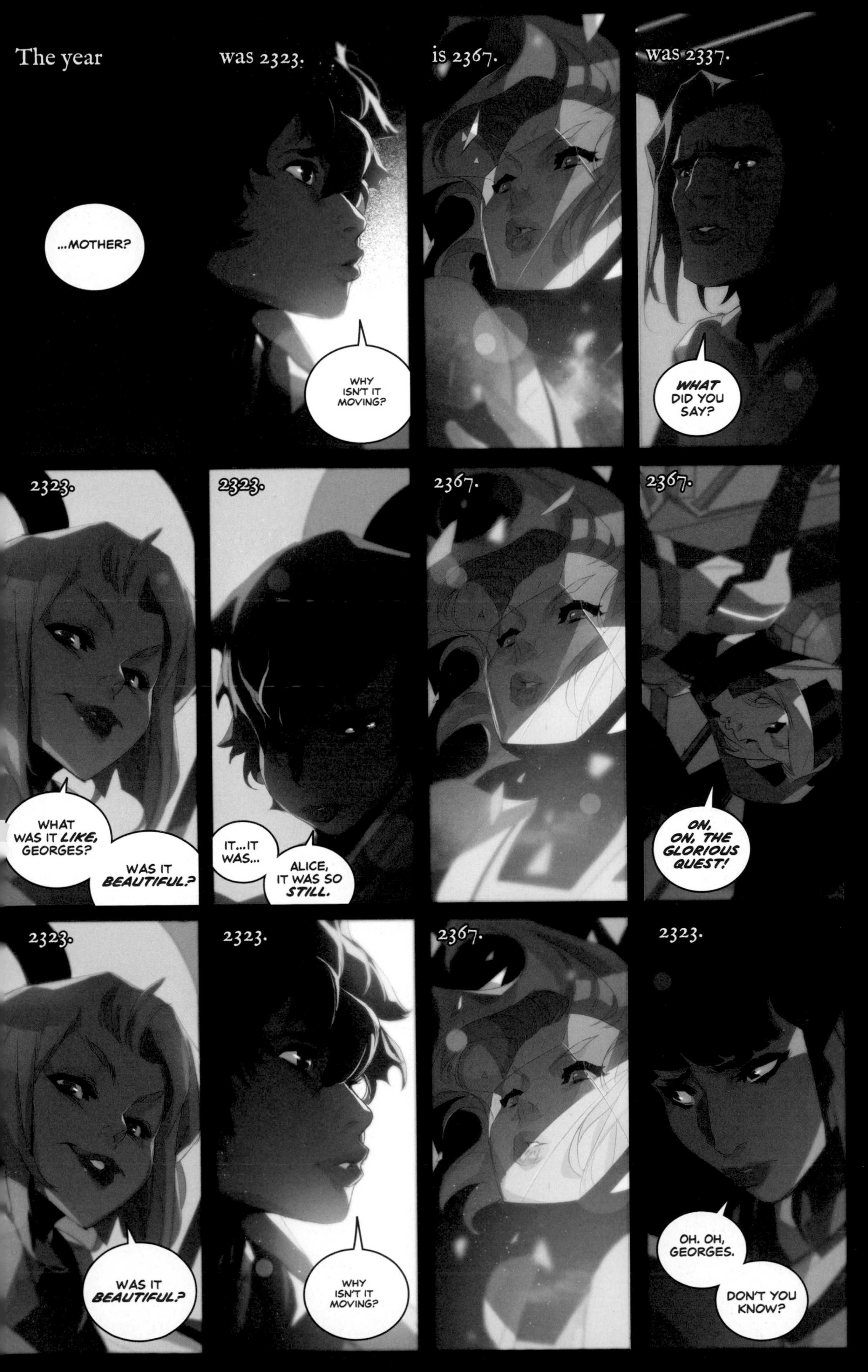

The year
...MOTHER?
was 2323.
WHY ISN'T IT MOVING?
is 2367.
was 2337.
WHAT DID YOU SAY?
2323.
WHAT WAS IT LIKE, GEORGES?
WAS IT BEAUTIFUL?
2323.
IT...IT WAS...
ALICE, IT WAS SO STILL.
2367.
2367.
ON, ON, THE GLORIOUS QUEST!
2323.
WAS IT BEAUTIFUL?
2323.
WHY ISN'T IT MOVING?
2367.
2323.
OH. OH, GEORGES.
DON'T YOU KNOW?

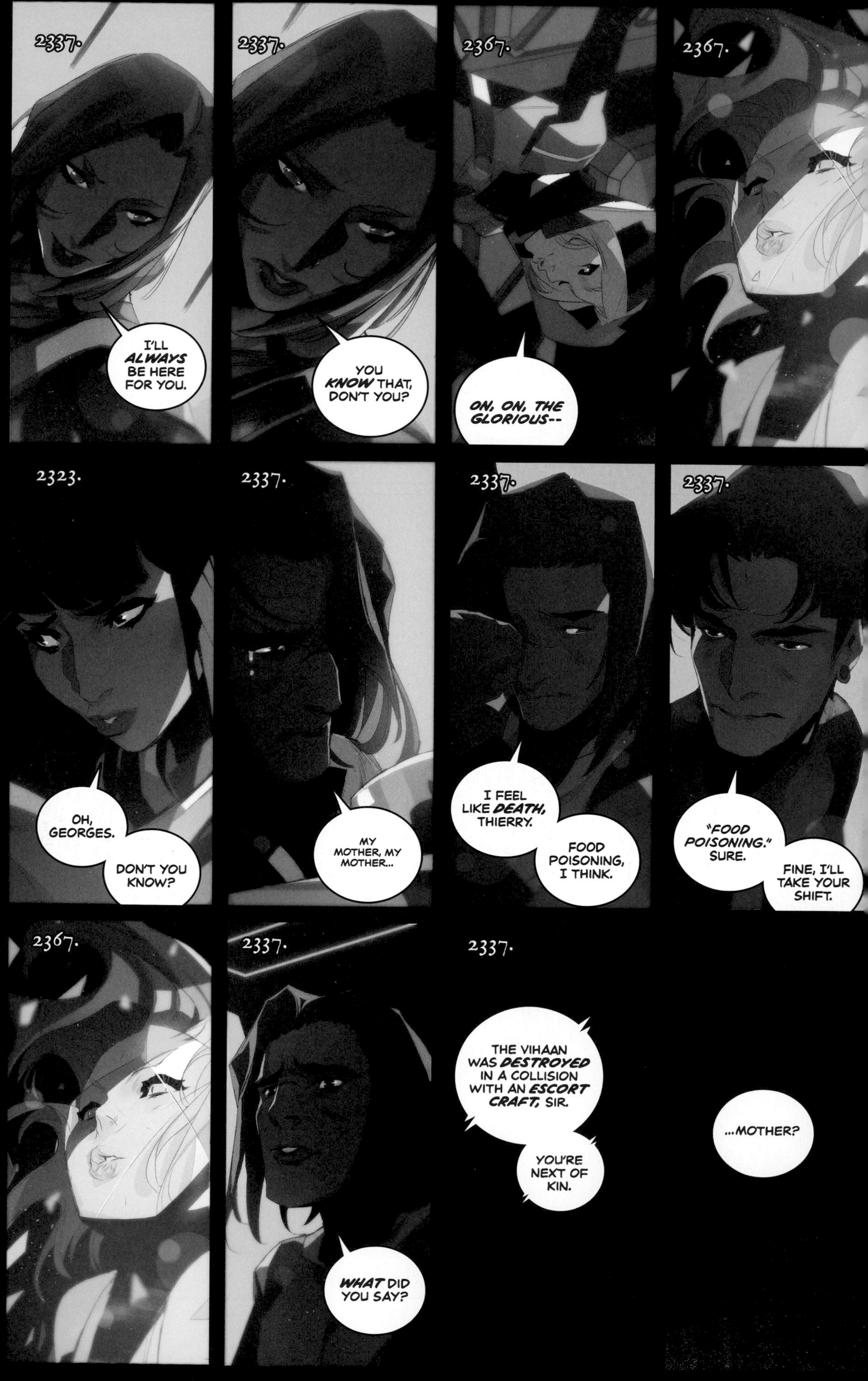
2337.
2337.
2367.
2367.
I'LL ALWAYS BE HERE FOR YOU.
YOU KNOW THAT, DON'T YOU?
ON, ON, THE GLORIOUS--
2323.
2337.
2337.
2337.
OH, GEORGES.
DON'T YOU KNOW?
MY MOTHER, MY MOTHER...
I FEEL LIKE DEATH, THIERRY.
FOOD POISONING, I THINK.
"FOOD POISONING." SURE.
FINE, I'LL TAKE YOUR SHIFT.
2367.
2337.
2337.
WHAT DID YOU SAY?
THE VIHAAN WAS DESTROYED IN A COLLISION WITH AN ESCORT CRAFT, SIR.
YOU'RE NEXT OF KIN.
...MOTHER?

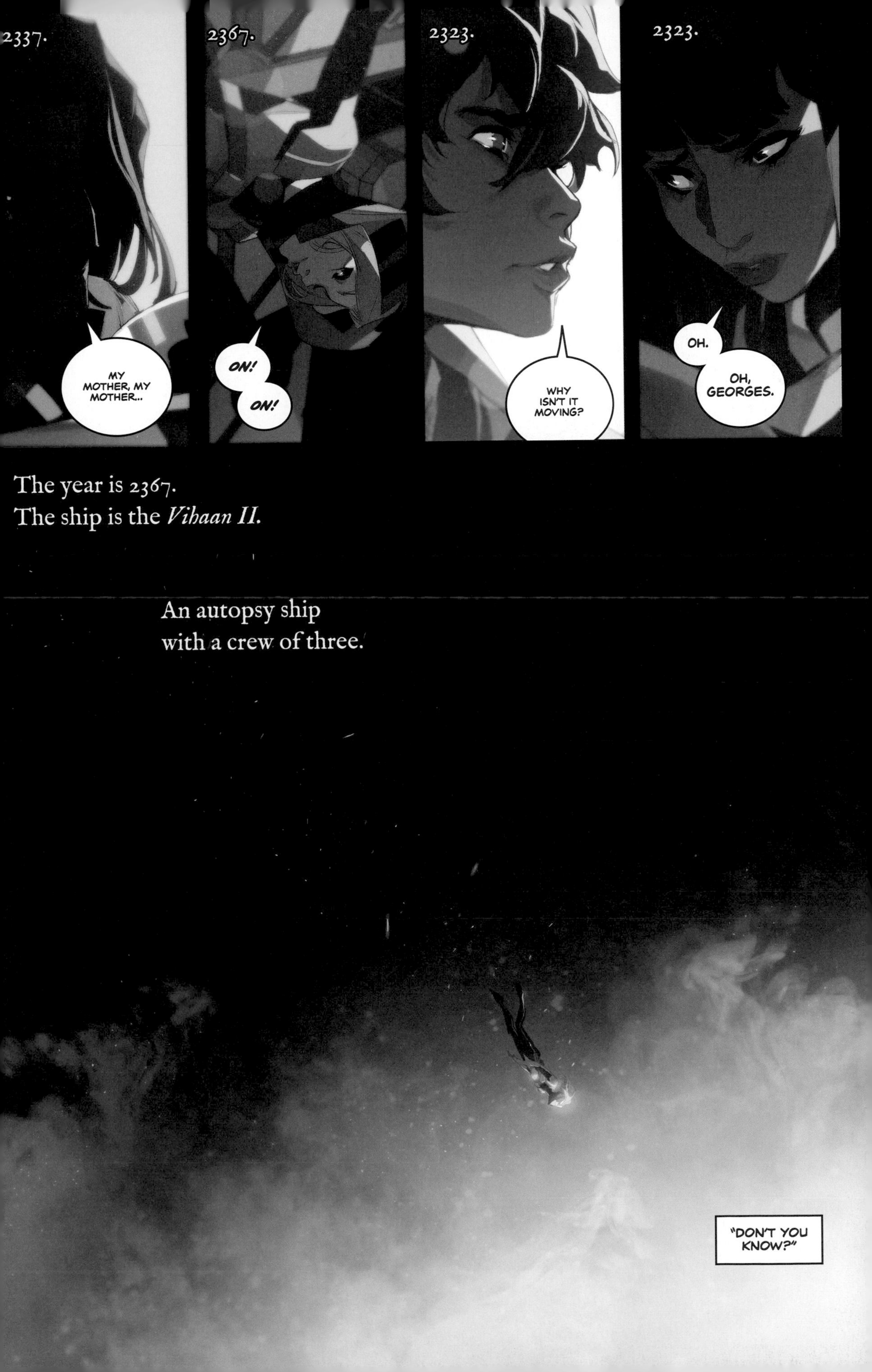

2337.
MY MOTHER, MY MOTHER...
2367.
ON!
ON!
2323.
WHY ISN'T IT MOVING?
2323.
OH.
OH, GEORGES.
The year is 2367.
The ship is the *Vihaan II.*
An autopsy ship
with a crew of three.
"DON'T YOU KNOW?"

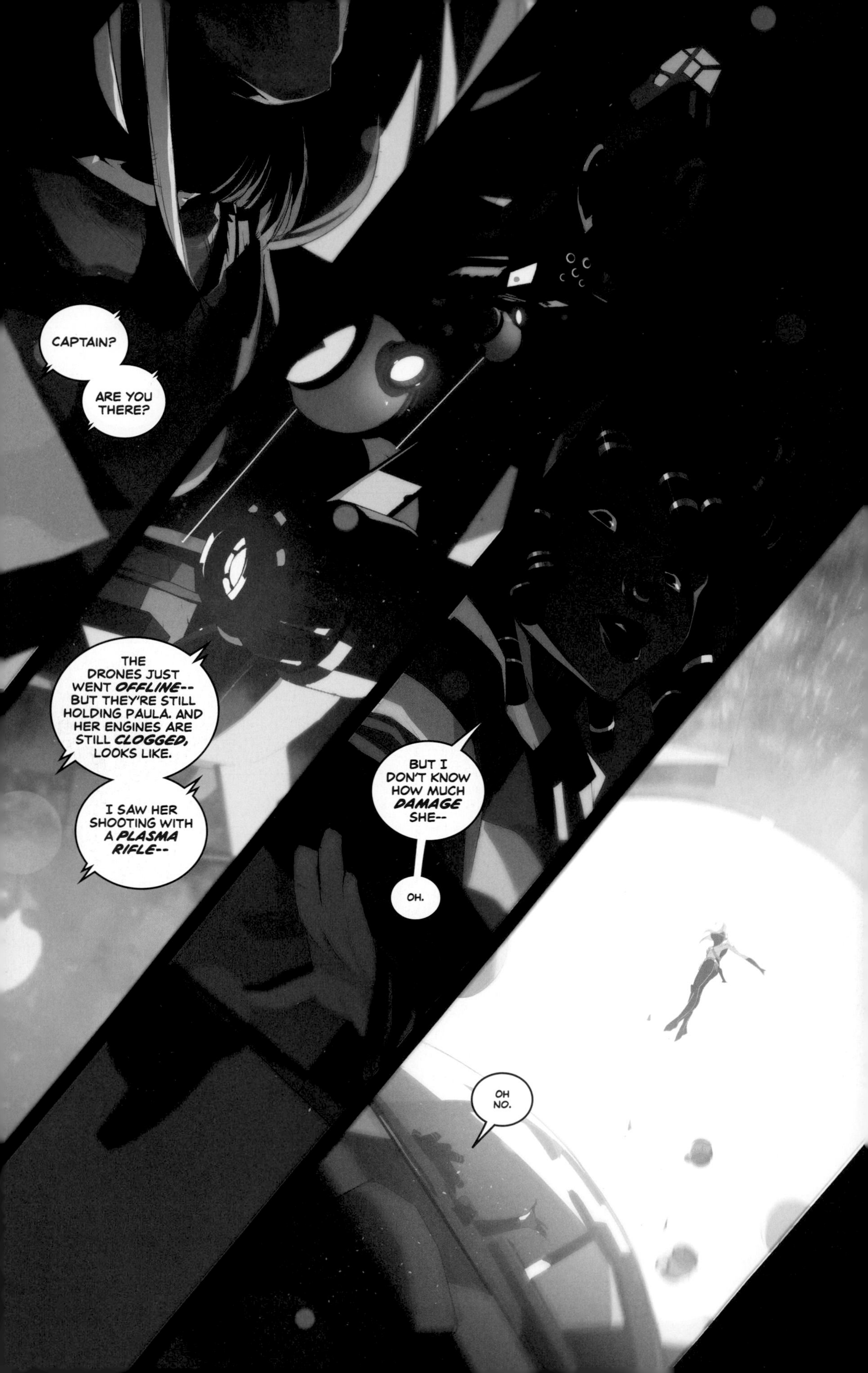
CAPTAIN?
ARE YOU THERE?
THE DRONES JUST WENT OFFLINE-- BUT THEY'RE STILL HOLDING PAULA. AND HER ENGINES ARE STILL CLOGGED, LOOKS LIKE.
I SAW HER SHOOTING WITH A PLASMA RIFLE--
BUT I DON'T KNOW HOW MUCH DAMAGE SHE--
OH.
OH NO.

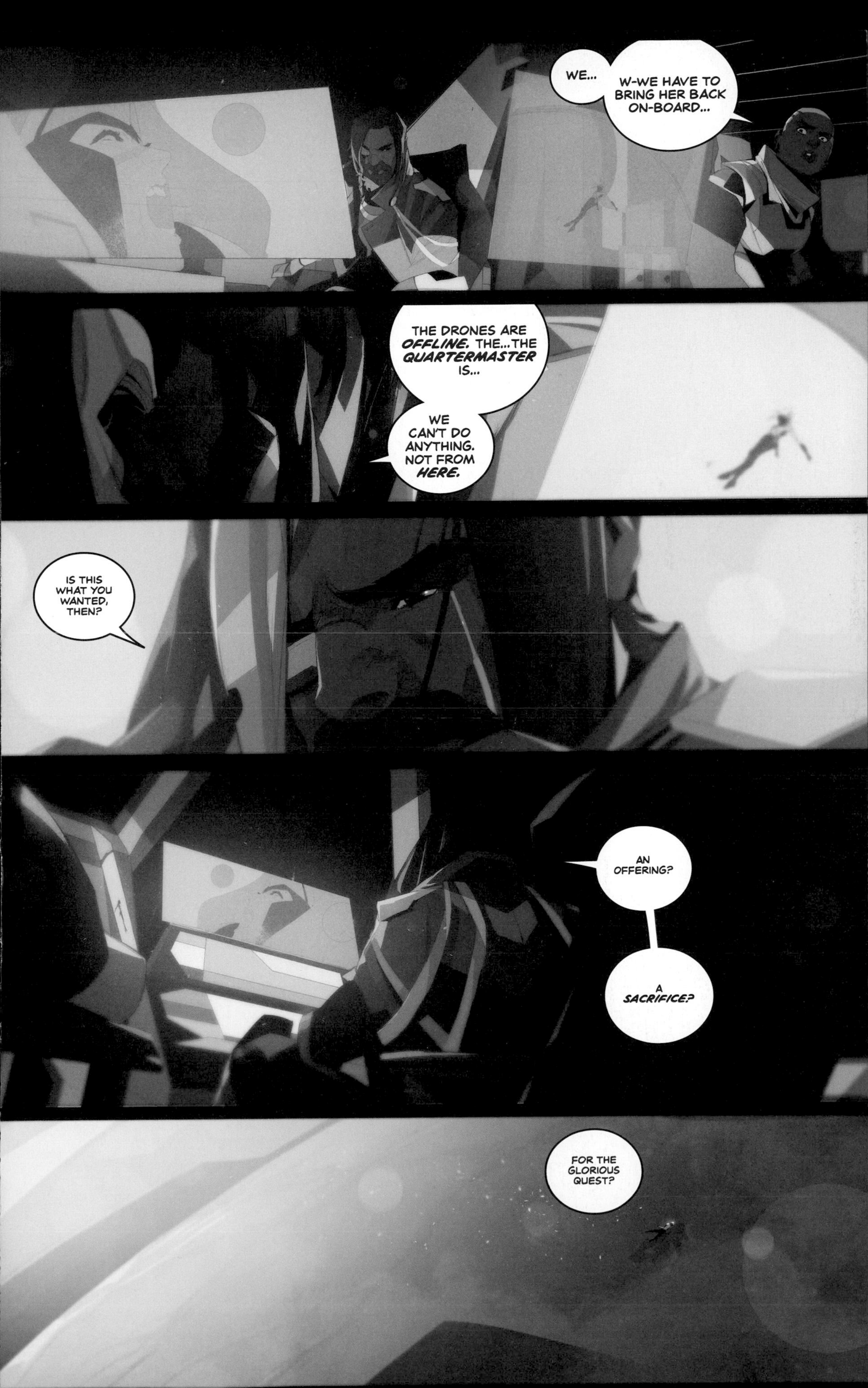
WE...
W-WE HAVE TO BRING HER BACK ON-BOARD...
THE DRONES ARE *OFFLINE.* THE...THE *QUARTERMASTER* IS...
WE CAN'T DO ANYTHING. NOT FROM *HERE.*
IS THIS WHAT YOU WANTED, THEN?
AN OFFERING?
A *SACRIFICE?*
FOR THE GLORIOUS QUEST?

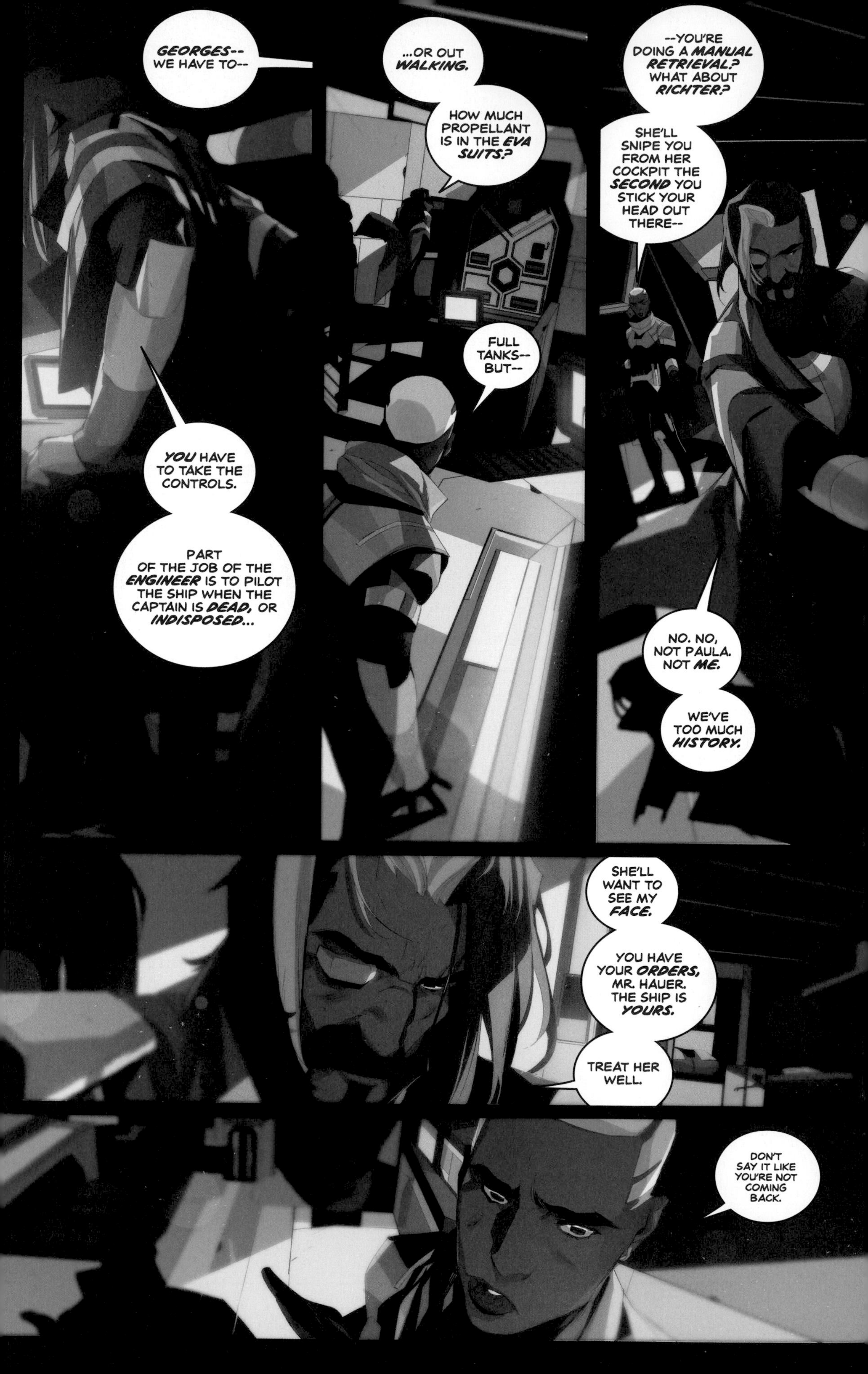
GEORGES-- WE HAVE TO--
YOU HAVE TO TAKE THE CONTROLS.
PART OF THE JOB OF THE ENGINEER IS TO PILOT THE SHIP WHEN THE CAPTAIN IS DEAD, OR INDISPOSED...
...OR OUT WALKING.
HOW MUCH PROPELLANT IS IN THE EVA SUITS?
FULL TANKS-- BUT--
--YOU'RE DOING A MANUAL RETRIEVAL? WHAT ABOUT RICHTER?
SHE'LL SNIPE YOU FROM HER COCKPIT THE SECOND YOU STICK YOUR HEAD OUT THERE--
NO. NO, NOT PAULA. NOT ME.
WE'VE TOO MUCH HISTORY.
SHE'LL WANT TO SEE MY FACE.
YOU HAVE YOUR ORDERS, MR. HAUER. THE SHIP IS YOURS.
TREAT HER WELL.
DON'T SAY IT LIKE YOU'RE NOT COMING BACK.

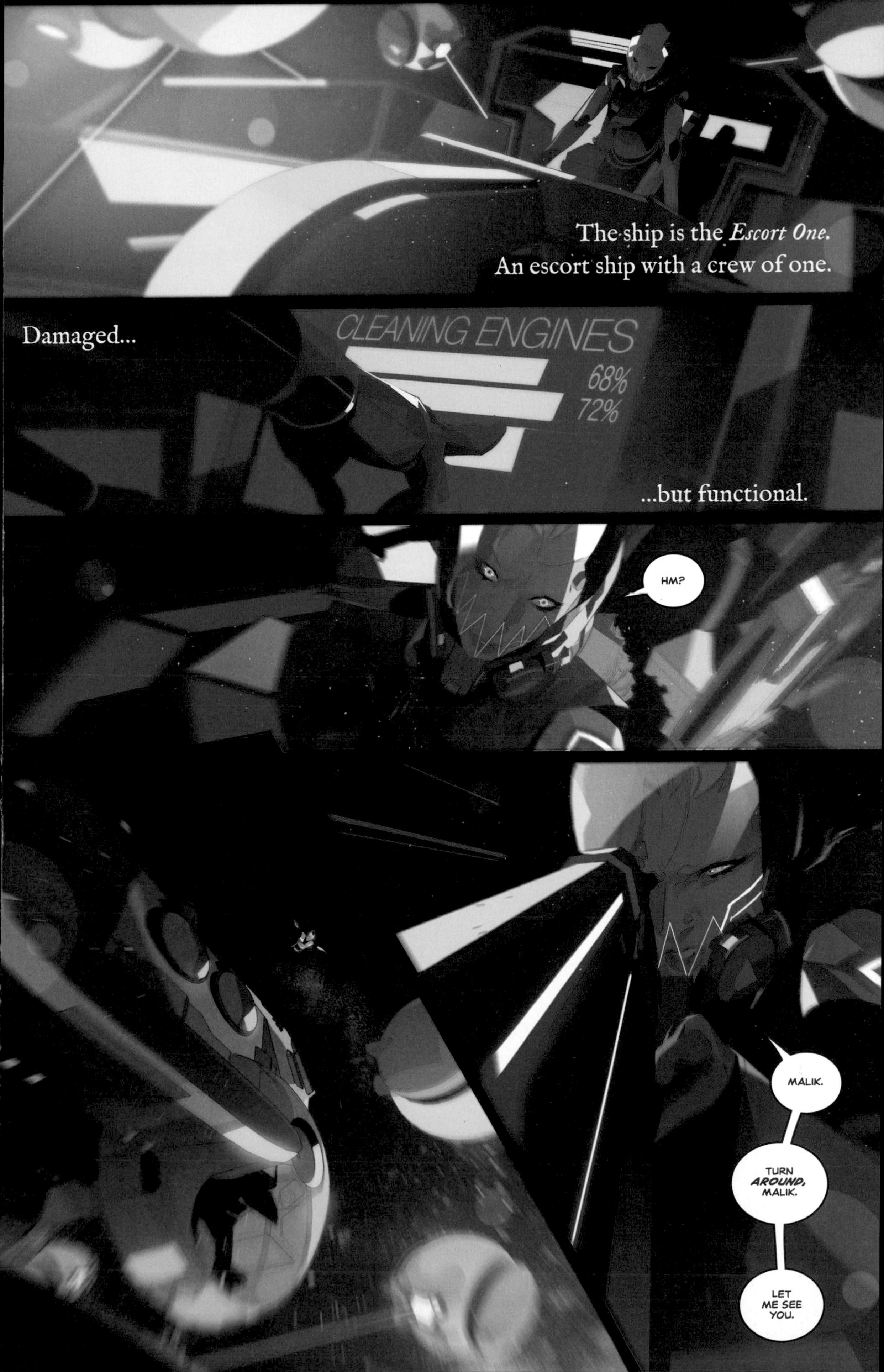
The ship is the *Escort One*.
An escort ship with a crew of one.
Damaged...
CLEANING ENGINES
68%
72%
...but functional.
HM?
MALIK.
TURN ***AROUND***, MALIK.
LET ME SEE YOU.

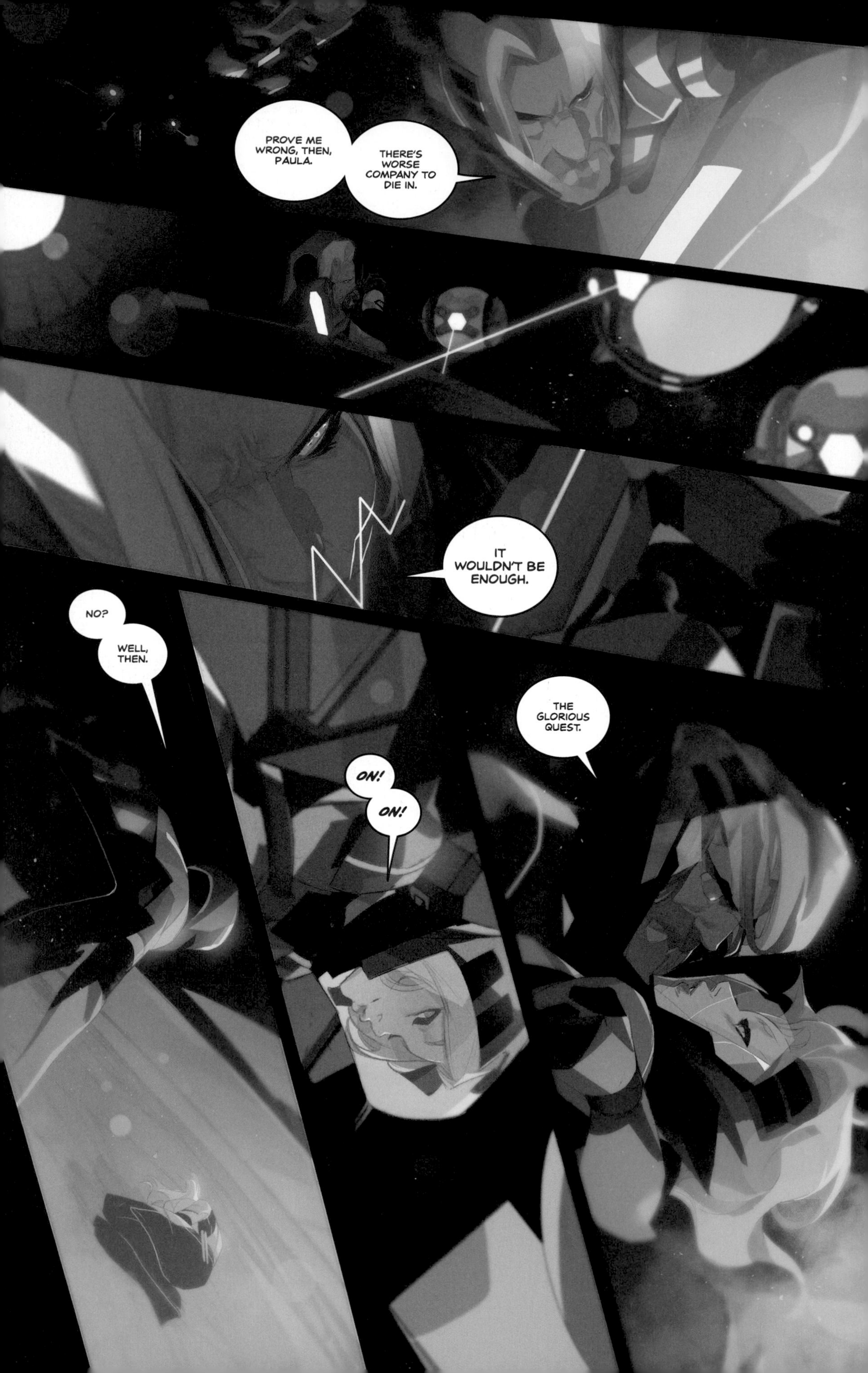
PROVE ME WRONG, THEN, PAULA.
THERE'S WORSE COMPANY TO DIE IN.
IT WOULDN'T BE ENOUGH.
NO?
WELL, THEN.
ON!
ON!
THE GLORIOUS QUEST.

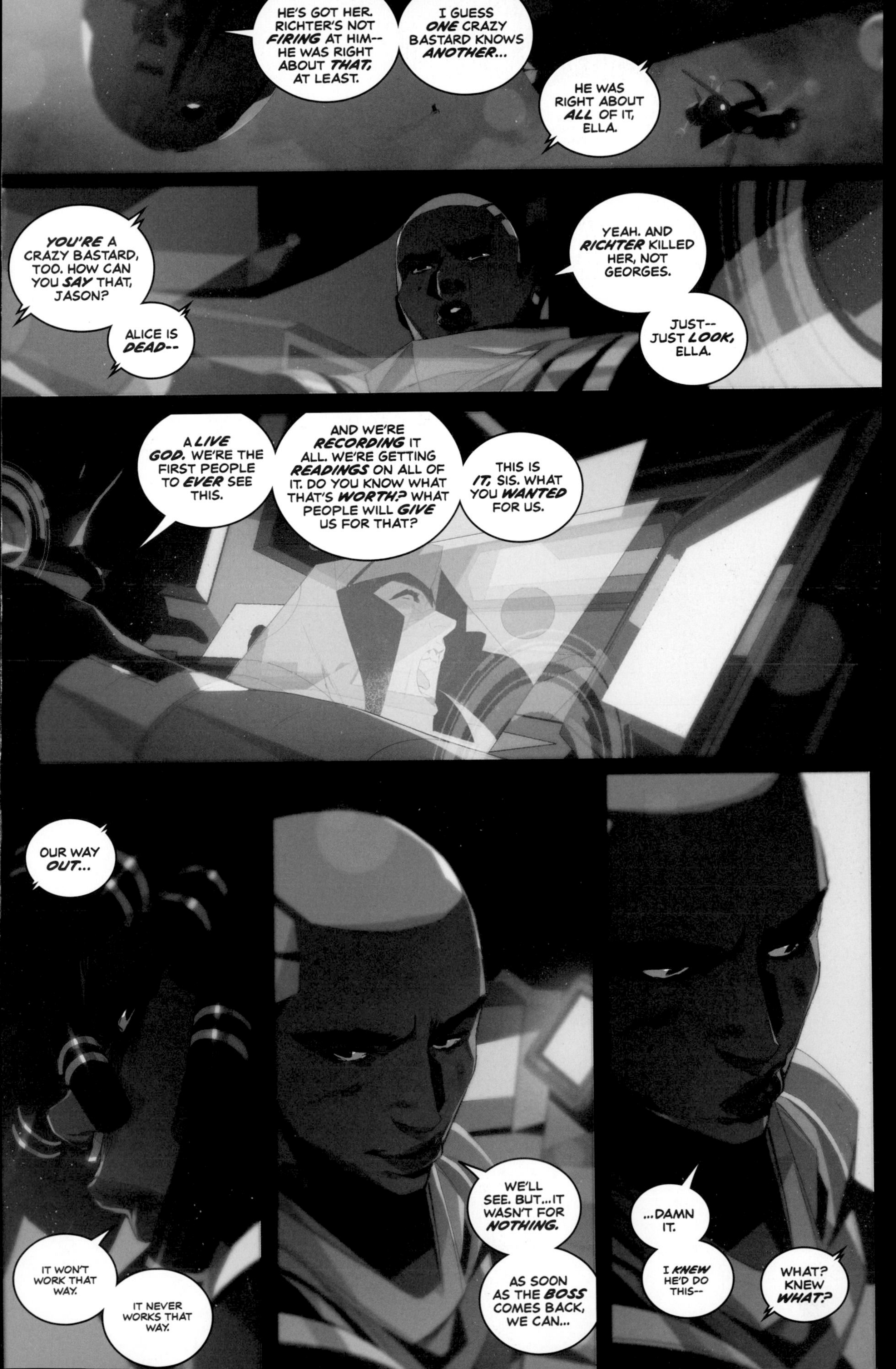
HE'S GOT HER. RICHTER'S NOT FIRING AT HIM-- HE WAS RIGHT ABOUT THAT, AT LEAST.
I GUESS ONE CRAZY BASTARD KNOWS ANOTHER...
HE WAS RIGHT ABOUT ALL OF IT, ELLA.
YOU'RE A CRAZY BASTARD, TOO. HOW CAN YOU SAY THAT, JASON?
ALICE IS DEAD--
YEAH. AND RICHTER KILLED HER, NOT GEORGES.
JUST-- JUST LOOK, ELLA.
A LIVE GOD. WE'RE THE FIRST PEOPLE TO EVER SEE THIS.
AND WE'RE RECORDING IT ALL. WE'RE GETTING READINGS ON ALL OF IT. DO YOU KNOW WHAT THAT'S WORTH? WHAT PEOPLE WILL GIVE US FOR THAT?
THIS IS IT, SIS. WHAT YOU WANTED FOR US.
OUR WAY OUT...
IT WON'T WORK THAT WAY.
IT NEVER WORKS THAT WAY.
WE'LL SEE. BUT...IT WASN'T FOR NOTHING.
AS SOON AS THE BOSS COMES BACK, WE CAN...
...DAMN IT.
I KNEW HE'D DO THIS--
WHAT? KNEW WHAT?

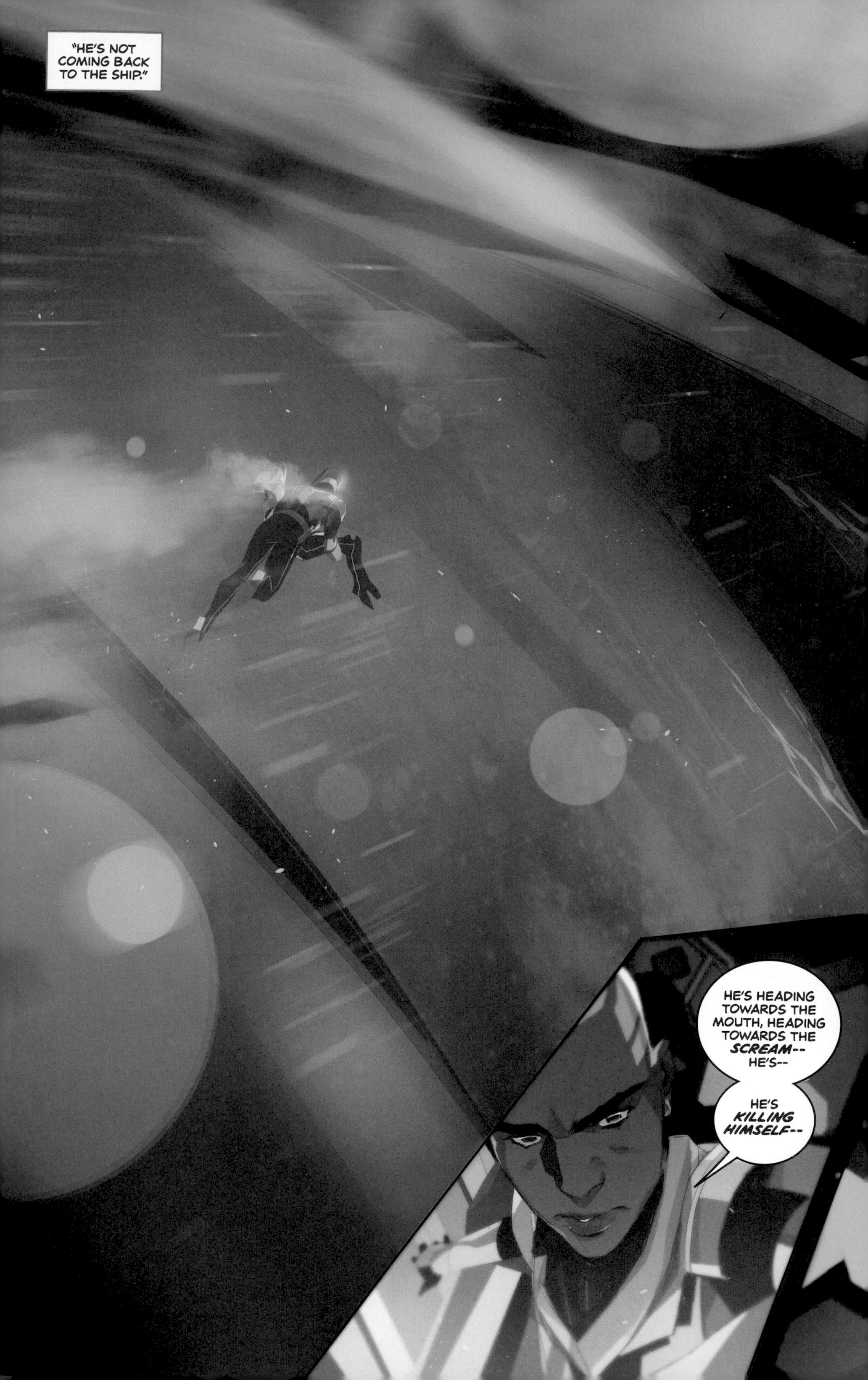
"HE'S NOT COMING BACK TO THE SHIP."
HE'S HEADING TOWARDS THE MOUTH, HEADING TOWARDS THE *SCREAM*-- HE'S--
HE'S *KILLING HIMSELF*--

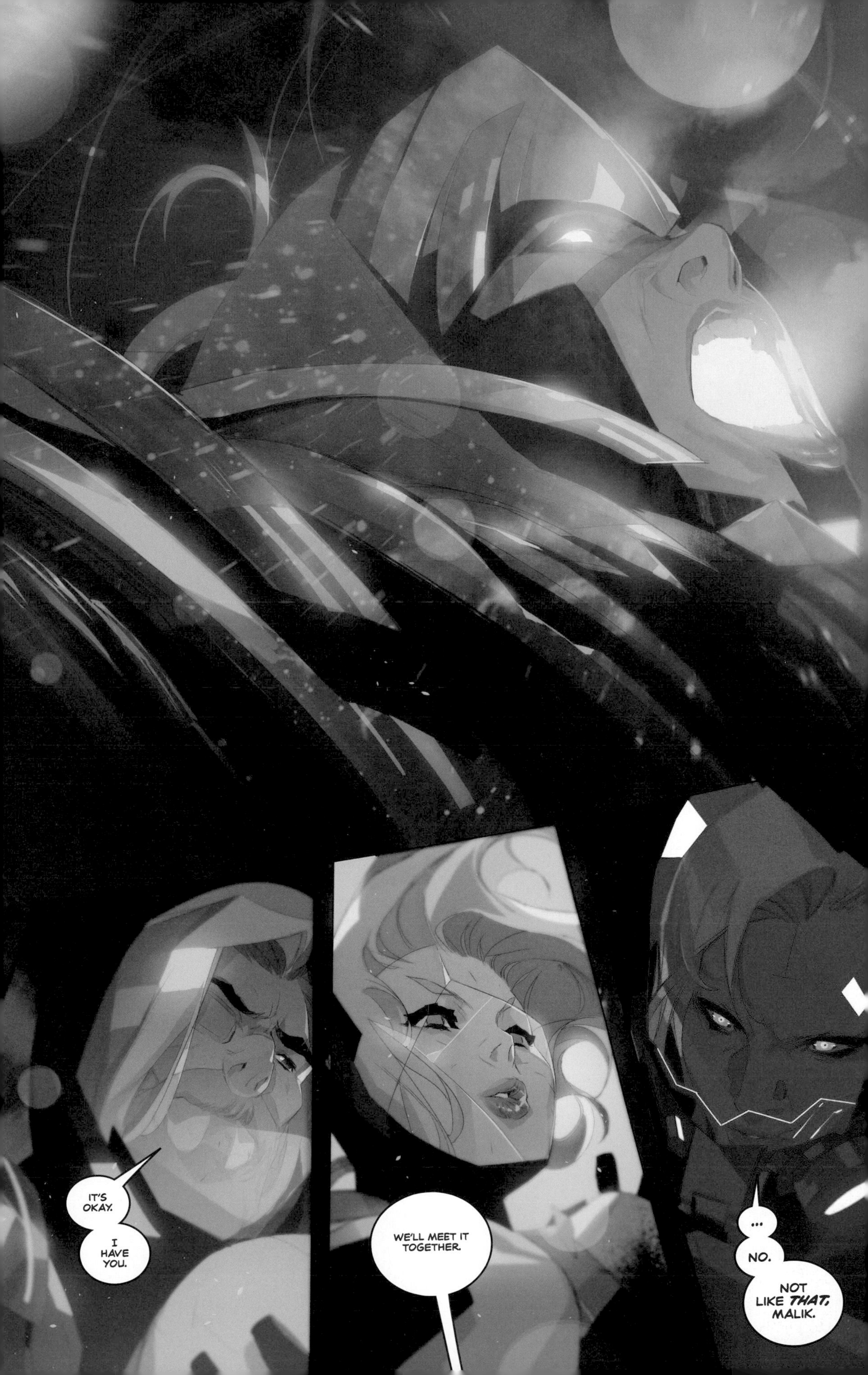
IT'S OKAY.
I HAVE YOU.
WE'LL MEET IT TOGETHER.
...
NO.
NOT LIKE *THAT,* MALIK.

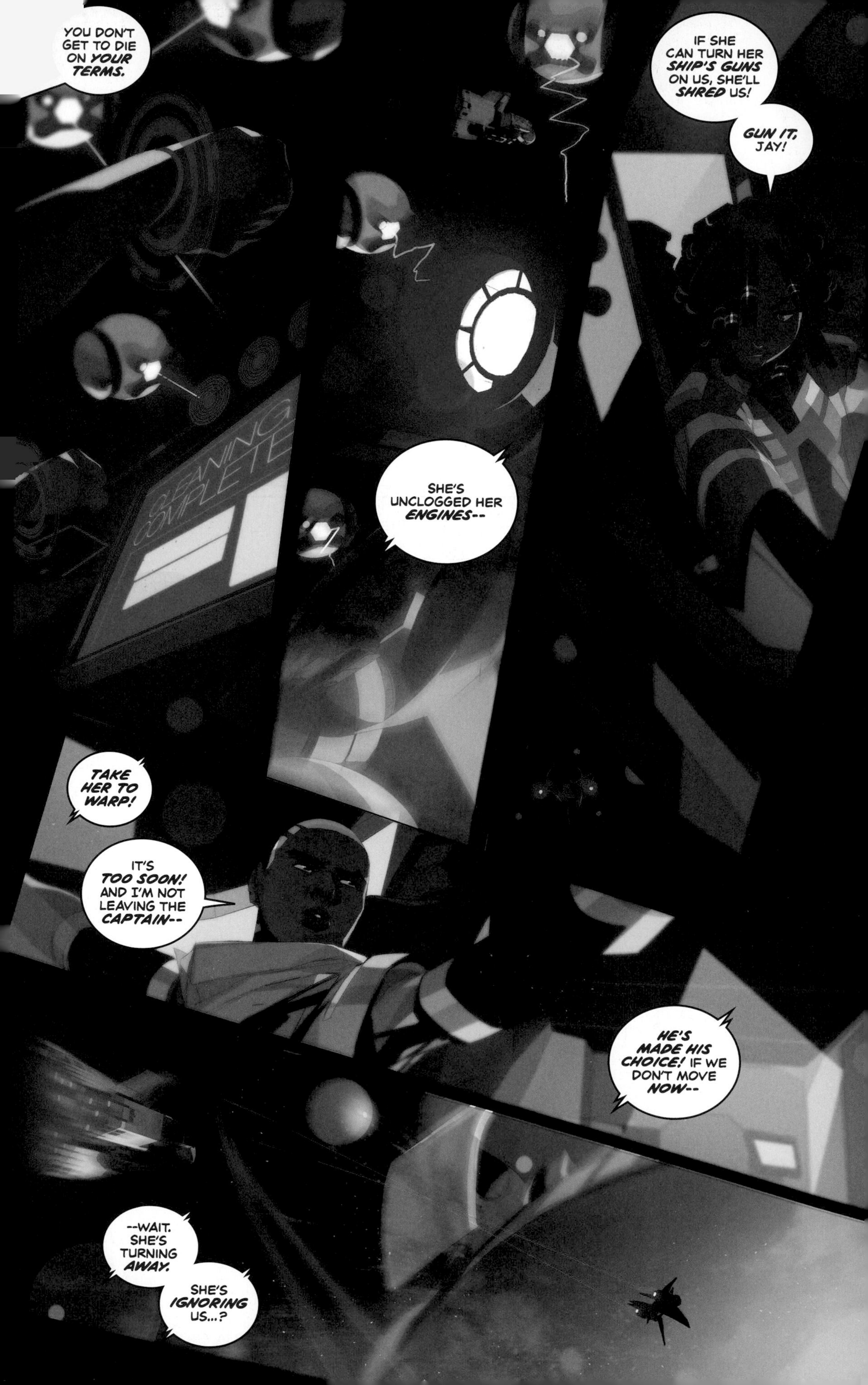
YOU DON'T GET TO DIE ON *YOUR TERMS.*
IF SHE CAN TURN HER *SHIP'S GUNS* ON US, SHE'LL *SHRED* US!
GUN IT, JAY!
CLEANING COMPLETE
SHE'S UNCLOGGED HER *ENGINES--*
TAKE HER TO WARP!
IT'S *TOO SOON!* AND I'M NOT LEAVING THE *CAPTAIN--*
HE'S MADE HIS CHOICE! IF WE DON'T MOVE *NOW--*
--WAIT. SHE'S TURNING *AWAY.*
SHE'S *IGNORING* US...?

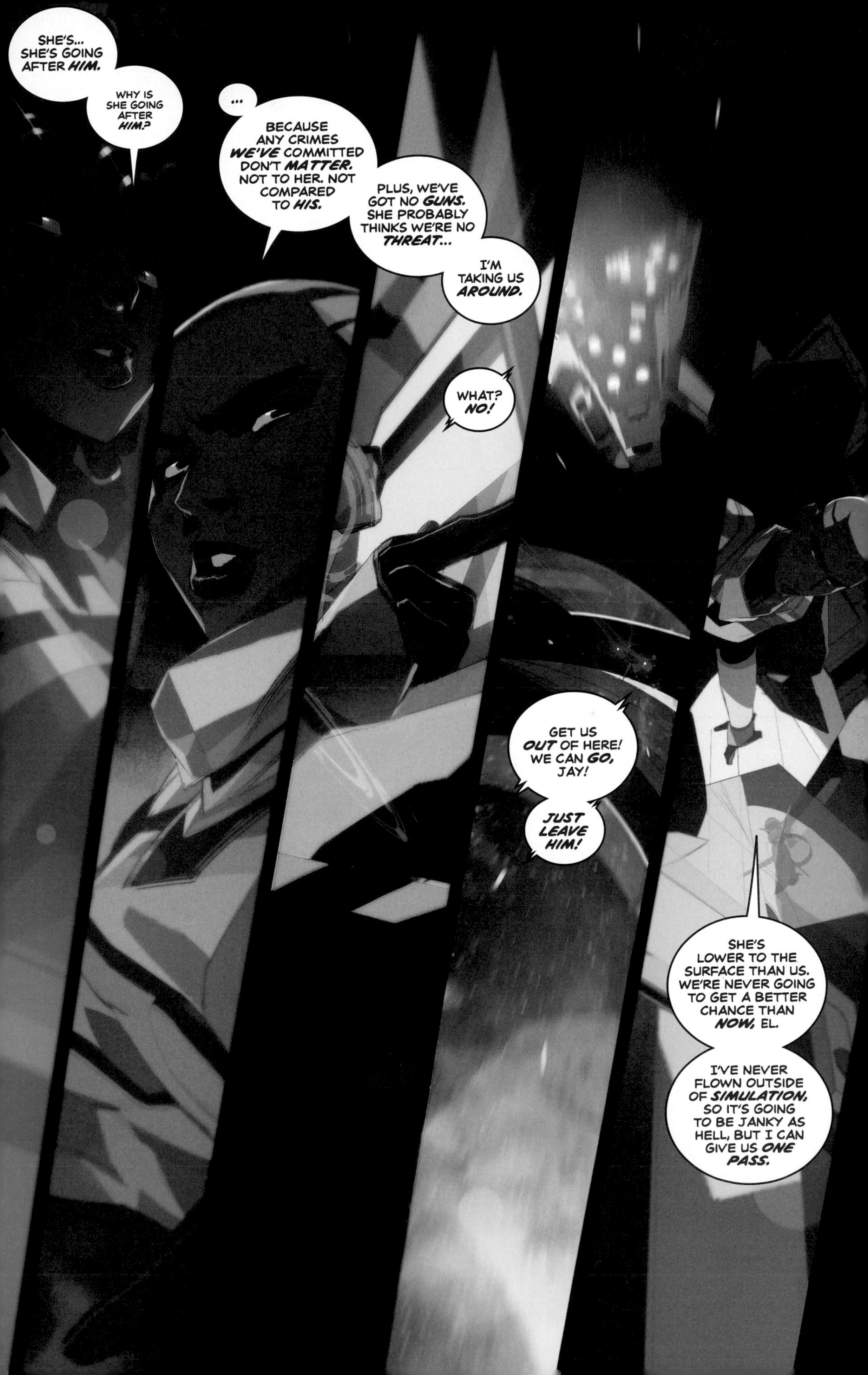
SHE'S... SHE'S GOING AFTER HIM.
WHY IS SHE GOING AFTER HIM?
...
BECAUSE ANY CRIMES WE'VE COMMITTED DON'T MATTER. NOT TO HER. NOT COMPARED TO HIS.
PLUS, WE'VE GOT NO GUNS. SHE PROBABLY THINKS WE'RE NO THREAT...
I'M TAKING US AROUND.
WHAT? NO!
GET US OUT OF HERE! WE CAN GO, JAY!
JUST LEAVE HIM!
SHE'S LOWER TO THE SURFACE THAN US. WE'RE NEVER GOING TO GET A BETTER CHANCE THAN NOW, EL.
I'VE NEVER FLOWN OUTSIDE OF SIMULATION, SO IT'S GOING TO BE JANKY AS HELL, BUT I CAN GIVE US ONE PASS.

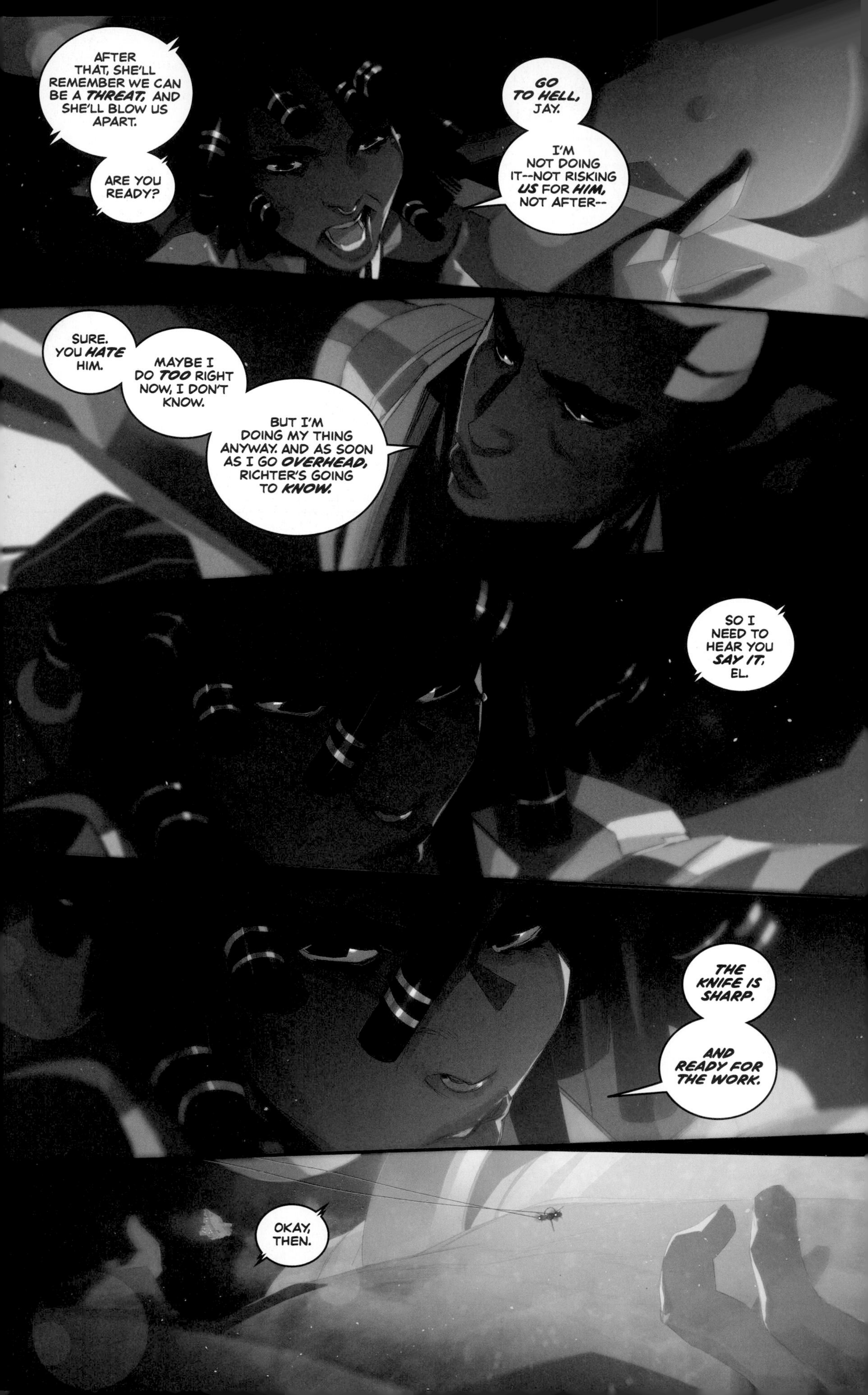
AFTER THAT, SHE'LL REMEMBER WE CAN BE A THREAT, AND SHE'LL BLOW US APART.
ARE YOU READY?
GO TO HELL, JAY.
I'M NOT DOING IT--NOT RISKING US FOR HIM, NOT AFTER--
SURE. YOU HATE HIM.
MAYBE I DO TOO RIGHT NOW, I DON'T KNOW.
BUT I'M DOING MY THING ANYWAY. AND AS SOON AS I GO OVERHEAD, RICHTER'S GOING TO KNOW.
SO I NEED TO HEAR YOU SAY IT, EL.
THE KNIFE IS SHARP.
AND READY FOR THE WORK.
OKAY, THEN.

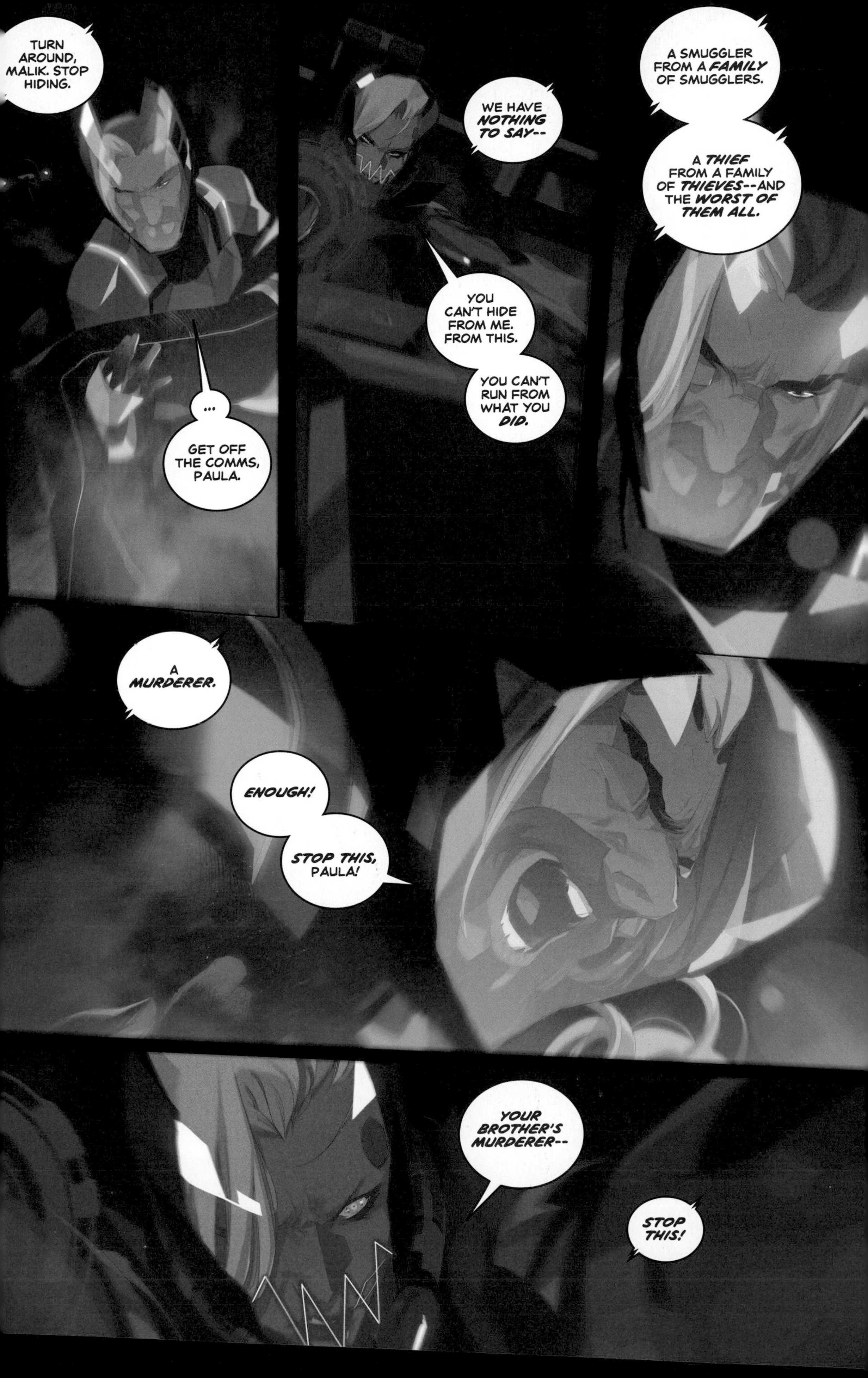

TURN AROUND, MALIK. STOP HIDING.
...
GET OFF THE COMMS, PAULA.
WE HAVE *NOTHING* TO SAY--
YOU CAN'T HIDE FROM ME. FROM THIS.
YOU CAN'T RUN FROM WHAT YOU *DID.*
A SMUGGLER FROM A *FAMILY* OF SMUGGLERS.
A *THIEF* FROM A FAMILY OF *THIEVES*--AND THE *WORST OF THEM ALL.*
A *MURDERER.*
ENOUGH!
STOP THIS, PAULA!
YOUR BROTHER'S MURDERER--
STOP THIS!

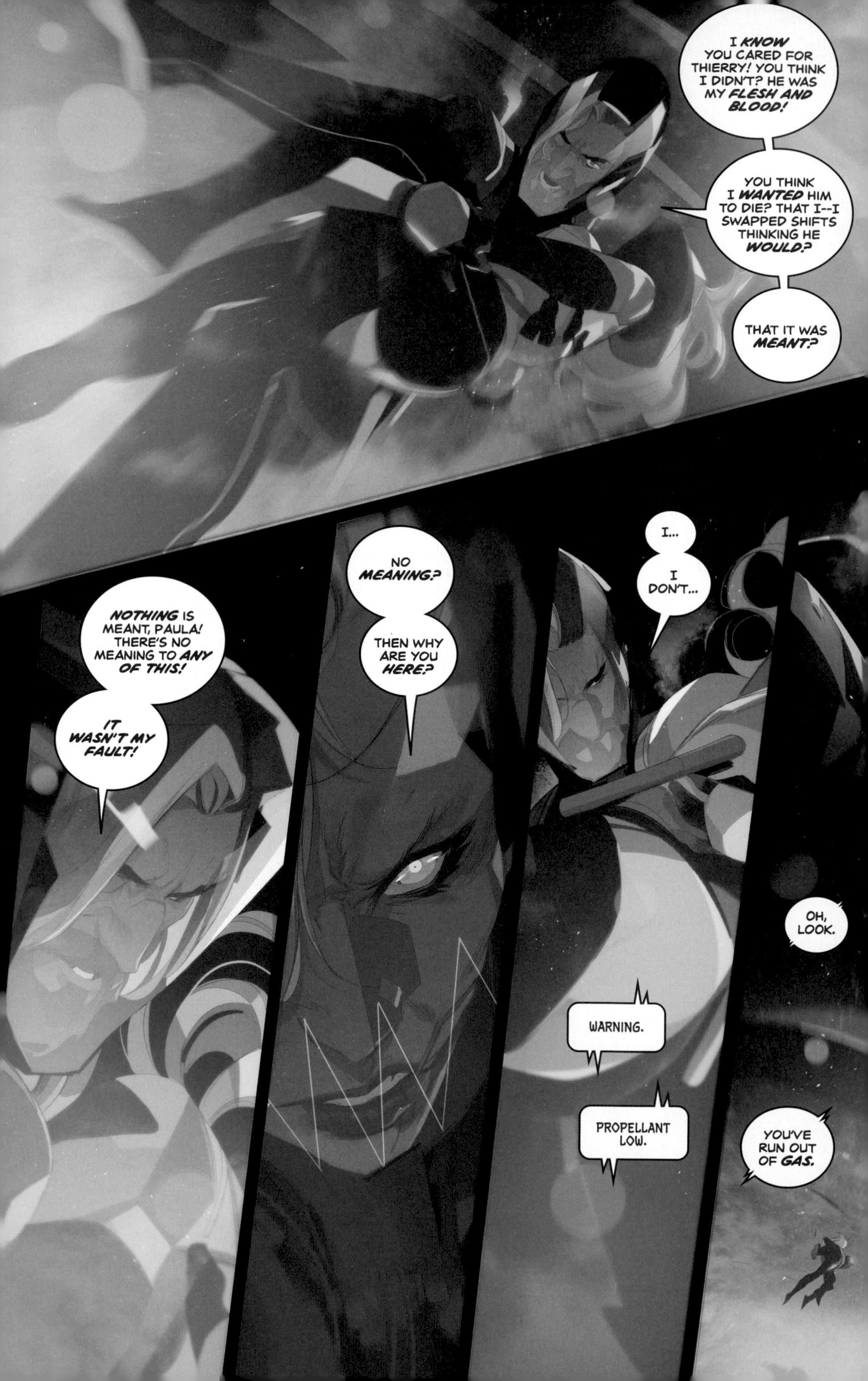

I *KNOW* YOU CARED FOR THIERRY! YOU THINK I DIDN'T? HE WAS MY *FLESH AND BLOOD!*
YOU THINK I *WANTED* HIM TO DIE? THAT I--I SWAPPED SHIFTS THINKING HE *WOULD?*
THAT IT WAS *MEANT?*
NOTHING IS MEANT, PAULA! THERE'S NO MEANING TO *ANY OF THIS!*
IT WASN'T MY FAULT!
NO *MEANING?*
THEN WHY ARE YOU *HERE?*
I...
I DON'T...
OH, LOOK.
WARNING.
PROPELLANT LOW.
YOU'VE RUN OUT OF *GAS.*

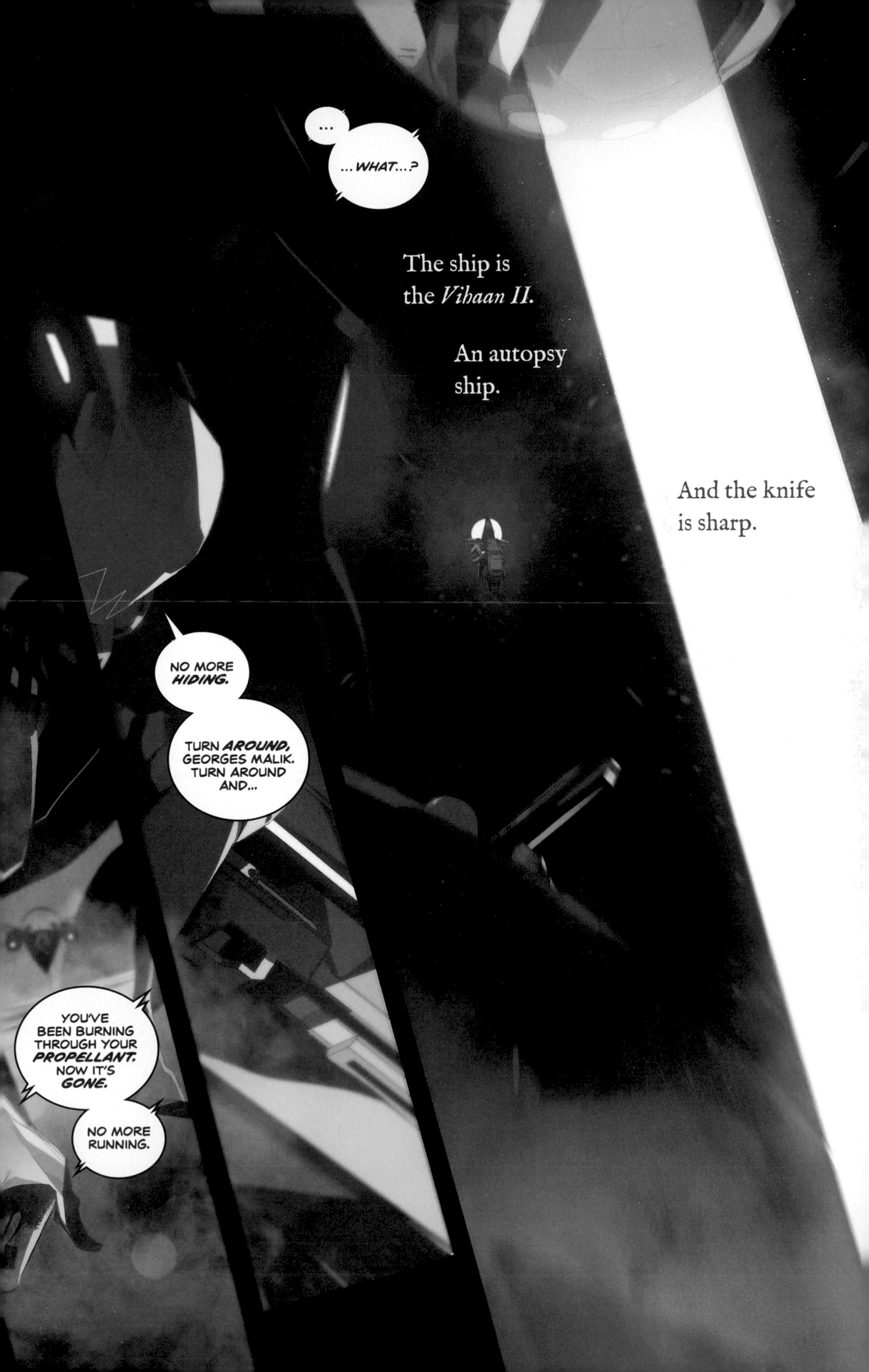
...
...WHAT...?
The ship is the *Vihaan II*.
An autopsy ship.
And the knife is sharp.
NO MORE *HIDING.*
TURN *AROUND,* GEORGES MALIK. TURN AROUND AND...
YOU'VE BEEN BURNING THROUGH YOUR *PROPELLANT.* NOW IT'S *GONE.*
NO MORE RUNNING.

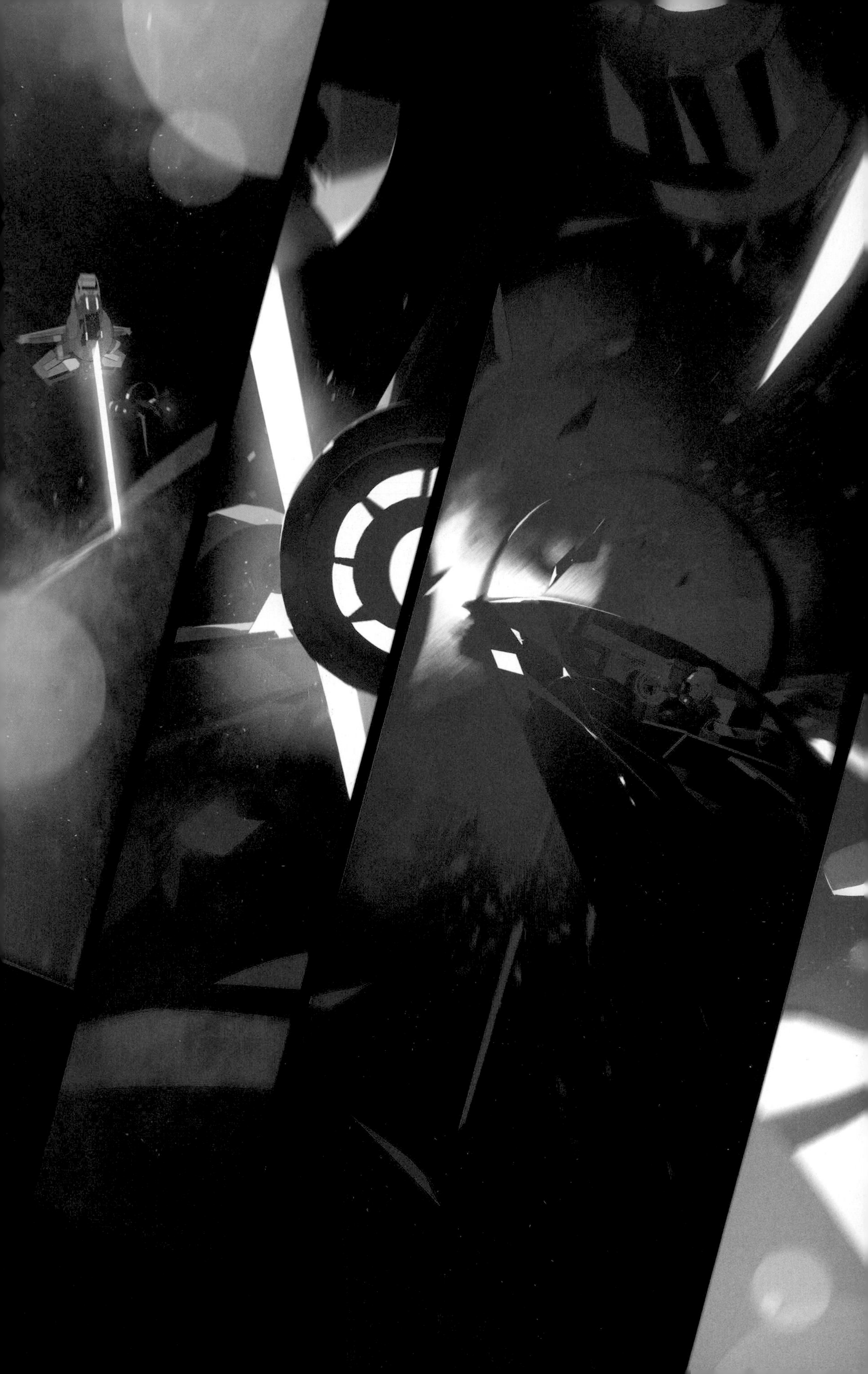

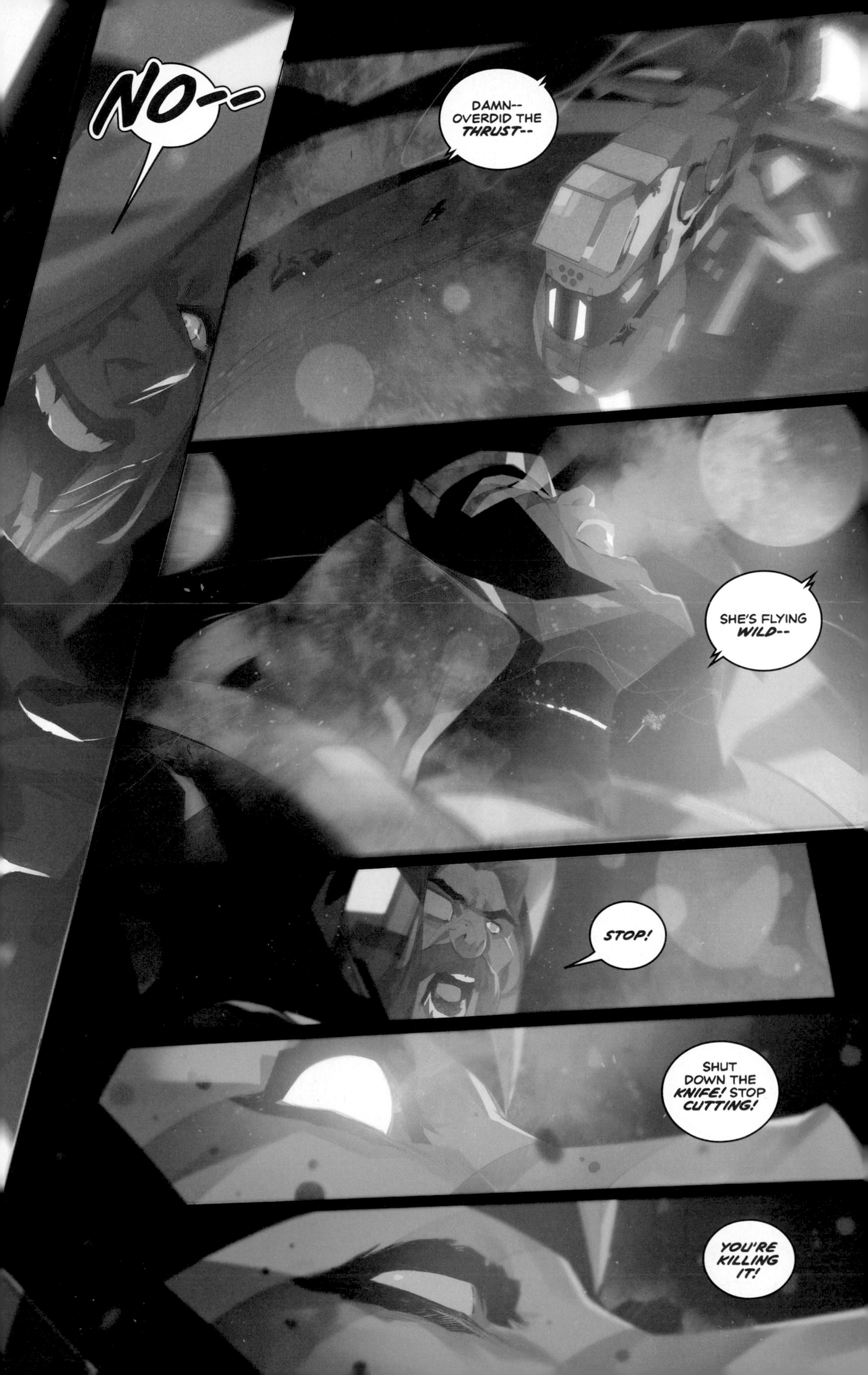
NO--
DAMN-- OVERDID THE THRUST--
SHE'S FLYING WILD--
STOP!
SHUT DOWN THE KNIFE! STOP CUTTING!
YOU'RE KILLING IT!

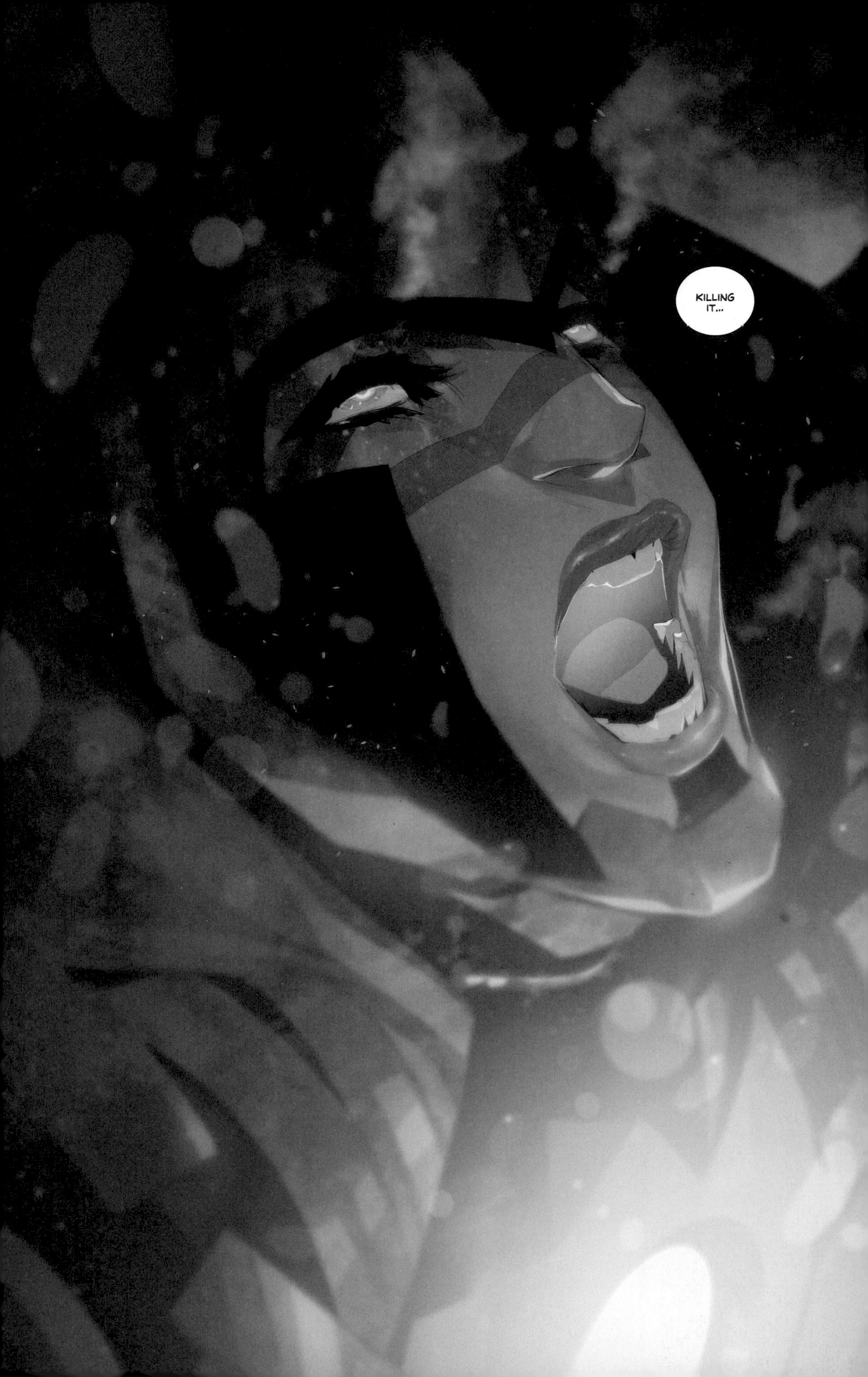
KILLING IT...

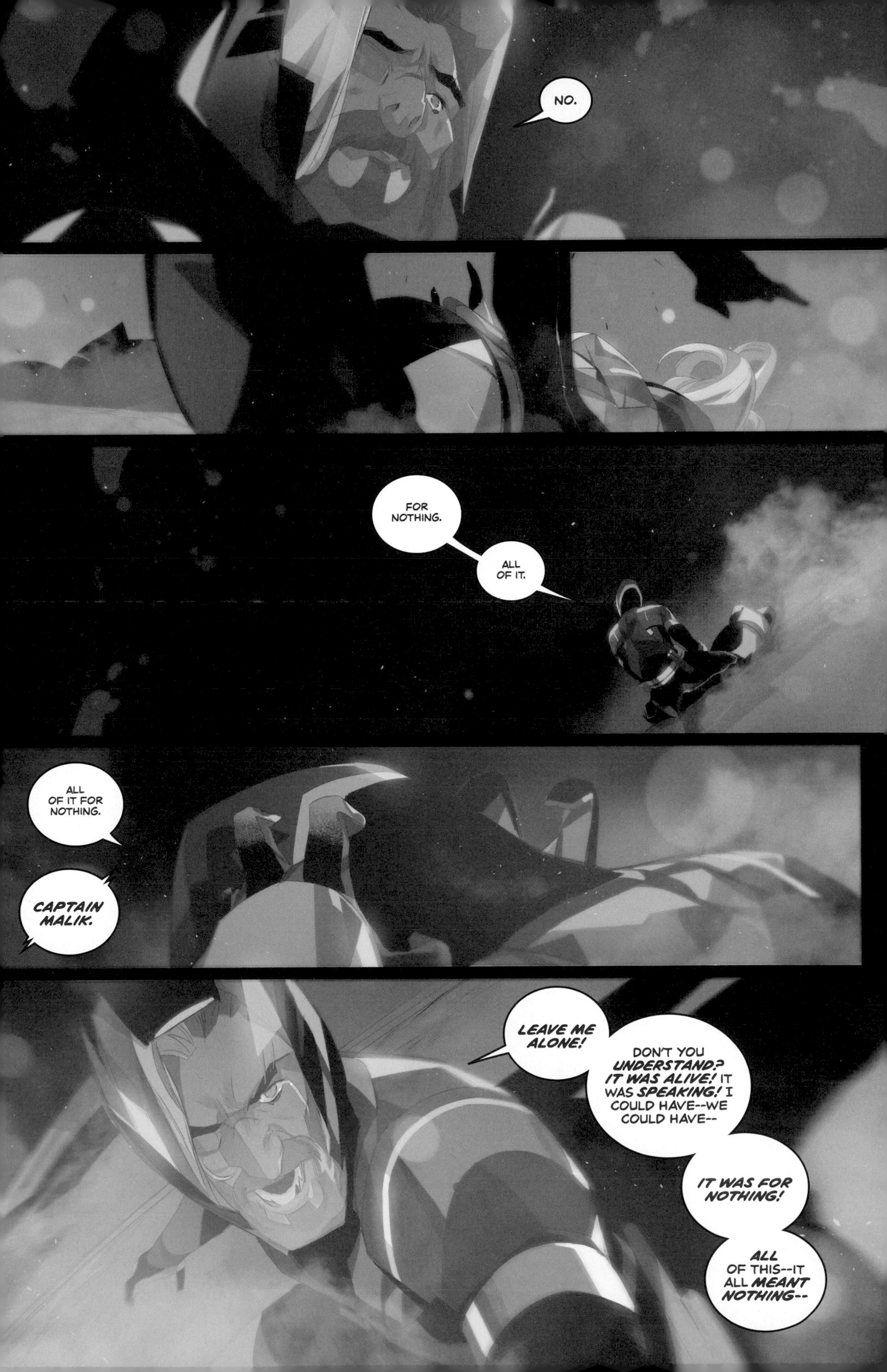
NO.
FOR NOTHING.
ALL OF IT.
ALL OF IT FOR NOTHING.
CAPTAIN MALIK.
LEAVE ME ALONE!
DON'T YOU UNDERSTAND? IT WAS ALIVE! IT WAS SPEAKING! I COULD HAVE--WE COULD HAVE--
IT WAS FOR NOTHING!
ALL OF THIS--IT ALL MEANT NOTHING--

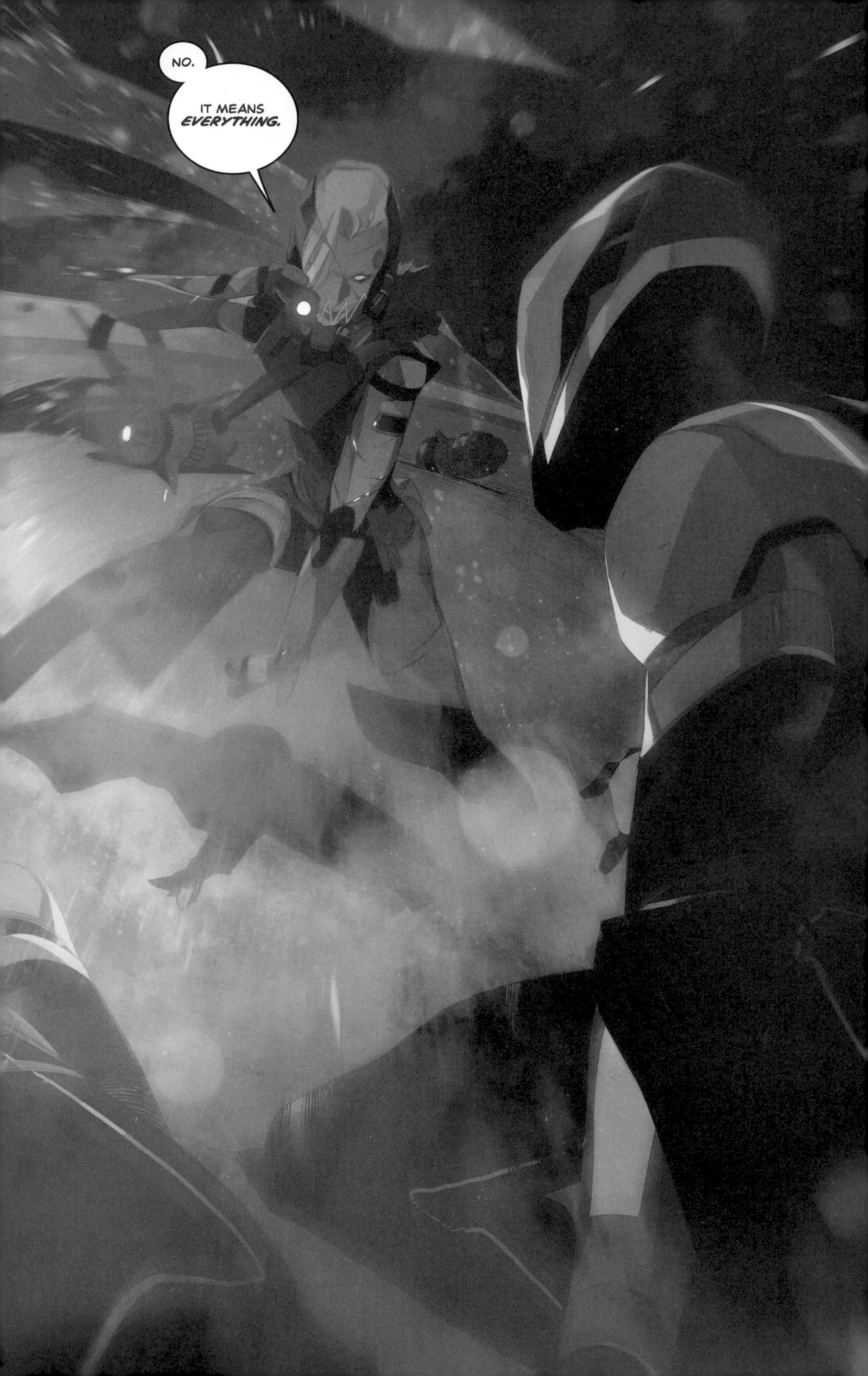
NO.
IT MEANS *EVERYTHING.*

Chapter Five

Look, and You Find Them

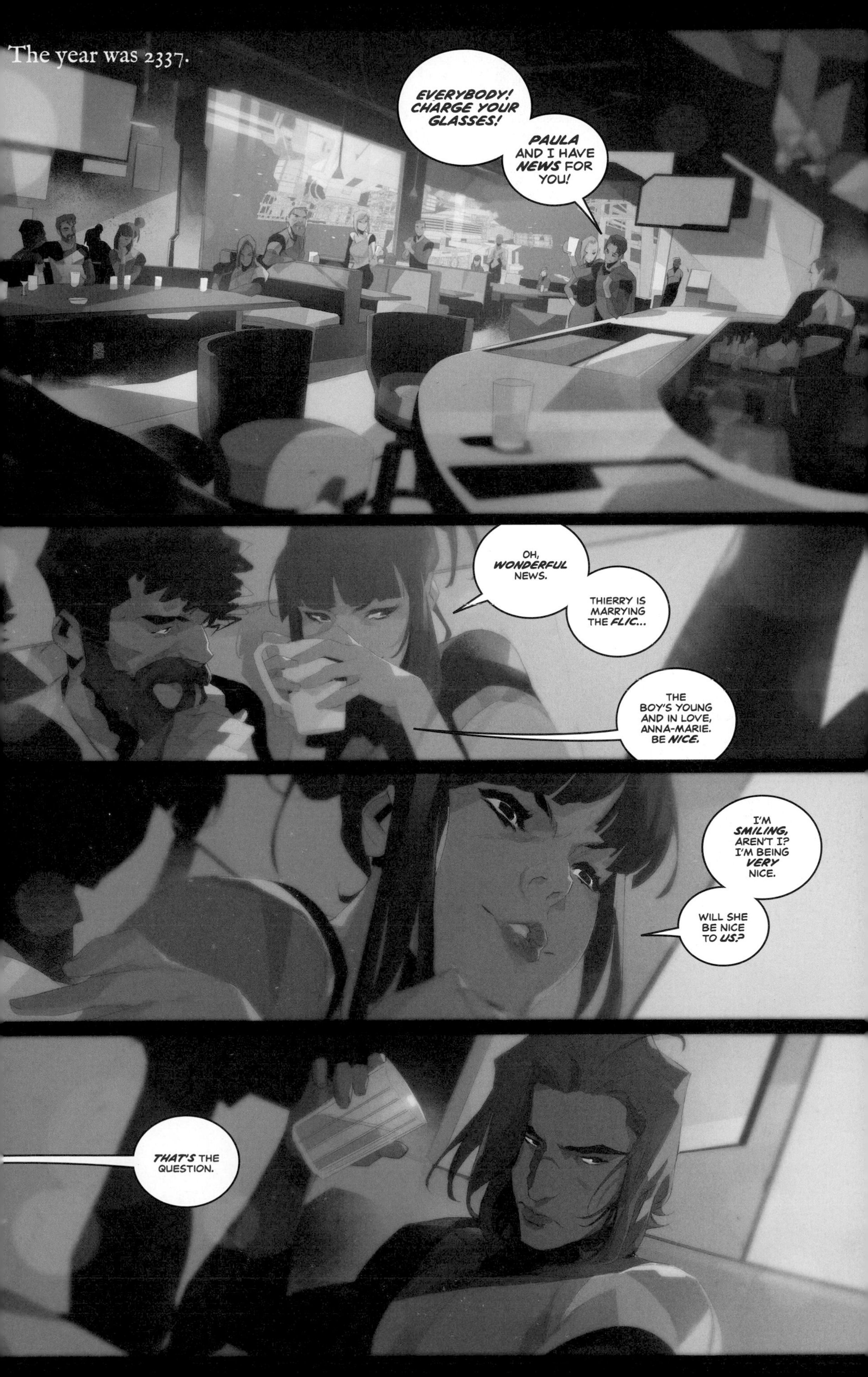
The year was 2337.
EVERYBODY! CHARGE YOUR GLASSES!
PAULA AND I HAVE NEWS FOR YOU!
OH, WONDERFUL NEWS.
THIERRY IS MARRYING THE FLIC...
THE BOY'S YOUNG AND IN LOVE, ANNA-MARIE. BE NICE.
I'M SMILING, AREN'T I? I'M BEING VERY NICE.
WILL SHE BE NICE TO US?
THAT'S THE QUESTION.

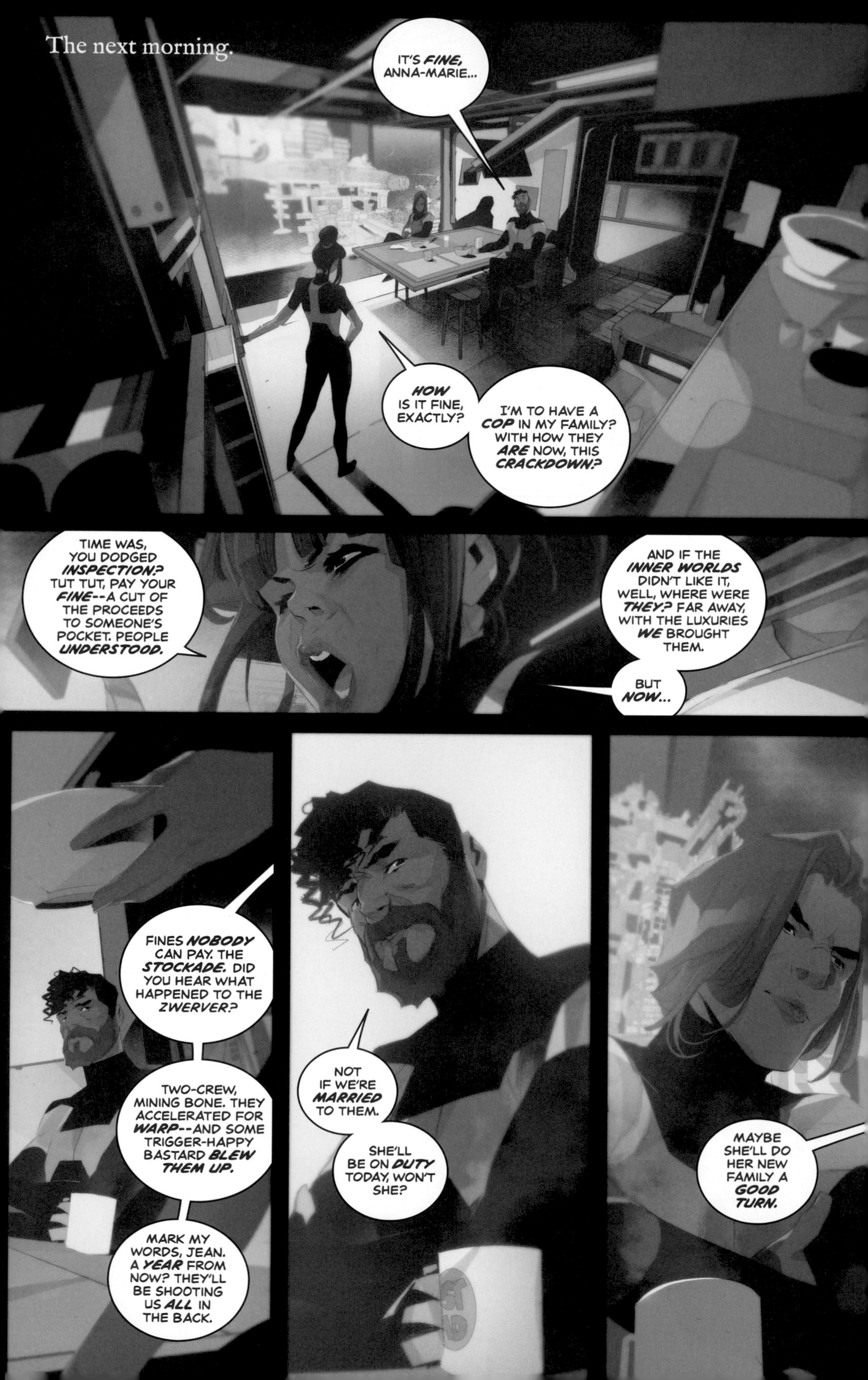

The next morning.
IT'S FINE, ANNA-MARIE...
HOW IS IT FINE, EXACTLY?
I'M TO HAVE A COP IN MY FAMILY? WITH HOW THEY ARE NOW, THIS CRACKDOWN?
TIME WAS, YOU DODGED INSPECTION? TUT TUT, PAY YOUR FINE--A CUT OF THE PROCEEDS TO SOMEONE'S POCKET. PEOPLE UNDERSTOOD.
AND IF THE INNER WORLDS DIDN'T LIKE IT, WELL, WHERE WERE THEY? FAR AWAY, WITH THE LUXURIES WE BROUGHT THEM.
BUT NOW...
FINES NOBODY CAN PAY. THE STOCKADE. DID YOU HEAR WHAT HAPPENED TO THE ZWERVER?
TWO-CREW, MINING BONE. THEY ACCELERATED FOR WARP--AND SOME TRIGGER-HAPPY BASTARD BLEW THEM UP.
MARK MY WORDS, JEAN. A YEAR FROM NOW? THEY'LL BE SHOOTING US ALL IN THE BACK.
NOT IF WE'RE MARRIED TO THEM.
SHE'LL BE ON DUTY TODAY, WON'T SHE?
MAYBE SHE'LL DO HER NEW FAMILY A GOOD TURN.

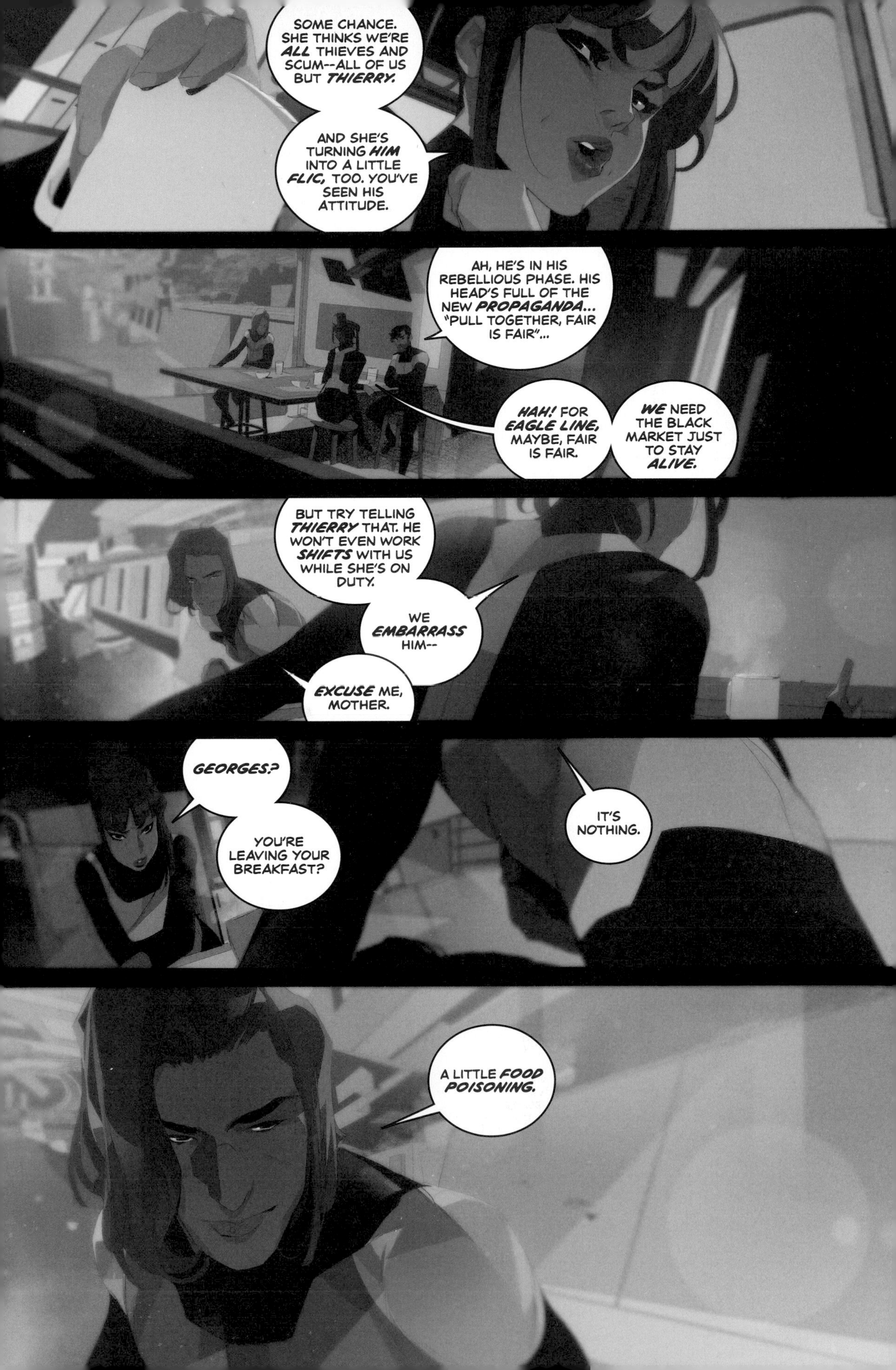
SOME CHANCE. SHE THINKS WE'RE *ALL* THIEVES AND SCUM--ALL OF US BUT *THIERRY.*
AND SHE'S TURNING *HIM* INTO A LITTLE *FLIC,* TOO. YOU'VE SEEN HIS ATTITUDE.
AH, HE'S IN HIS REBELLIOUS PHASE. HIS HEAD'S FULL OF THE NEW *PROPAGANDA...* "PULL TOGETHER, FAIR IS FAIR"...
HAH! FOR *EAGLE LINE,* MAYBE, FAIR IS FAIR.
WE NEED THE BLACK MARKET JUST TO STAY *ALIVE.*
BUT TRY TELLING *THIERRY* THAT. HE WON'T EVEN WORK *SHIFTS* WITH US WHILE SHE'S ON DUTY.
WE *EMBARRASS* HIM--
EXCUSE ME, MOTHER.
GEORGES?
YOU'RE LEAVING YOUR BREAKFAST?
IT'S NOTHING.
A LITTLE *FOOD POISONING.*

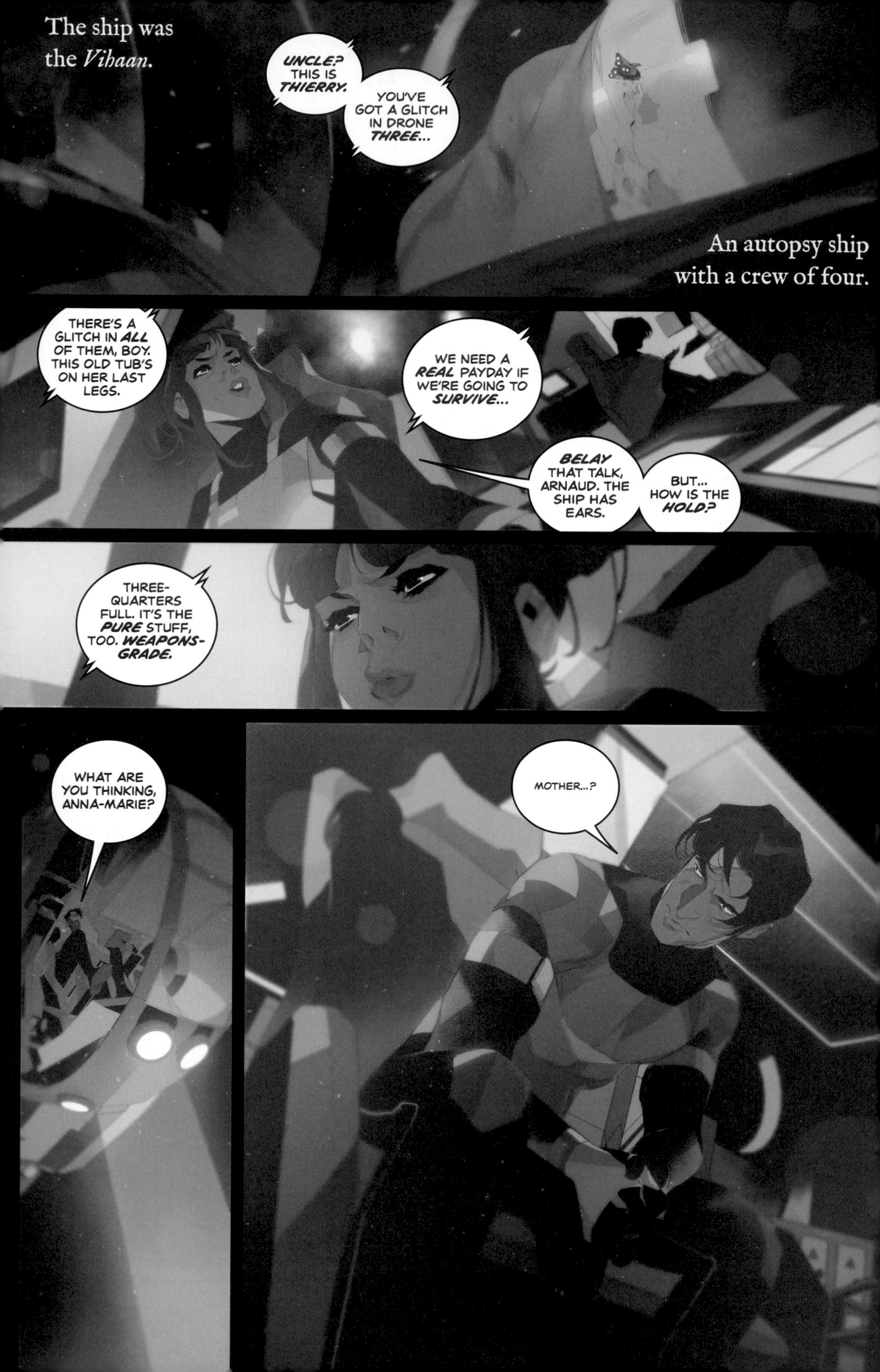
The ship was the *Vihaan*.
UNCLE? THIS IS THIERRY.
YOU'VE GOT A GLITCH IN DRONE THREE...
An autopsy ship with a crew of four.
THERE'S A GLITCH IN ALL OF THEM, BOY. THIS OLD TUB'S ON HER LAST LEGS.
WE NEED A REAL PAYDAY IF WE'RE GOING TO SURVIVE...
BELAY THAT TALK, ARNAUD. THE SHIP HAS EARS.
BUT... HOW IS THE HOLD?
THREE-QUARTERS FULL. IT'S THE PURE STUFF, TOO. WEAPONS-GRADE.
WHAT ARE YOU THINKING, ANNA-MARIE?
MOTHER...?

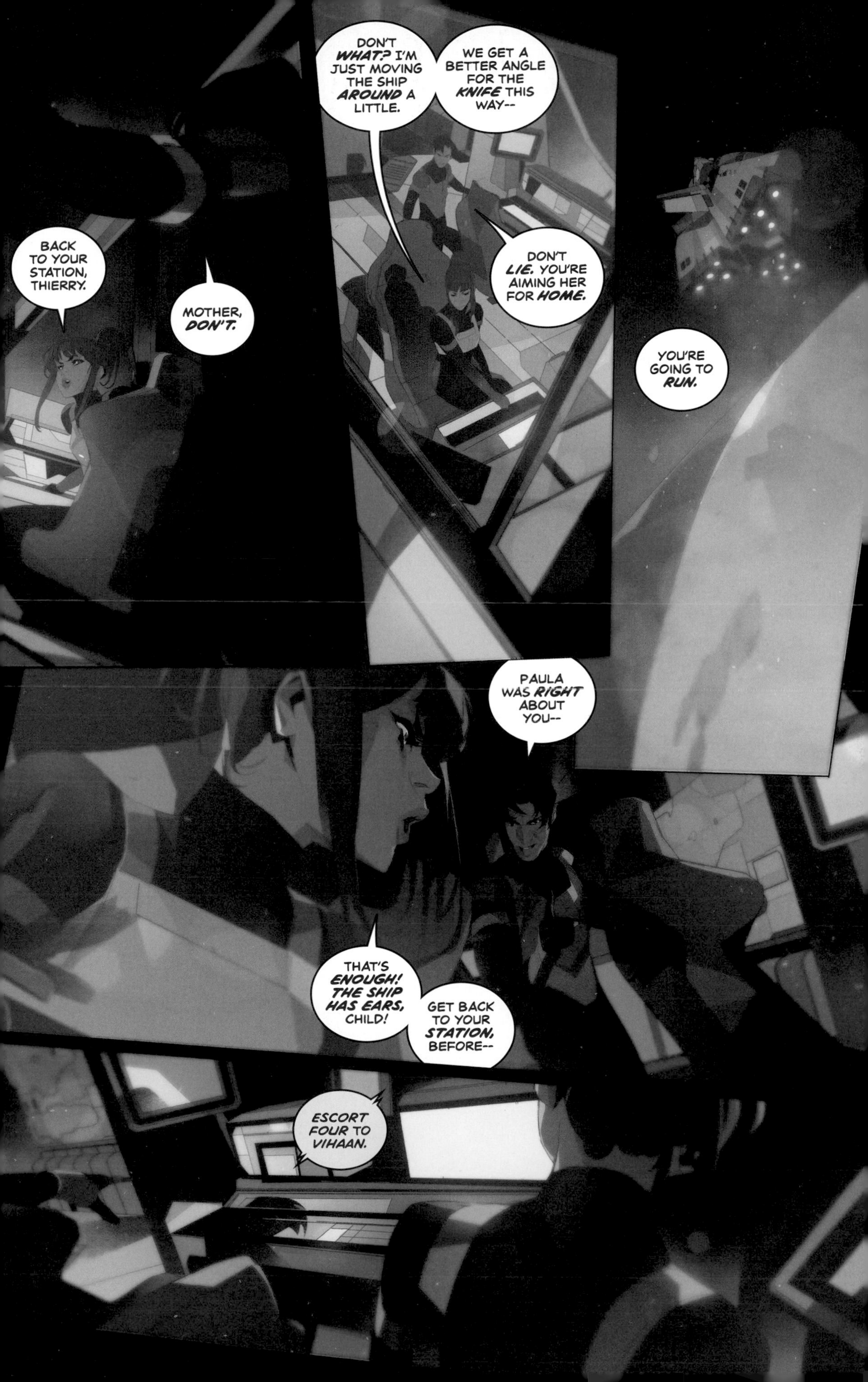
BACK TO YOUR STATION, THIERRY.
MOTHER, DON'T.
DON'T WHAT? I'M JUST MOVING THE SHIP AROUND A LITTLE.
WE GET A BETTER ANGLE FOR THE KNIFE THIS WAY--
DON'T LIE. YOU'RE AIMING HER FOR HOME.
YOU'RE GOING TO RUN.
PAULA WAS RIGHT ABOUT YOU--
THAT'S ENOUGH! THE SHIP HAS EARS, CHILD!
GET BACK TO YOUR STATION, BEFORE--
ESCORT FOUR TO VIHAAN.

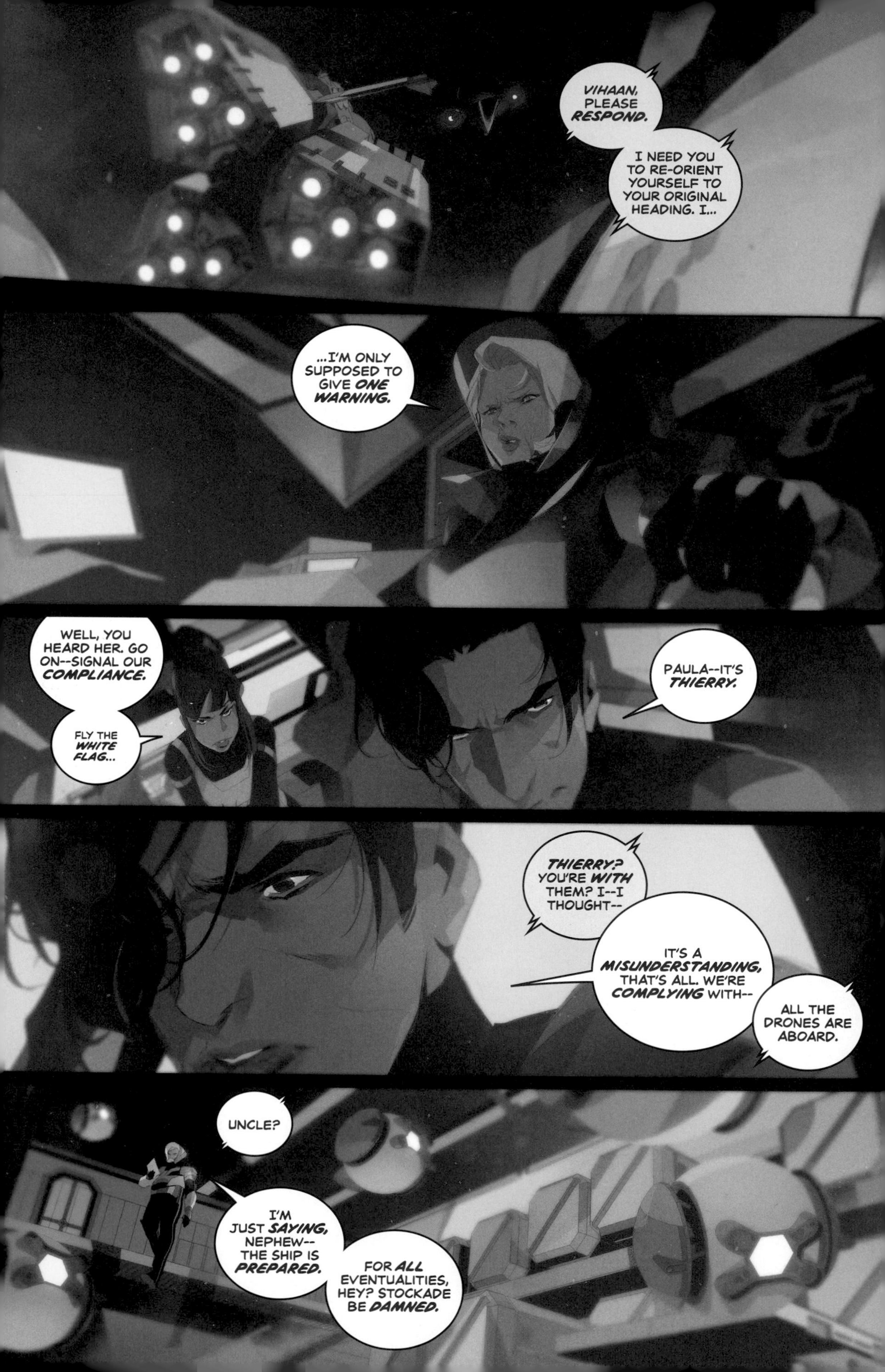
VIHAAN, PLEASE RESPOND.
I NEED YOU TO RE-ORIENT YOURSELF TO YOUR ORIGINAL HEADING. I...
...I'M ONLY SUPPOSED TO GIVE ONE WARNING.
WELL, YOU HEARD HER. GO ON--SIGNAL OUR COMPLIANCE.
FLY THE WHITE FLAG...
PAULA--IT'S THIERRY.
THIERRY? YOU'RE WITH THEM? I--I THOUGHT--
IT'S A MISUNDERSTANDING, THAT'S ALL. WE'RE COMPLYING WITH--
ALL THE DRONES ARE ABOARD.
UNCLE?
I'M JUST SAYING, NEPHEW-- THE SHIP IS PREPARED.
FOR ALL EVENTUALITIES, HEY? STOCKADE BE DAMNED.

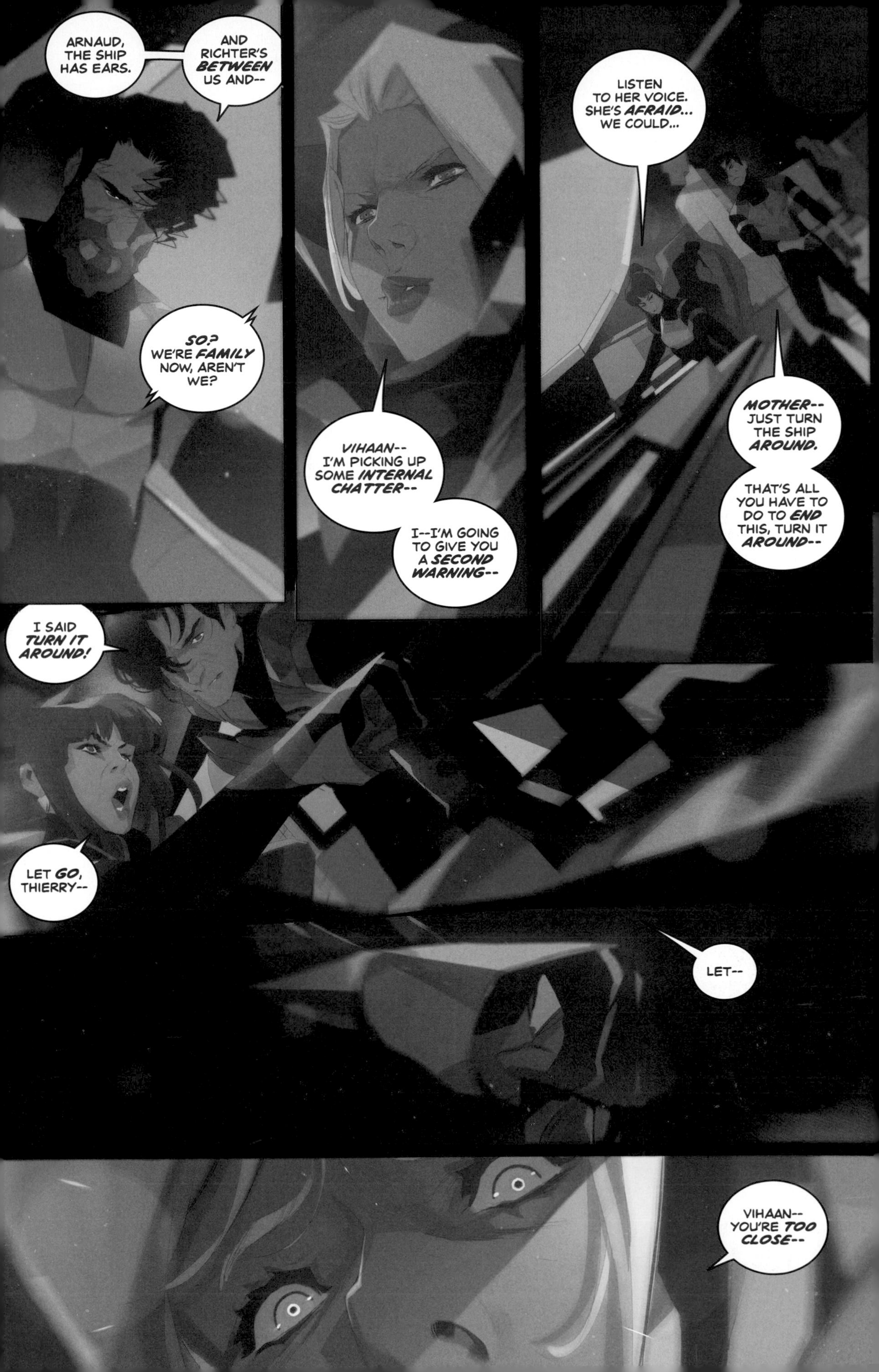
ARNAUD, THE SHIP HAS EARS.
AND RICHTER'S BETWEEN US AND--
SO? WE'RE FAMILY NOW, AREN'T WE?
VIHAAN-- I'M PICKING UP SOME INTERNAL CHATTER--
I--I'M GOING TO GIVE YOU A SECOND WARNING--
LISTEN TO HER VOICE. SHE'S AFRAID... WE COULD...
MOTHER-- JUST TURN THE SHIP AROUND.
THAT'S ALL YOU HAVE TO DO TO END THIS, TURN IT AROUND--
I SAID TURN IT AROUND!
LET GO, THIERRY--
LET--
VIHAAN-- YOU'RE TOO CLOSE--

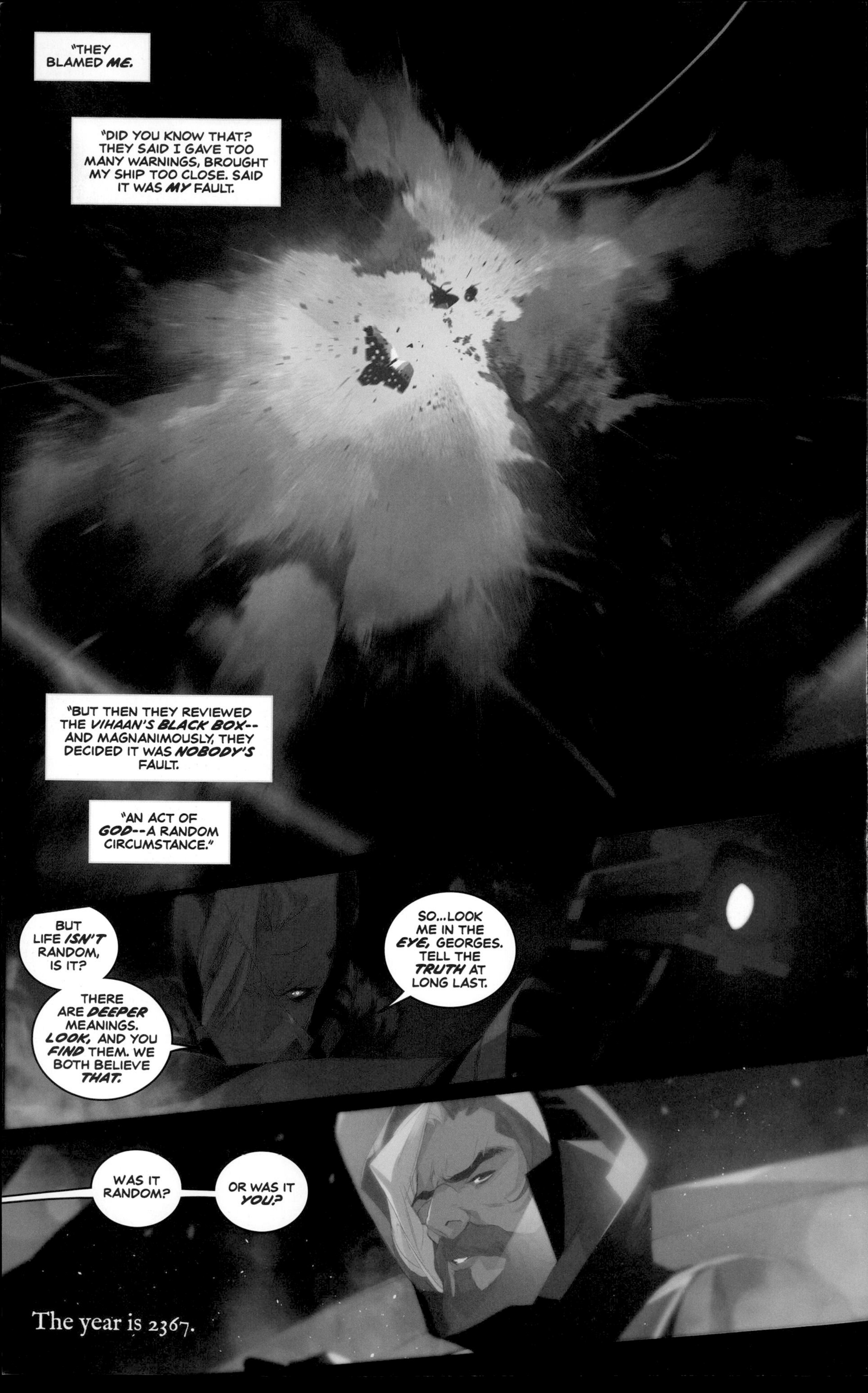
"THEY BLAMED *ME*.
"DID YOU KNOW THAT? THEY SAID I GAVE TOO MANY WARNINGS, BROUGHT MY SHIP TOO CLOSE. SAID IT WAS *MY* FAULT.
"BUT THEN THEY REVIEWED THE *VIHAAN'S BLACK BOX*-- AND MAGNANIMOUSLY, THEY DECIDED IT WAS *NOBODY'S* FAULT.
"AN ACT OF *GOD*--A RANDOM CIRCUMSTANCE."
BUT LIFE *ISN'T* RANDOM, IS IT?
THERE ARE *DEEPER* MEANINGS. *LOOK,* AND YOU *FIND* THEM. WE BOTH BELIEVE *THAT.*
SO...LOOK ME IN THE *EYE,* GEORGES. TELL THE *TRUTH* AT LONG LAST.
WAS IT RANDOM?
OR WAS IT *YOU?*
The year is 2367.

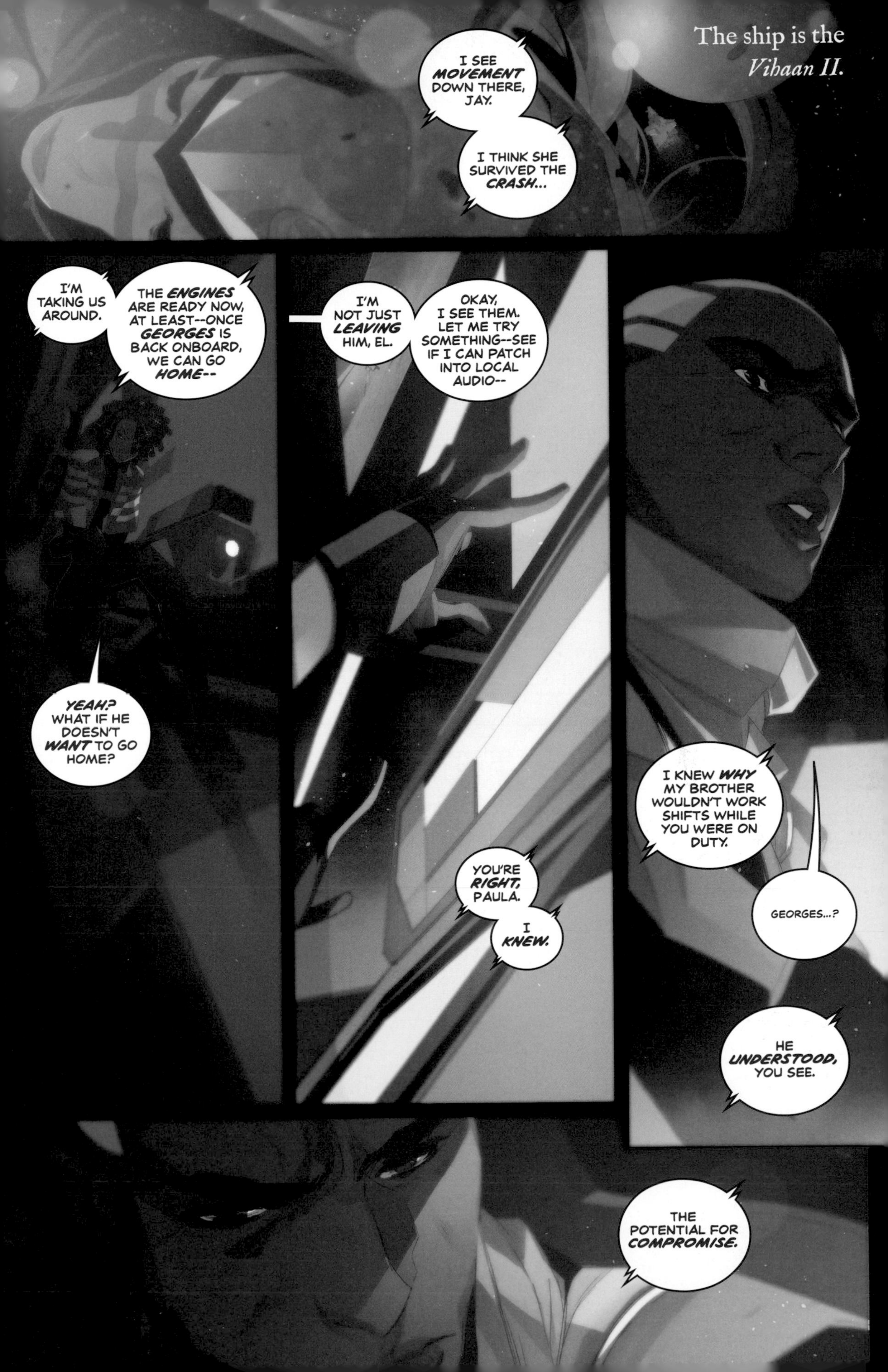
The ship is the *Vihaan II*.
I SEE MOVEMENT DOWN THERE, JAY.
I THINK SHE SURVIVED THE CRASH...
I'M TAKING US AROUND.
THE ENGINES ARE READY NOW, AT LEAST--ONCE GEORGES IS BACK ONBOARD, WE CAN GO HOME--
YEAH? WHAT IF HE DOESN'T WANT TO GO HOME?
I'M NOT JUST LEAVING HIM, EL.
OKAY, I SEE THEM. LET ME TRY SOMETHING--SEE IF I CAN PATCH INTO LOCAL AUDIO--
YOU'RE RIGHT, PAULA.
I KNEW.
I KNEW WHY MY BROTHER WOULDN'T WORK SHIFTS WHILE YOU WERE ON DUTY.
GEORGES...?
HE UNDERSTOOD, YOU SEE.
THE POTENTIAL FOR COMPROMISE.

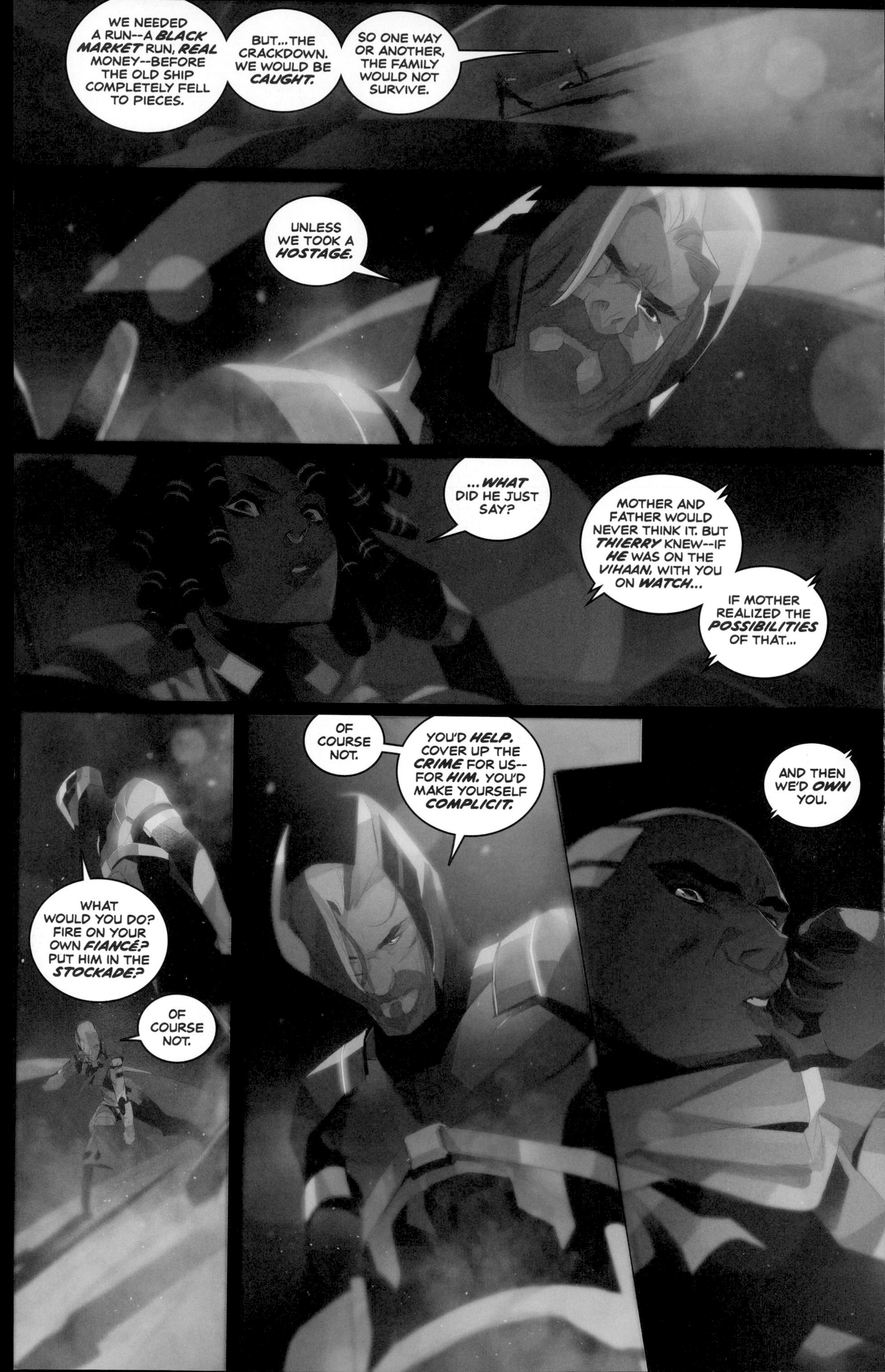
WE NEEDED A RUN--A BLACK MARKET RUN, REAL MONEY--BEFORE THE OLD SHIP COMPLETELY FELL TO PIECES.
BUT...THE CRACKDOWN. WE WOULD BE CAUGHT.
SO ONE WAY OR ANOTHER, THE FAMILY WOULD NOT SURVIVE.
UNLESS WE TOOK A HOSTAGE.
...WHAT DID HE JUST SAY?
MOTHER AND FATHER WOULD NEVER THINK IT. BUT THIERRY KNEW--IF HE WAS ON THE VIHAAN, WITH YOU ON WATCH...
IF MOTHER REALIZED THE POSSIBILITIES OF THAT...
WHAT WOULD YOU DO? FIRE ON YOUR OWN FIANCÉ? PUT HIM IN THE STOCKADE?
OF COURSE NOT.
OF COURSE NOT.
YOU'D HELP. COVER UP THE CRIME FOR US--FOR HIM. YOU'D MAKE YOURSELF COMPLICIT.
AND THEN WE'D OWN YOU.

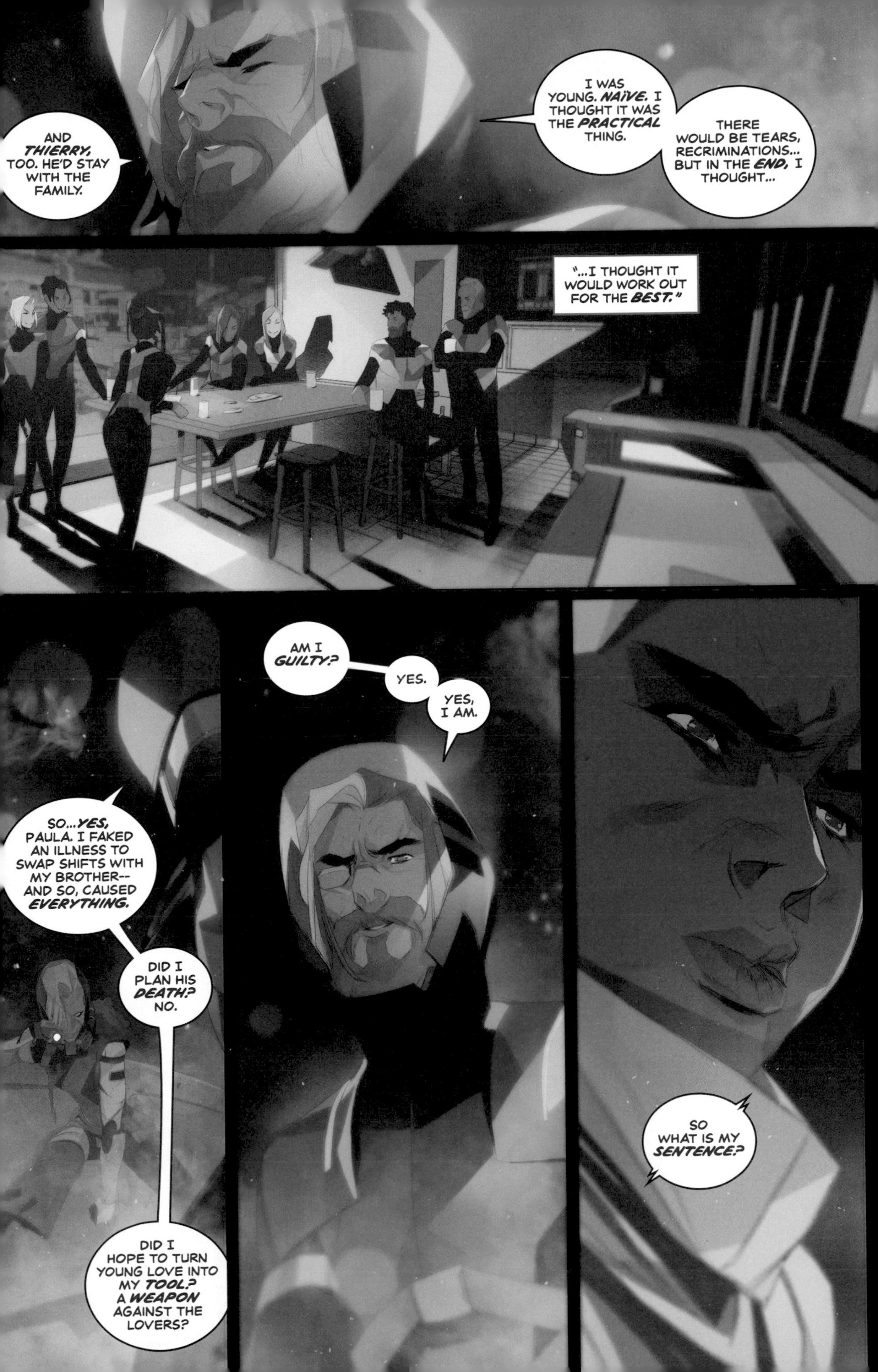
AND *THIERRY,* TOO. HE'D STAY WITH THE FAMILY.
I WAS YOUNG. *NAÏVE.* I THOUGHT IT WAS THE *PRACTICAL* THING.
THERE WOULD BE TEARS, RECRIMINATIONS... BUT IN THE *END,* I THOUGHT...
"...I THOUGHT IT WOULD WORK OUT FOR THE *BEST."*
AM I *GUILTY?*
YES.
YES, I AM.
SO...*YES,* PAULA. I FAKED AN ILLNESS TO SWAP SHIFTS WITH MY BROTHER-- AND SO, CAUSED *EVERYTHING.*
DID I PLAN HIS *DEATH?* NO.
DID I HOPE TO TURN YOUNG LOVE INTO MY *TOOL?* A *WEAPON* AGAINST THE LOVERS?
SO WHAT IS MY *SENTENCE?*

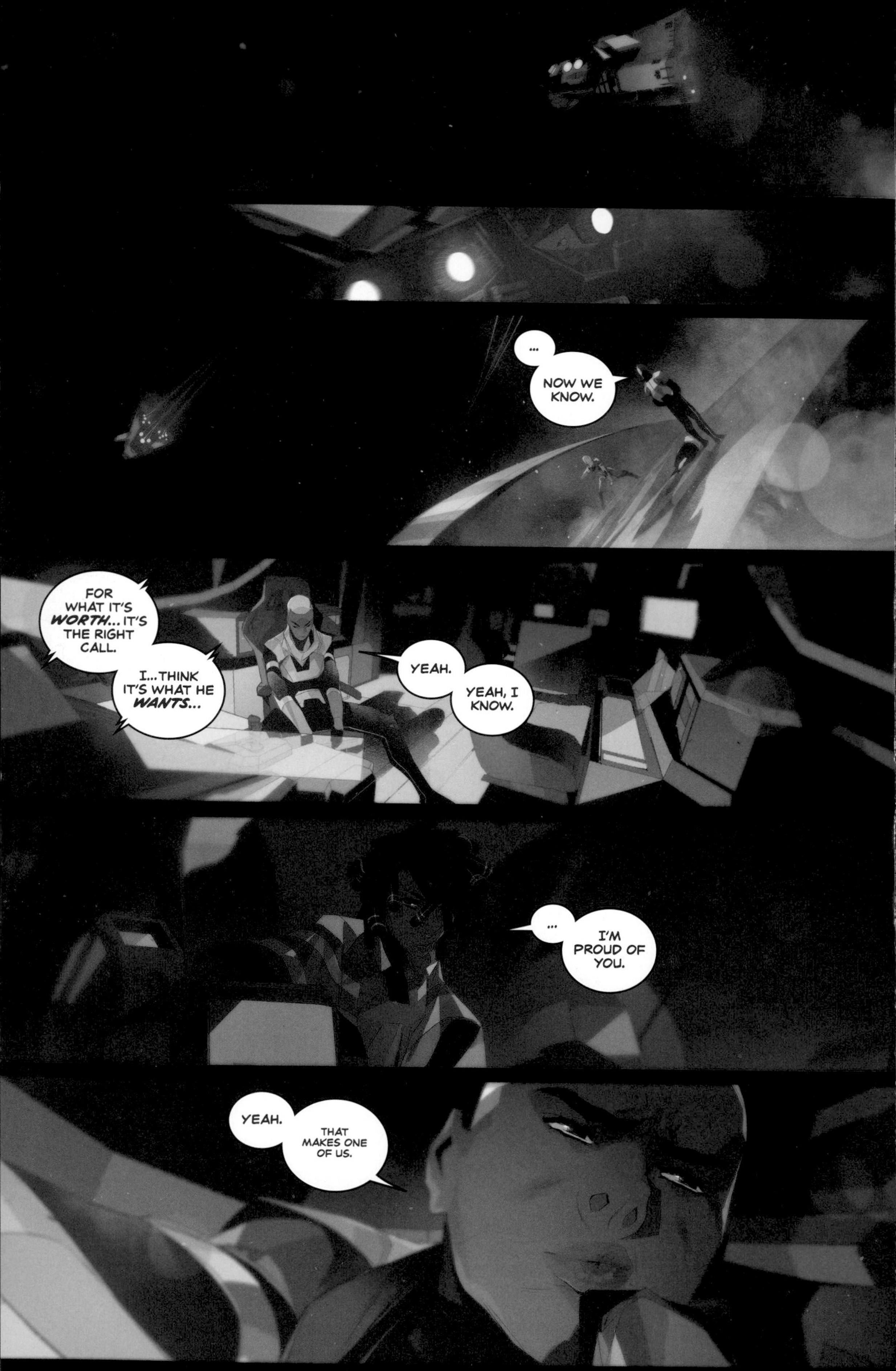
...
NOW WE KNOW.
FOR WHAT IT'S WORTH... IT'S THE RIGHT CALL.
I...THINK IT'S WHAT HE WANTS...
YEAH.
YEAH, I KNOW.
...
I'M PROUD OF YOU.
YEAH.
THAT MAKES ONE OF US.

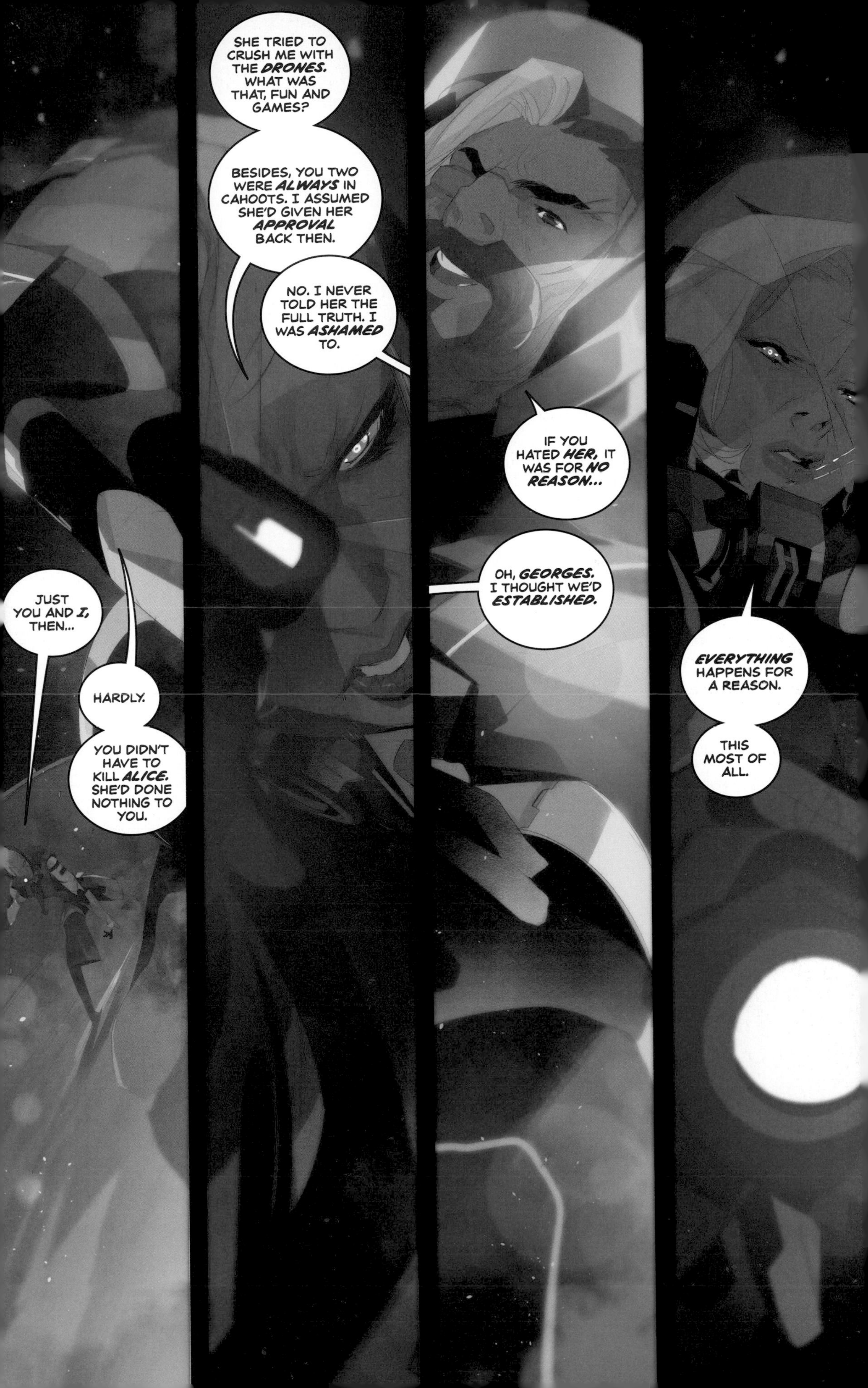
JUST YOU AND I, THEN...
HARDLY.
YOU DIDN'T HAVE TO KILL ALICE. SHE'D DONE NOTHING TO YOU.
SHE TRIED TO CRUSH ME WITH THE DRONES. WHAT WAS THAT, FUN AND GAMES?
BESIDES, YOU TWO WERE ALWAYS IN CAHOOTS. I ASSUMED SHE'D GIVEN HER APPROVAL BACK THEN.
NO. I NEVER TOLD HER THE FULL TRUTH. I WAS ASHAMED TO.
IF YOU HATED HER, IT WAS FOR NO REASON...
OH, GEORGES. I THOUGHT WE'D ESTABLISHED.
EVERYTHING HAPPENS FOR A REASON.
THIS MOST OF ALL.

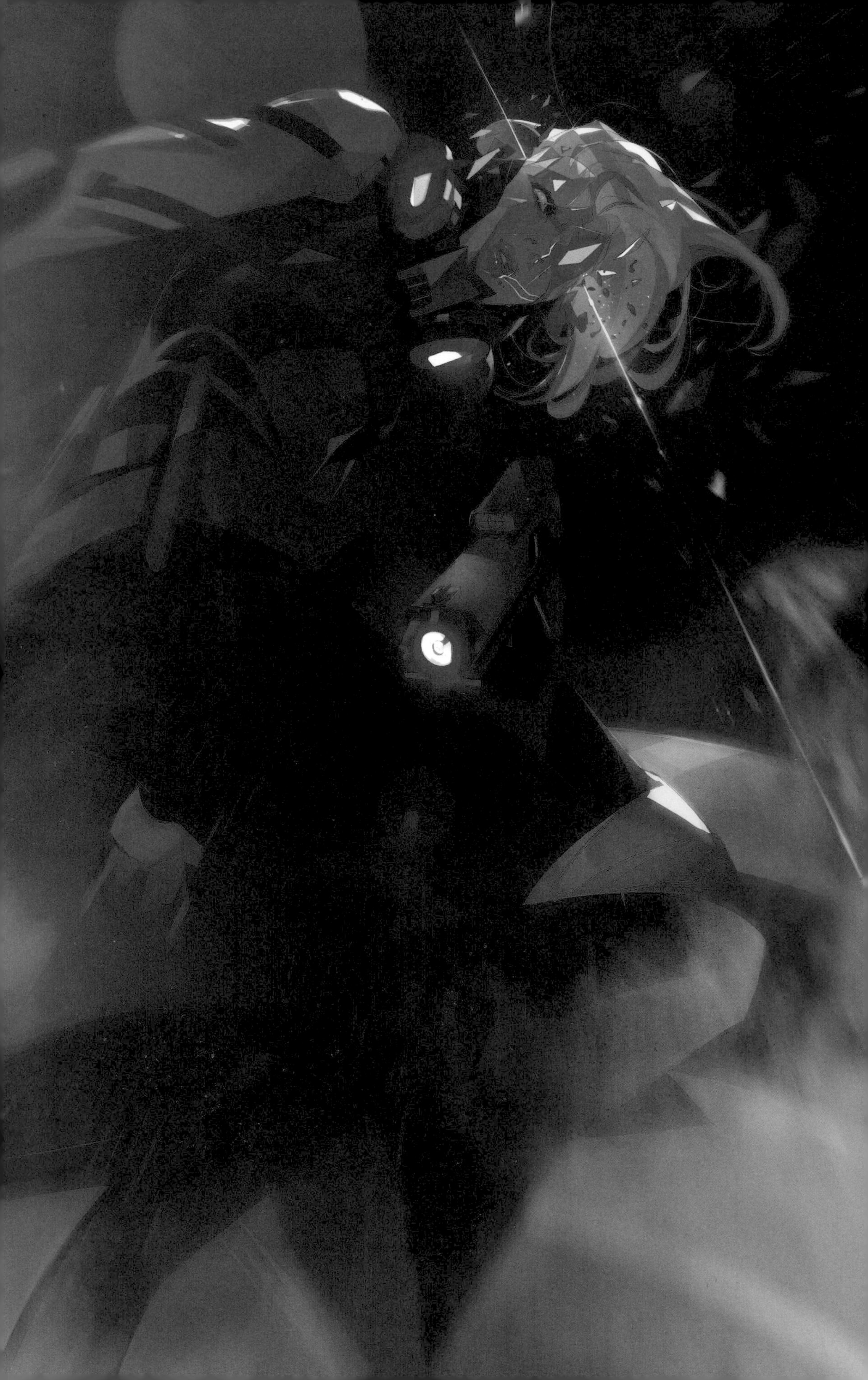

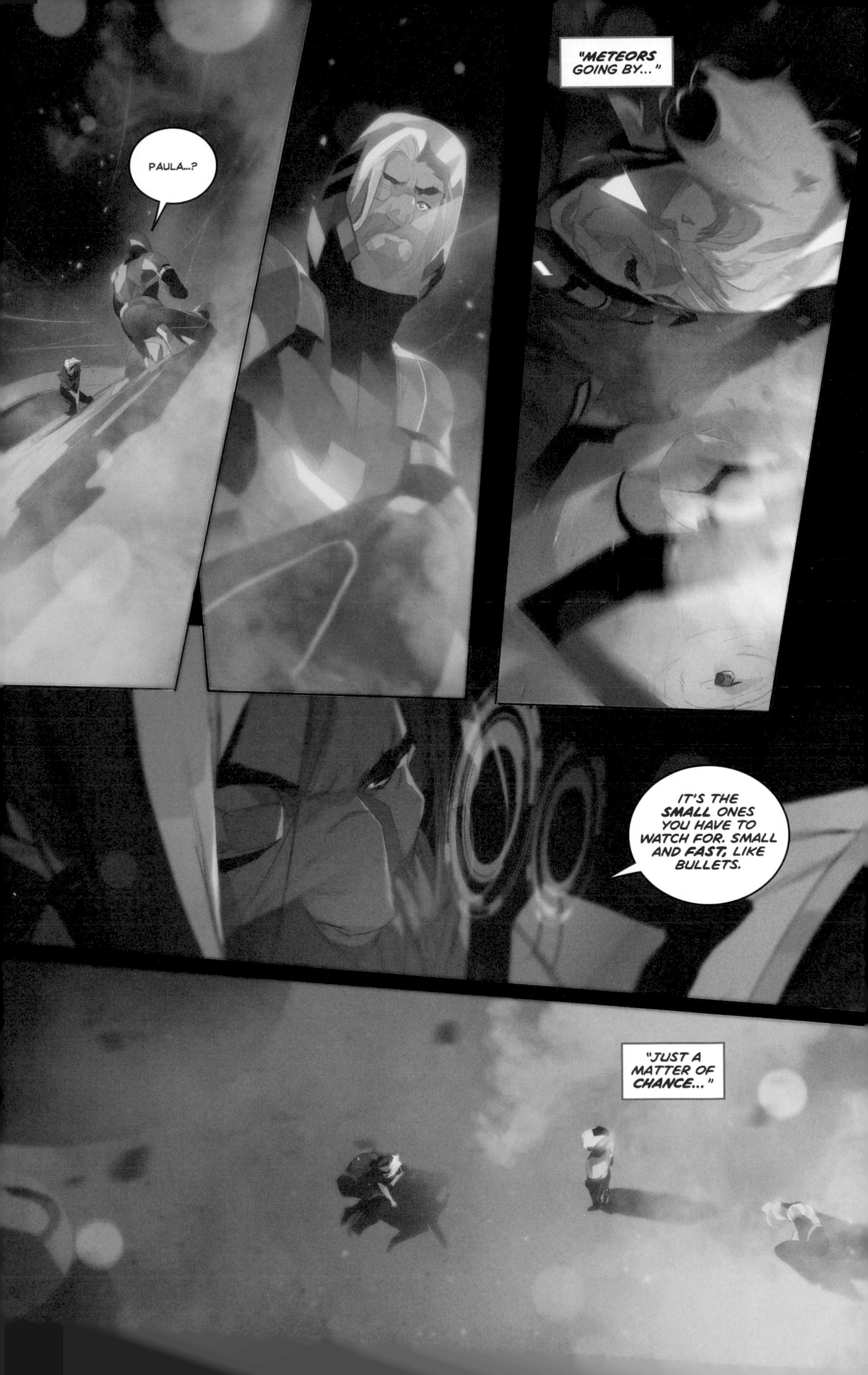
PAULA...?
"METEORS GOING BY..."
IT'S THE SMALL ONES YOU HAVE TO WATCH FOR. SMALL AND FAST, LIKE BULLETS.
"JUST A MATTER OF CHANCE..."

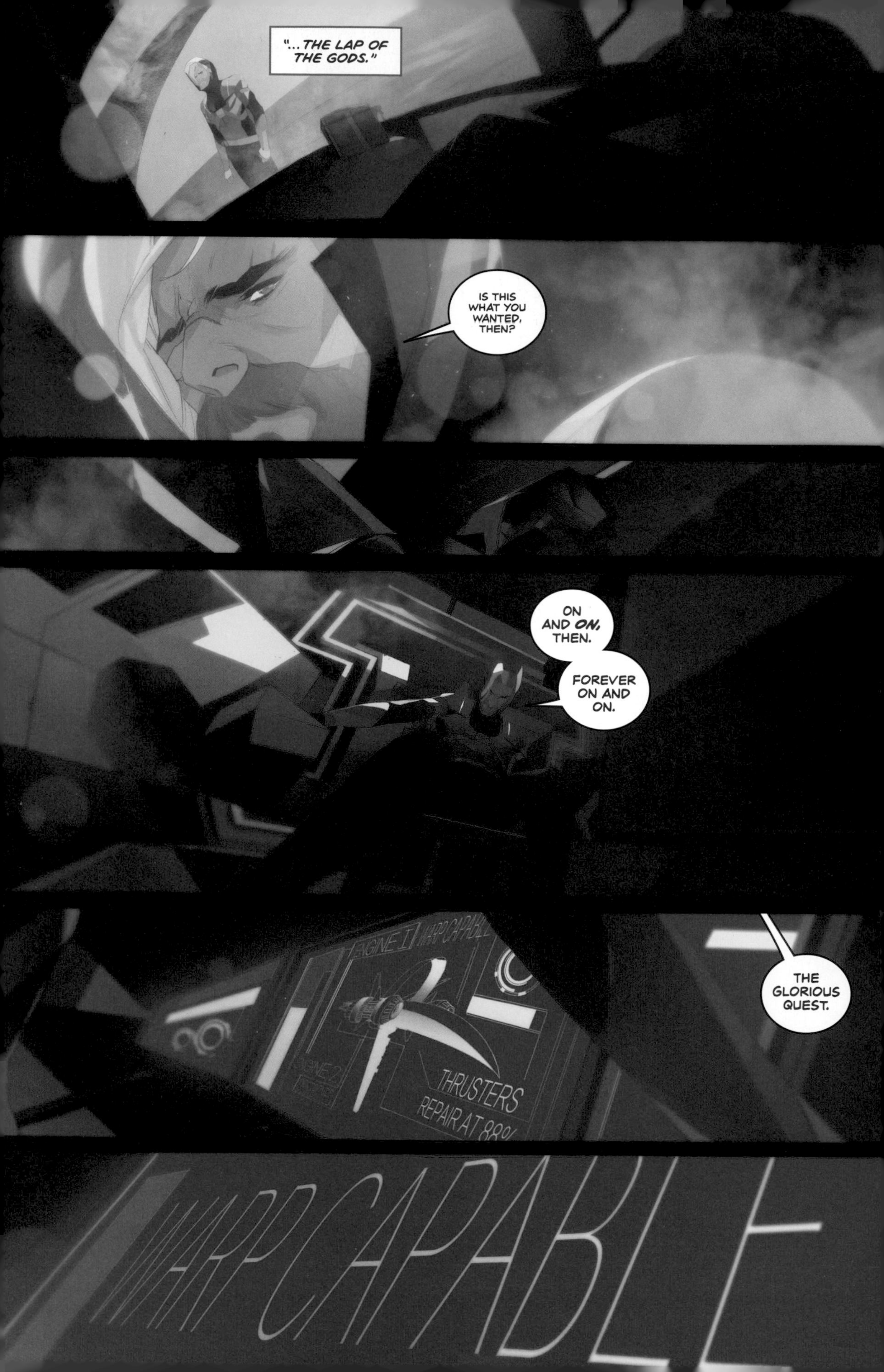
"...THE LAP OF THE GODS."
IS THIS WHAT YOU WANTED, THEN?
ON AND ON, THEN.
FOREVER ON AND ON.
ENGINE 1 WARP CAPABLE
ENGINE 2
THRUSTERS REPAIR AT 88%
THE GLORIOUS QUEST.
WARP CAPABLE

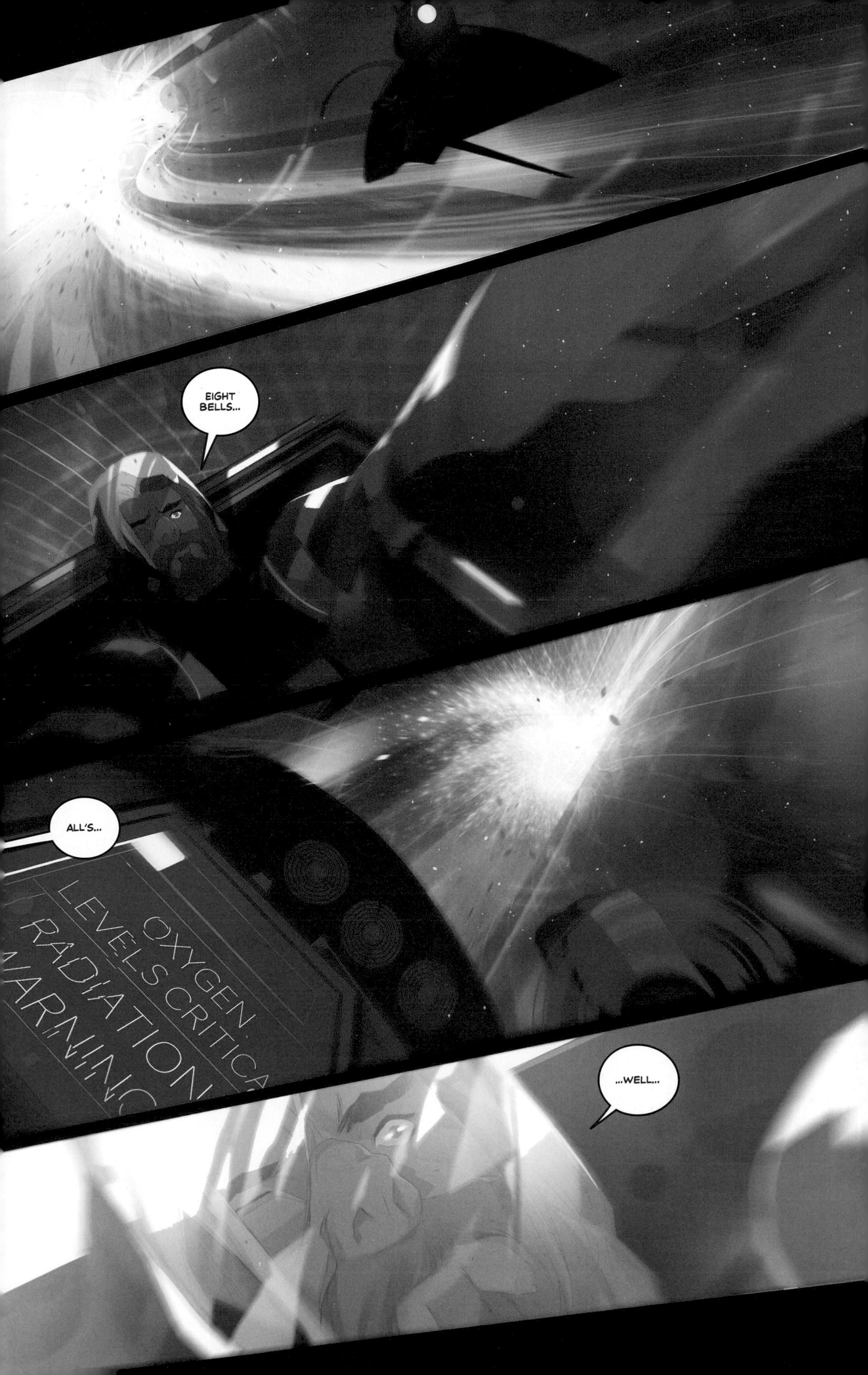
EIGHT BELLS...
ALL'S...
OXYGEN
LEVELS CRITICA
RADIATION
...WELL...

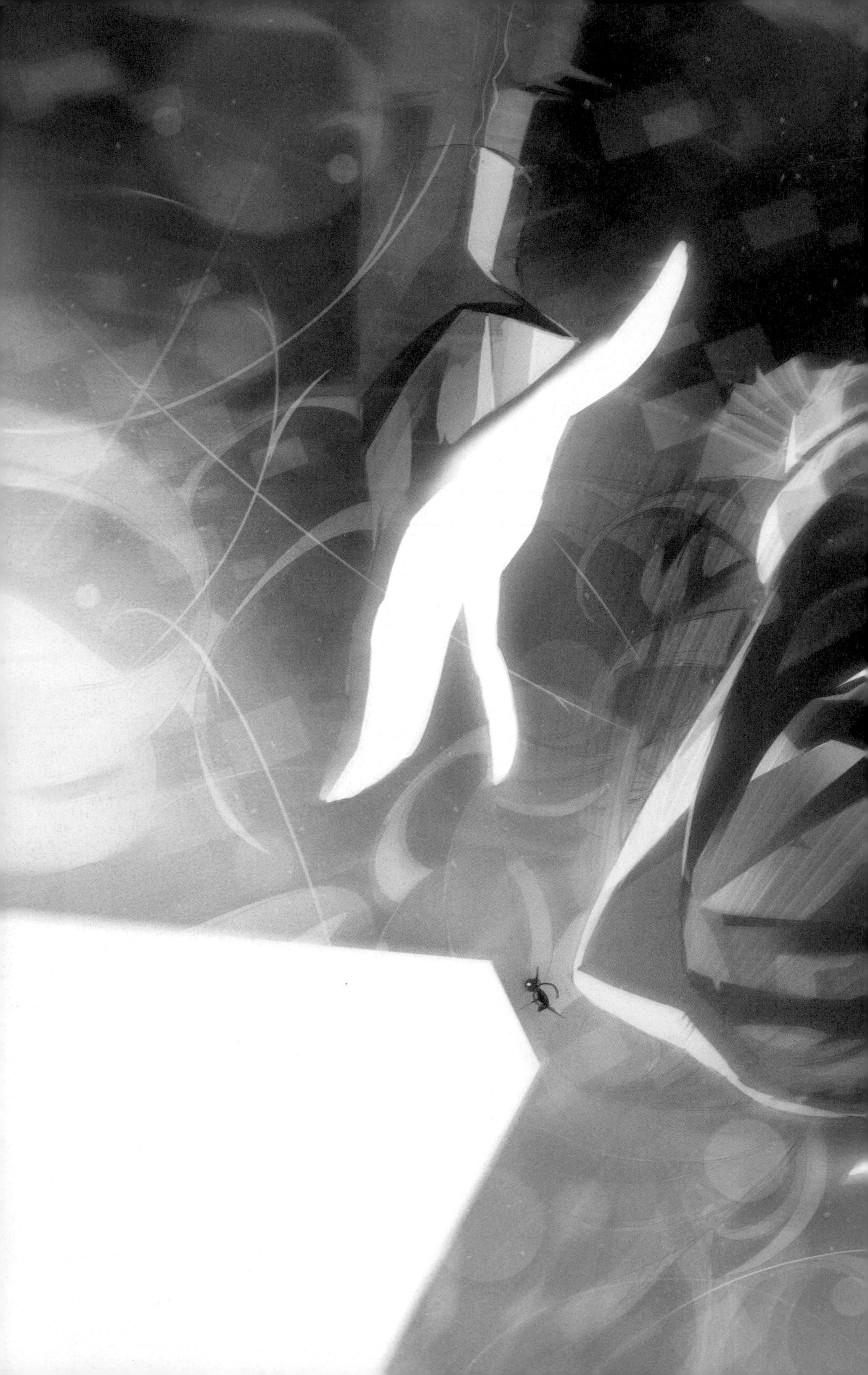

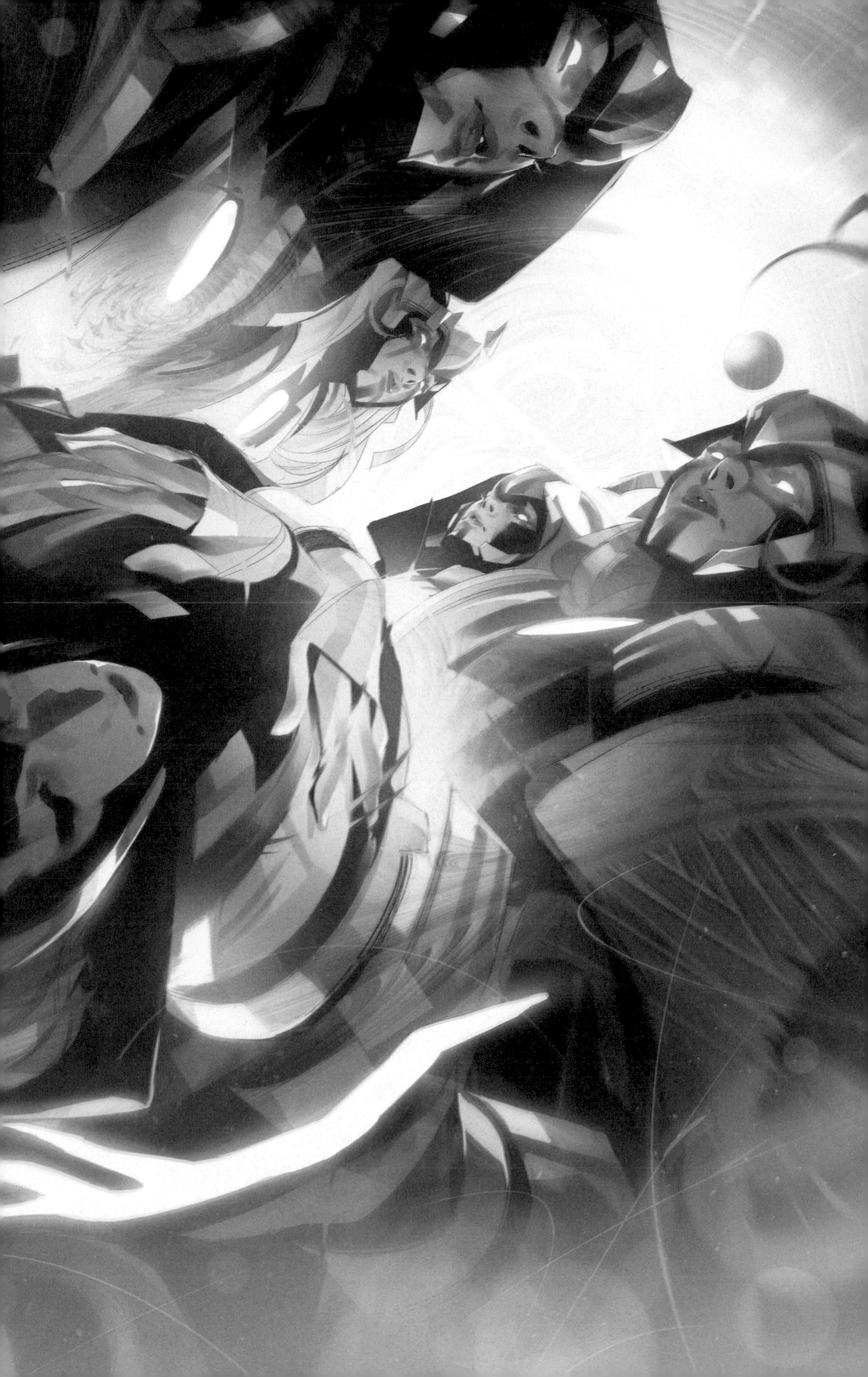

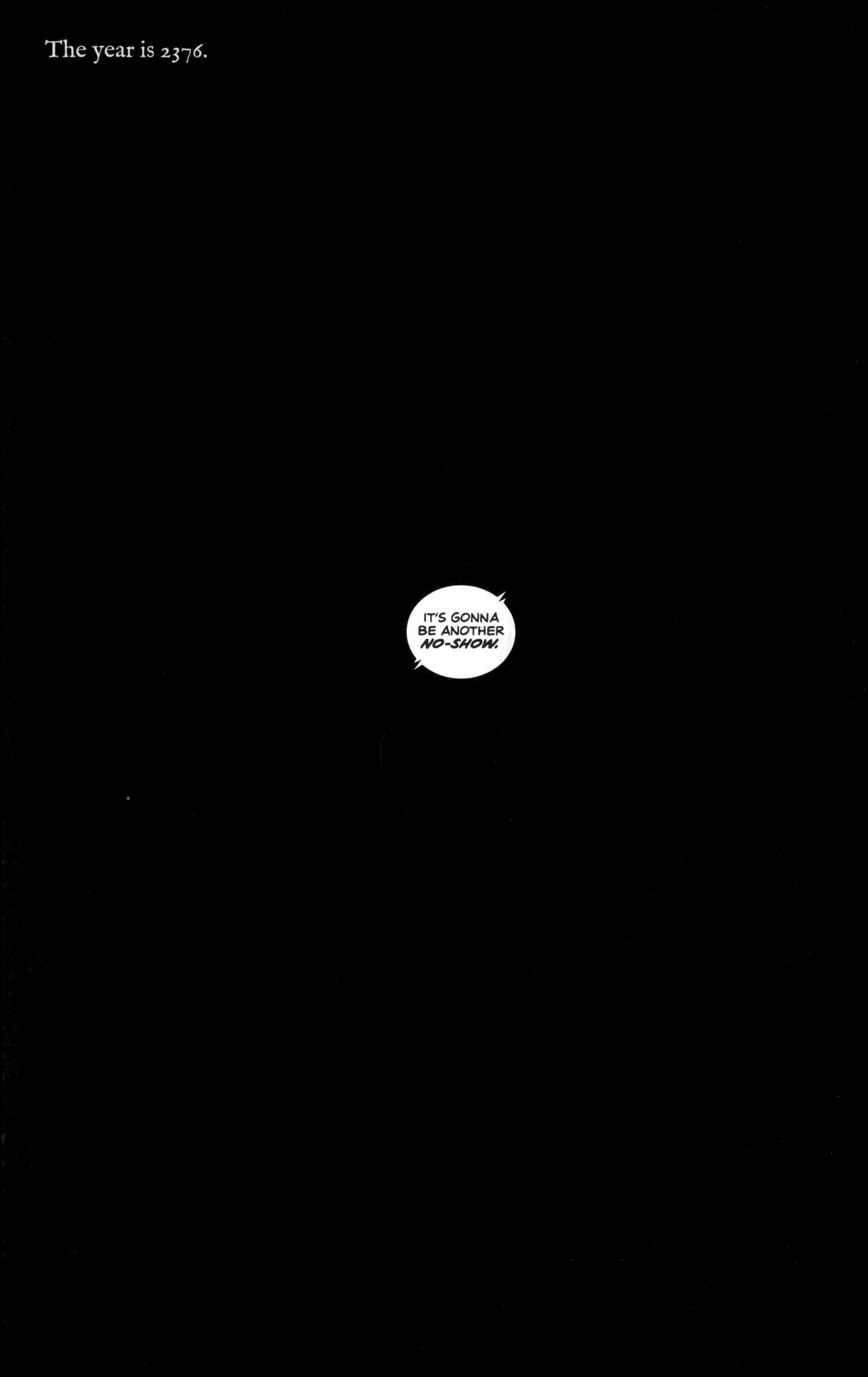
The year is 2376.
IT'S GONNA BE ANOTHER *NO-SHOW.*

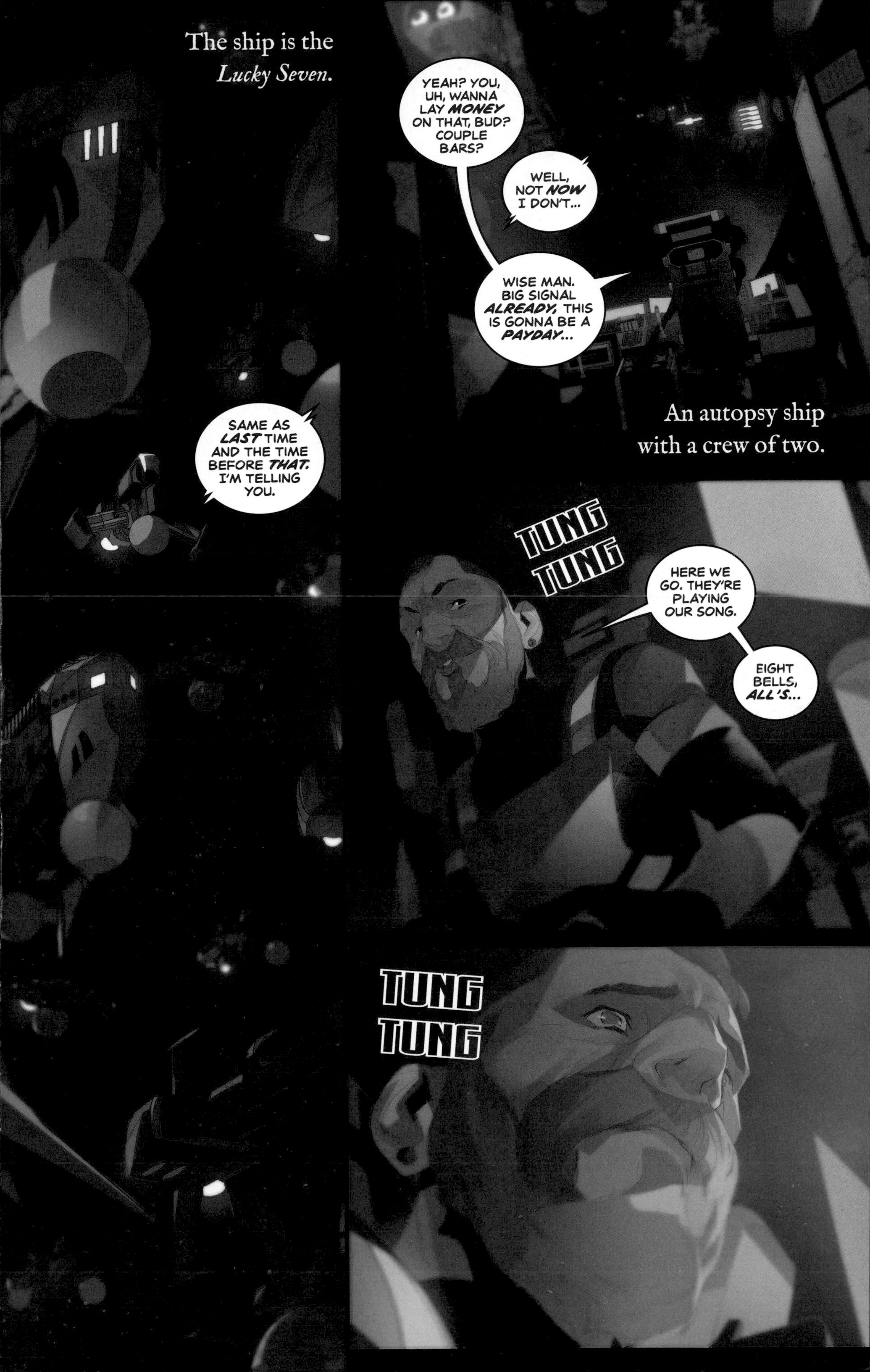
The ship is the *Lucky Seven*.
YEAH? YOU, UH, WANNA LAY MONEY ON THAT, BUD? COUPLE BARS?
WELL, NOT NOW I DON'T...
WISE MAN. BIG SIGNAL ALREADY, THIS IS GONNA BE A PAYDAY...
SAME AS LAST TIME AND THE TIME BEFORE THAT. I'M TELLING YOU.
An autopsy ship with a crew of two.
TUNG TUNG
HERE WE GO. THEY'RE PLAYING OUR SONG.
EIGHT BELLS, ALL'S...
TUNG TUNG

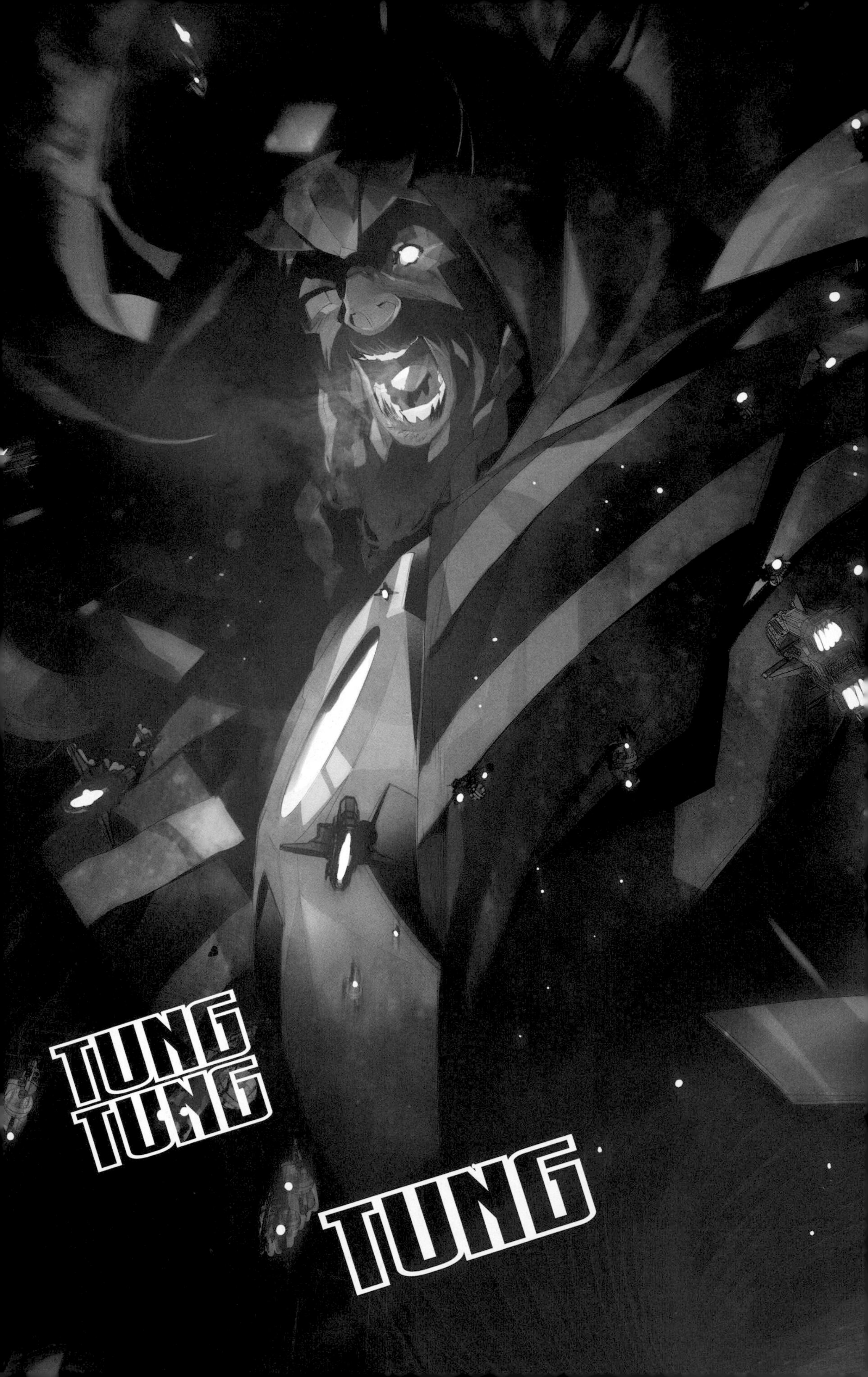
TUNG
TUNG
TUNG

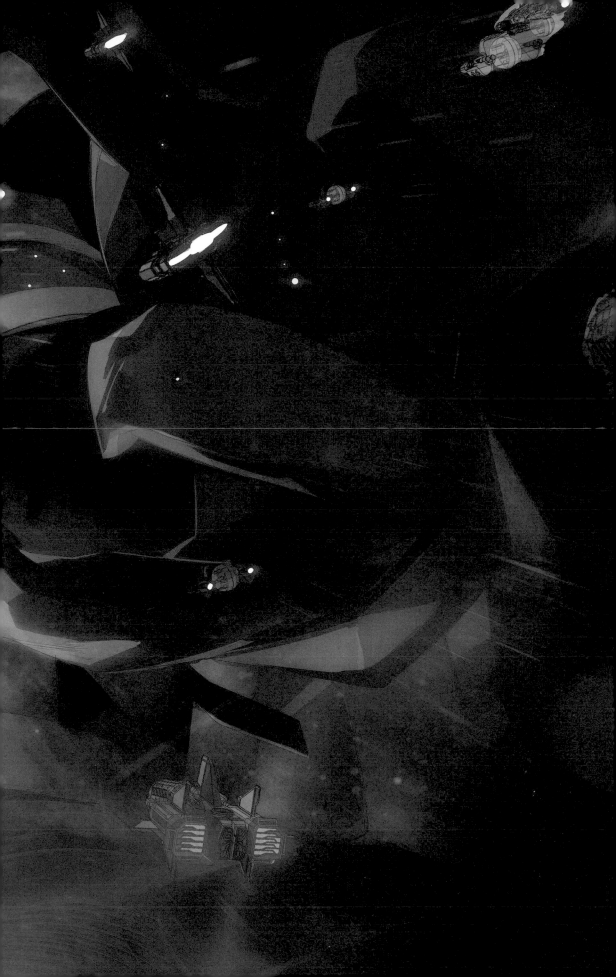

TUNG

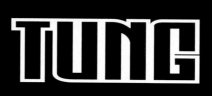

END OF BOOK ONE

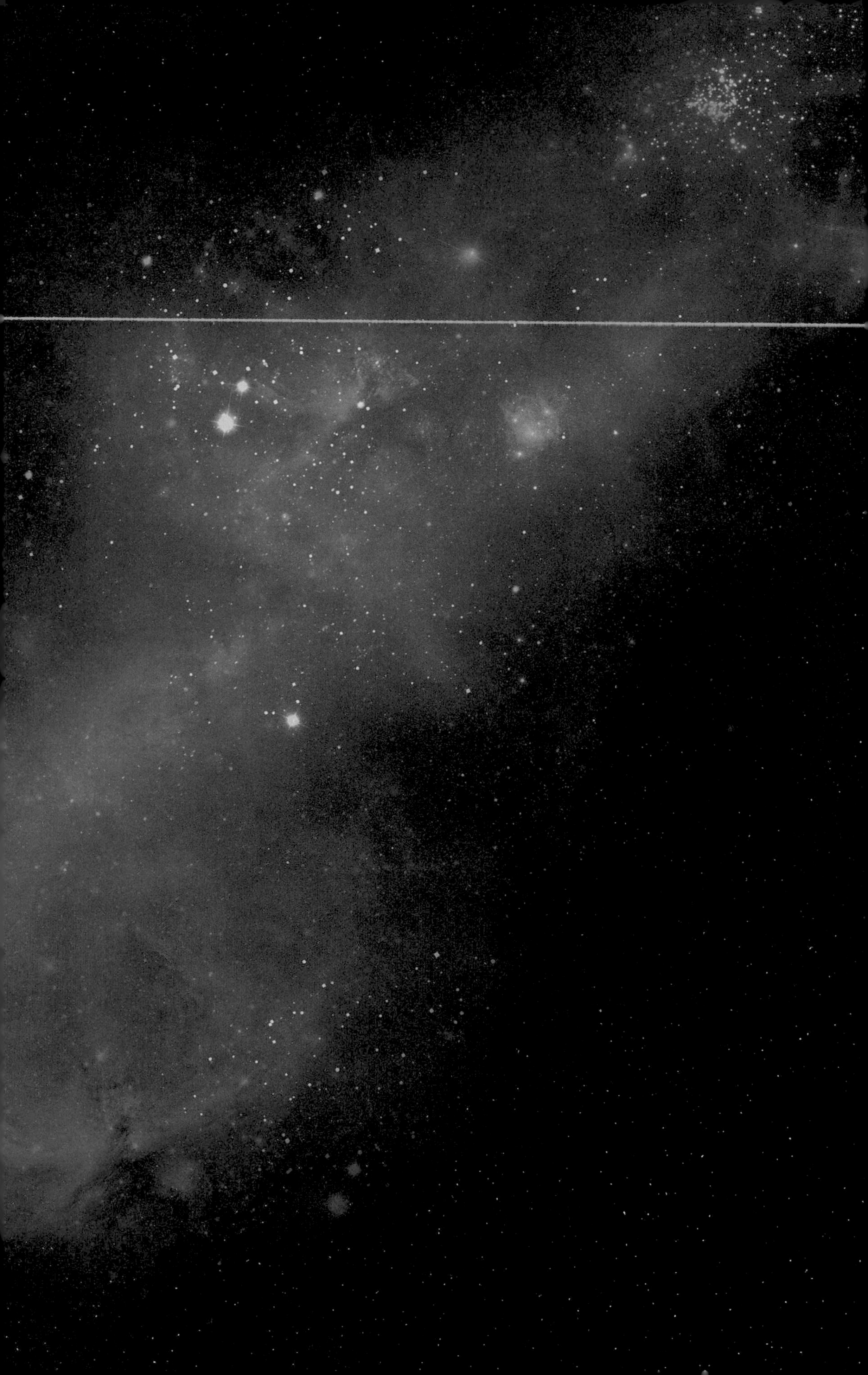

Cover Gallery

Issue One Cover by **Simone Di Meo**

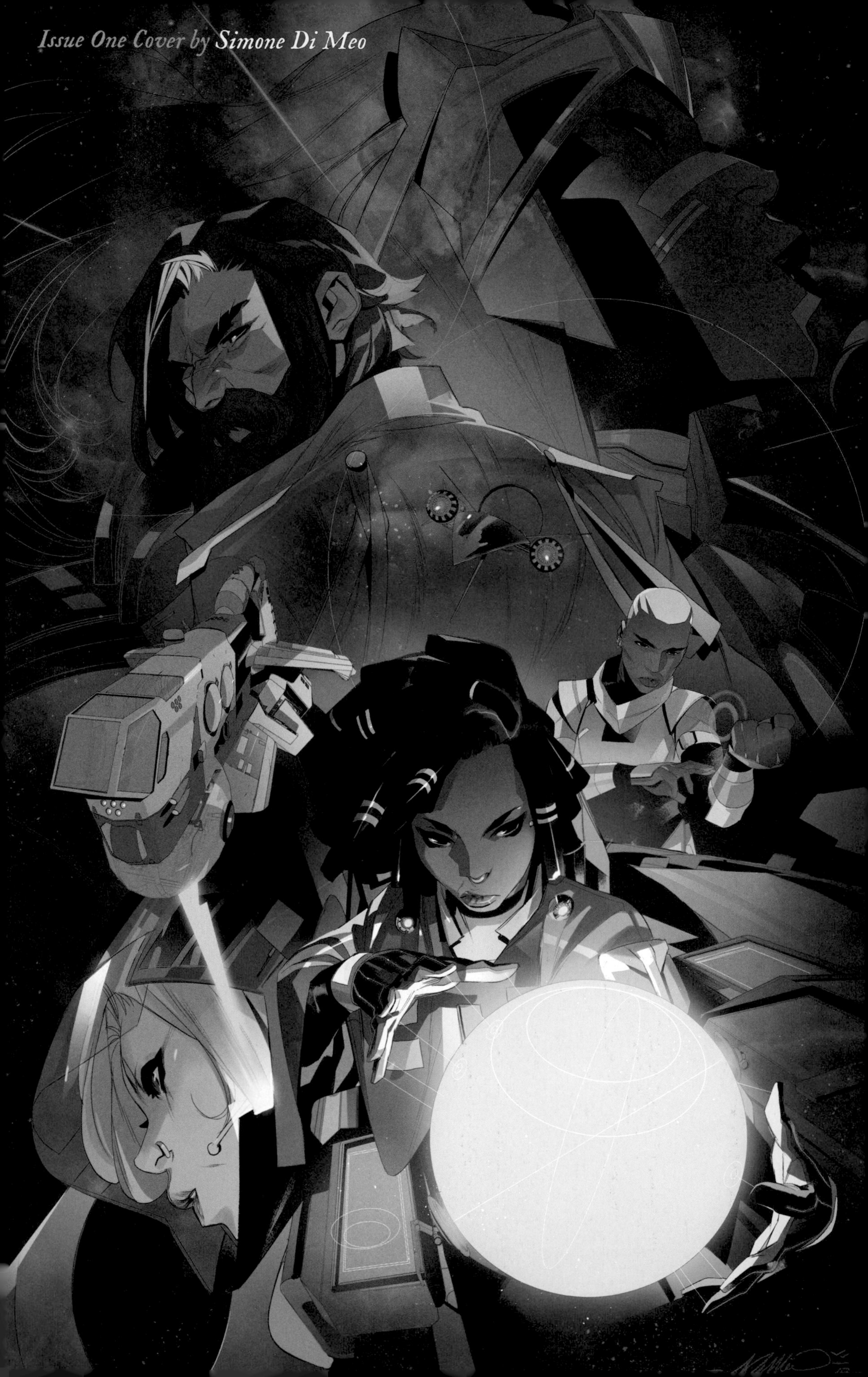

Issue One Cover by Toni Infante

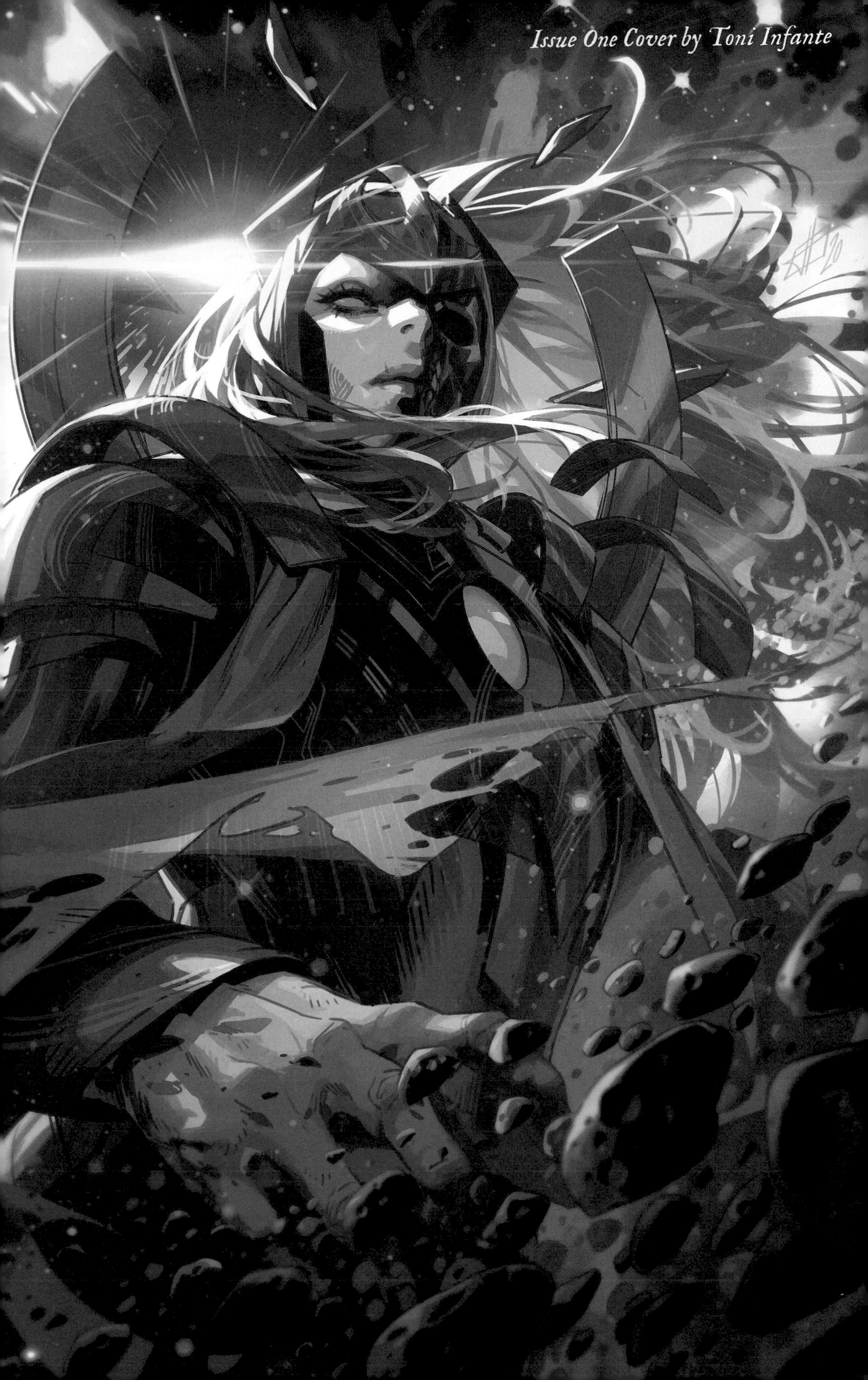

Issue Two Cover by **Simone Di Meo**

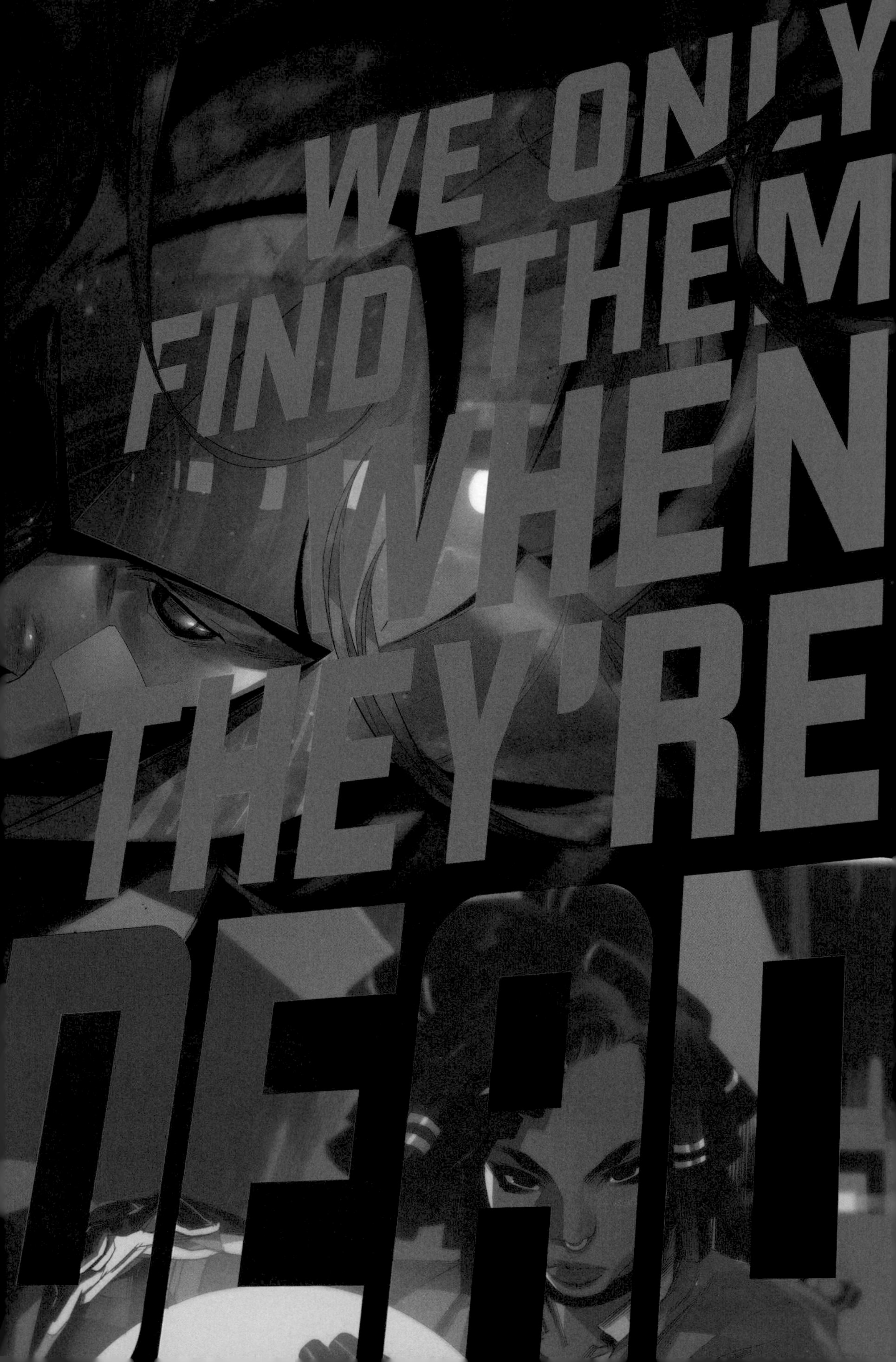
WE ONLY
FIND THEM
WHEN
THEY'RE
DEAD

Issue Two Cover by Toni Infante

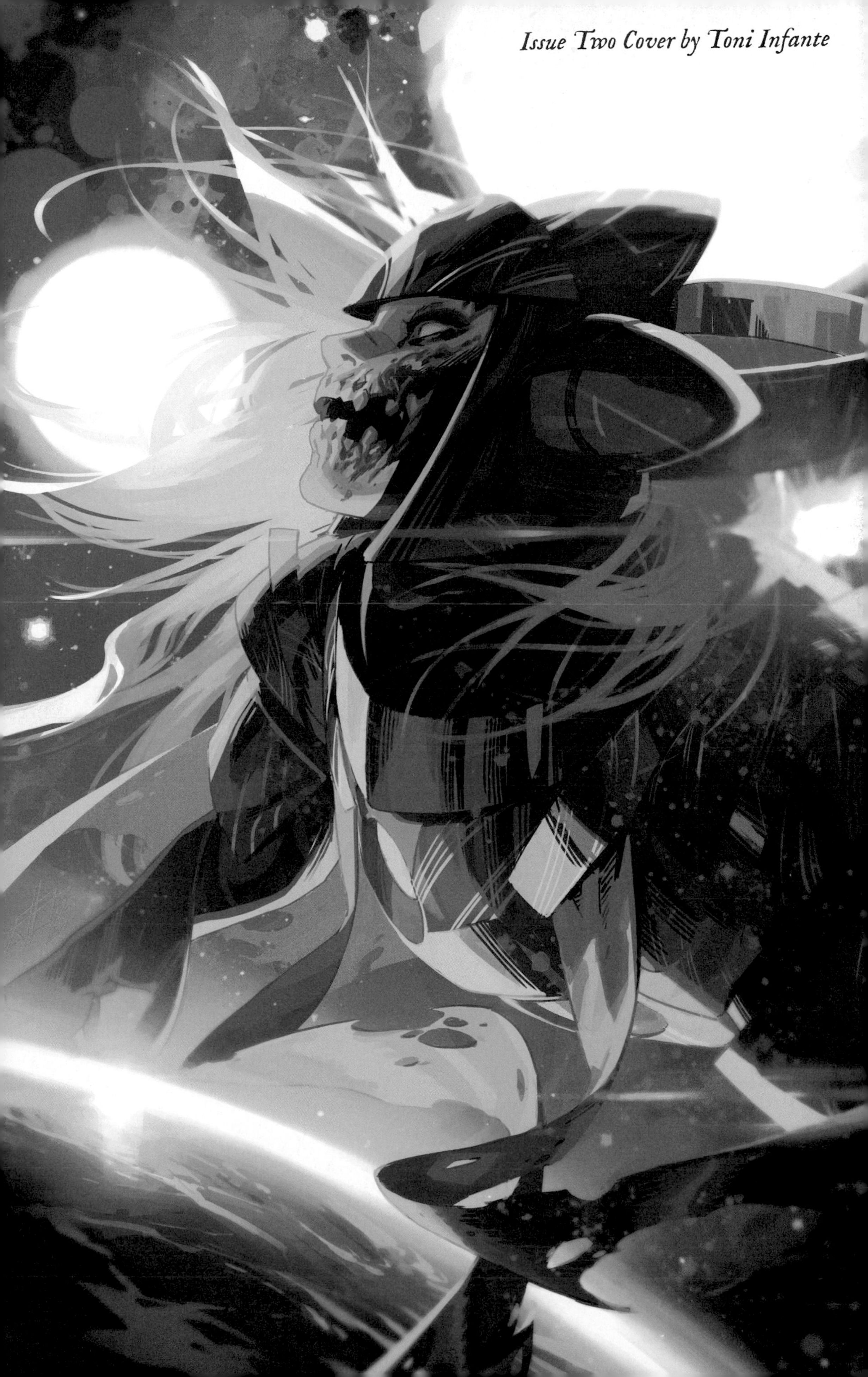

Issue Three Cover by Simone Di Meo

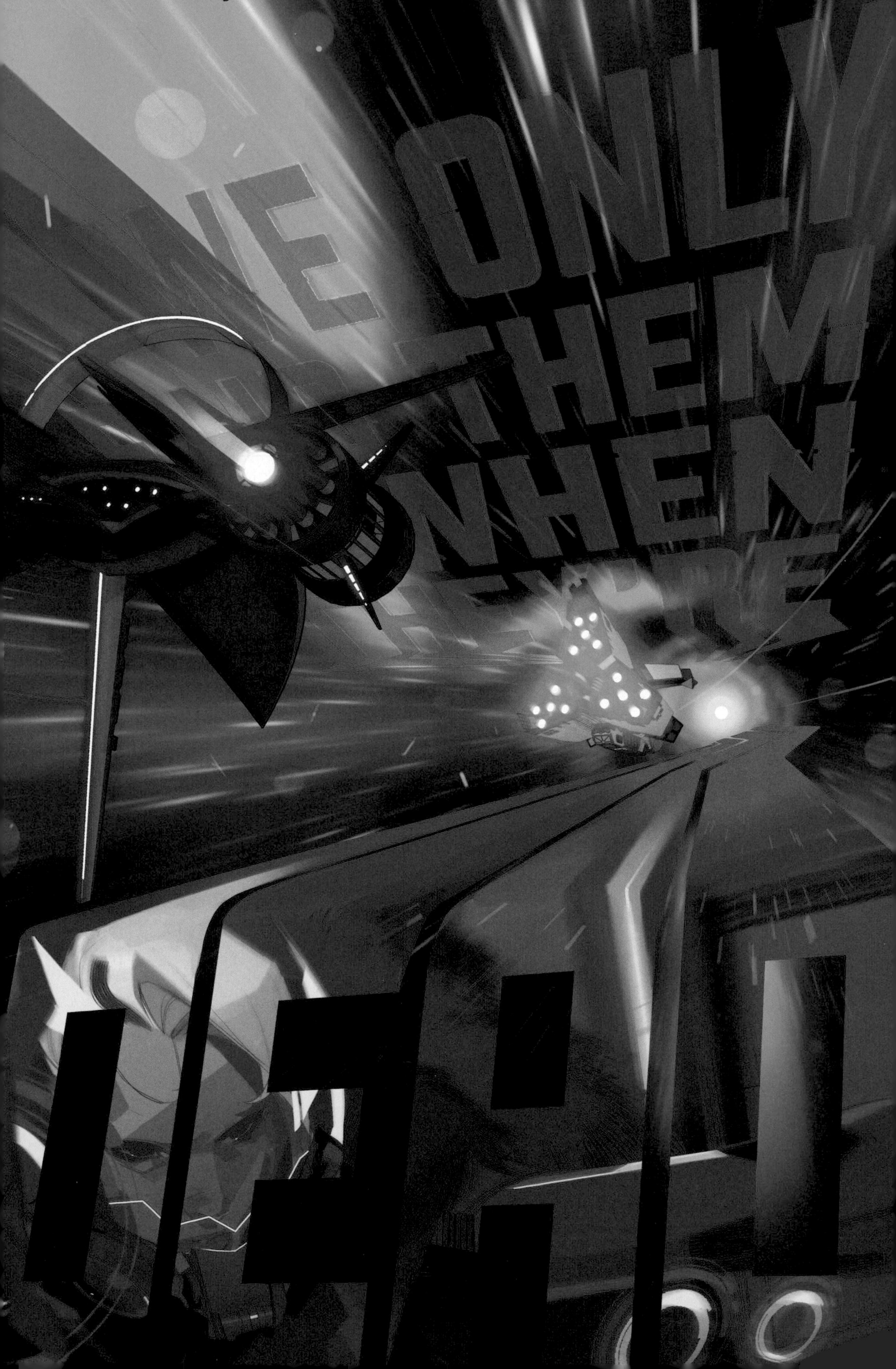
ONLY
THEM
WHEN

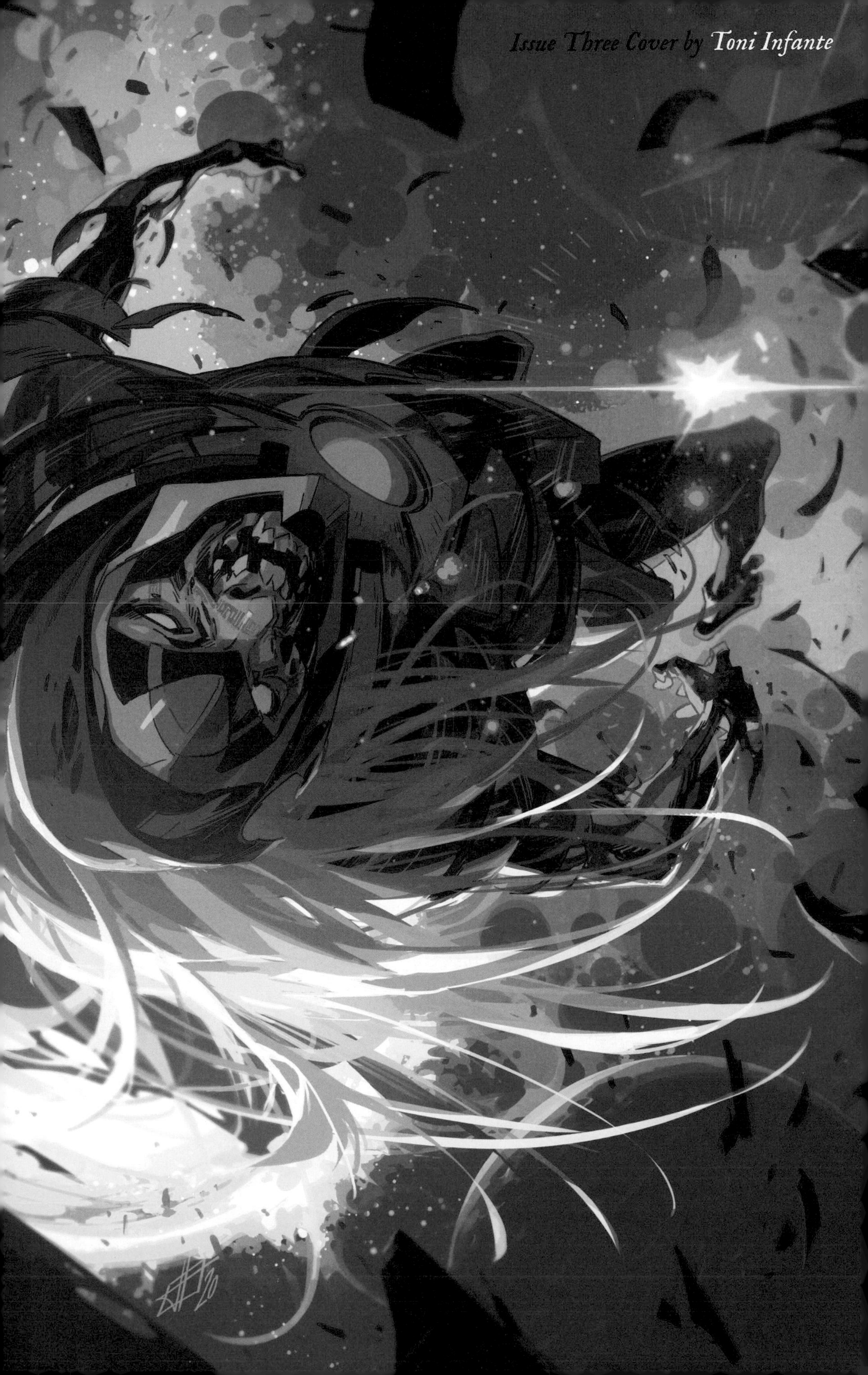

Issue Three Cover by Toni Infante

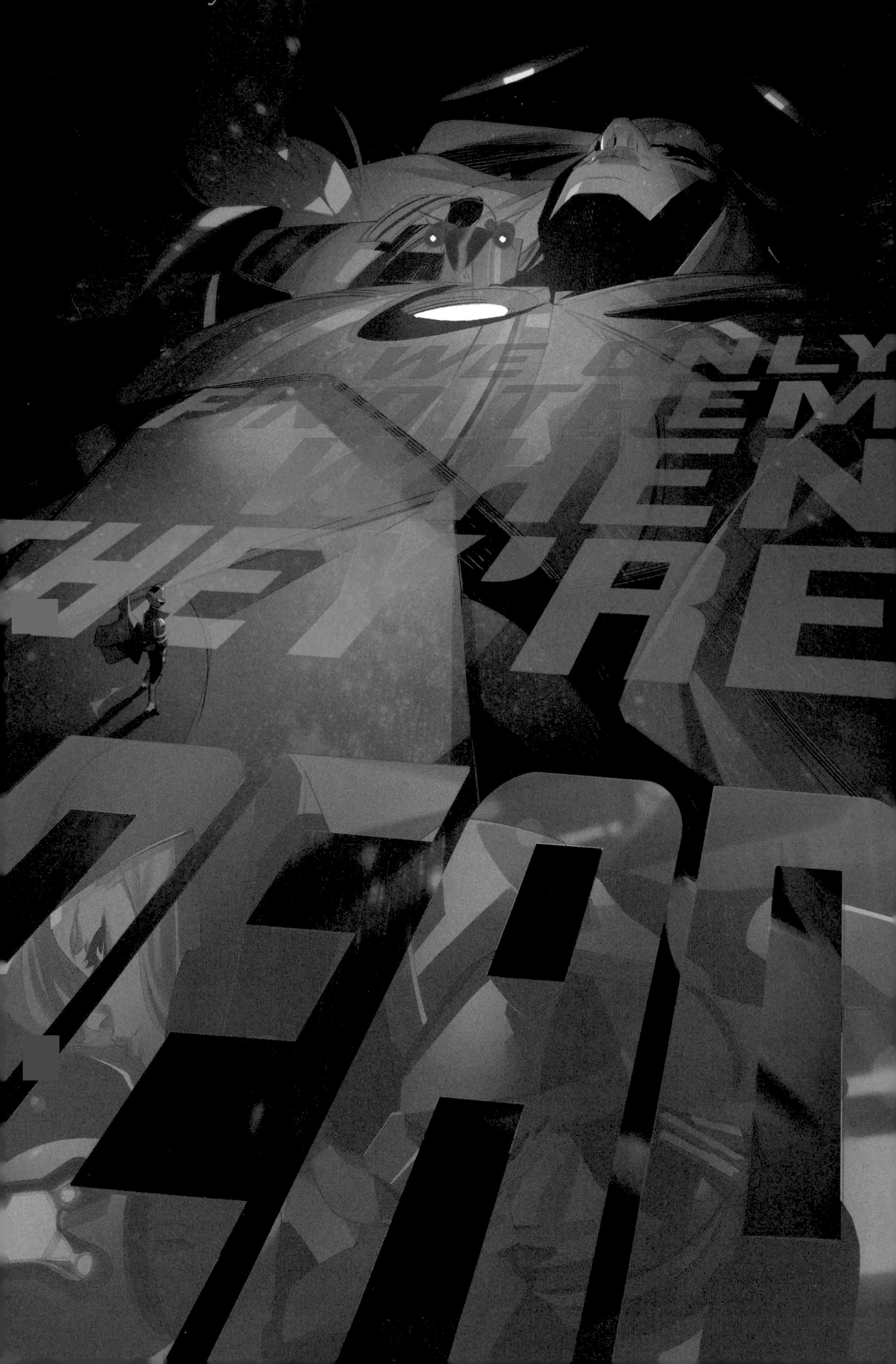

Issue Four Cover by Simone Di Meo

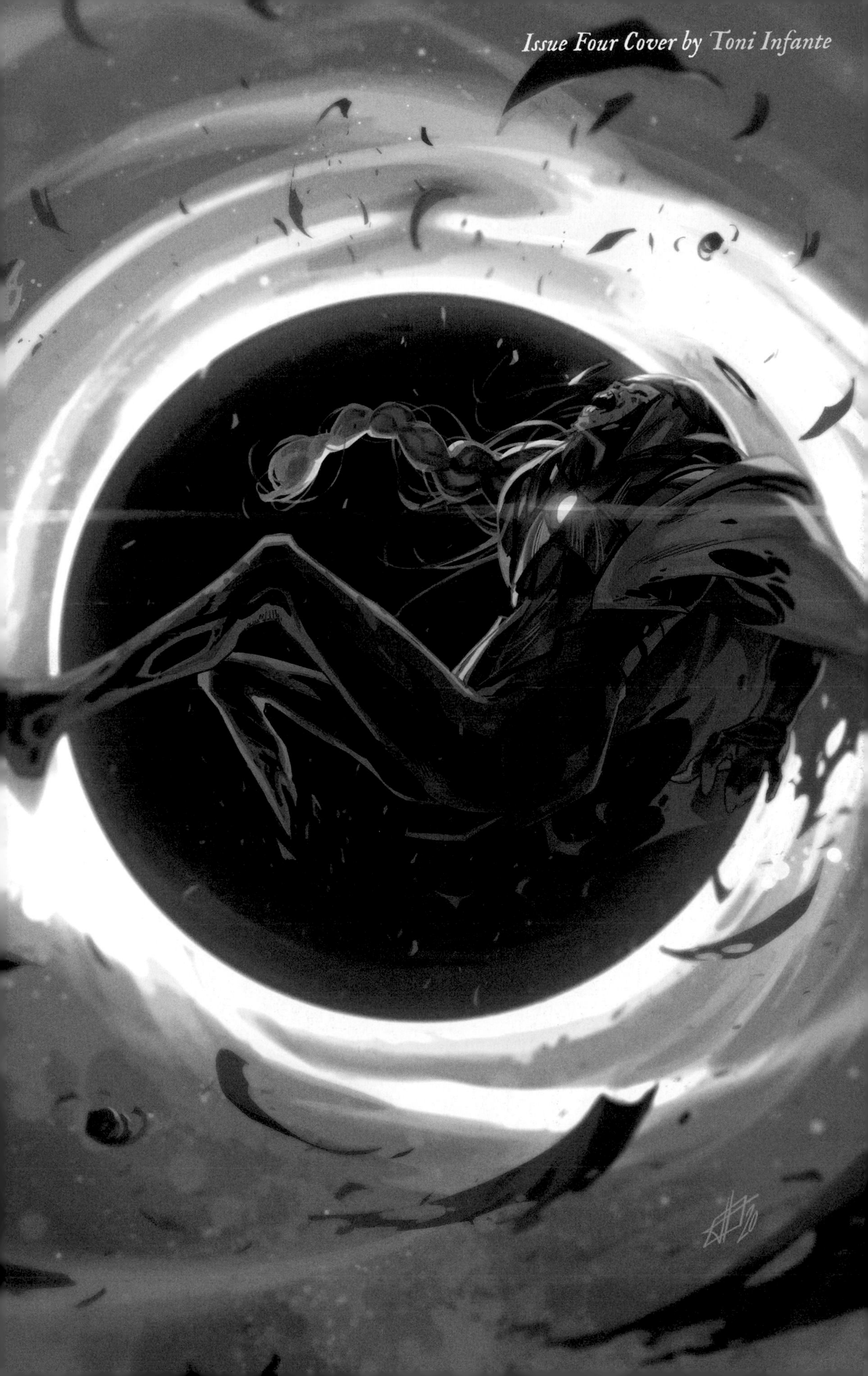

Issue Four Cover by Toni Infante

Issue Five Cover by **Simone Di Meo**

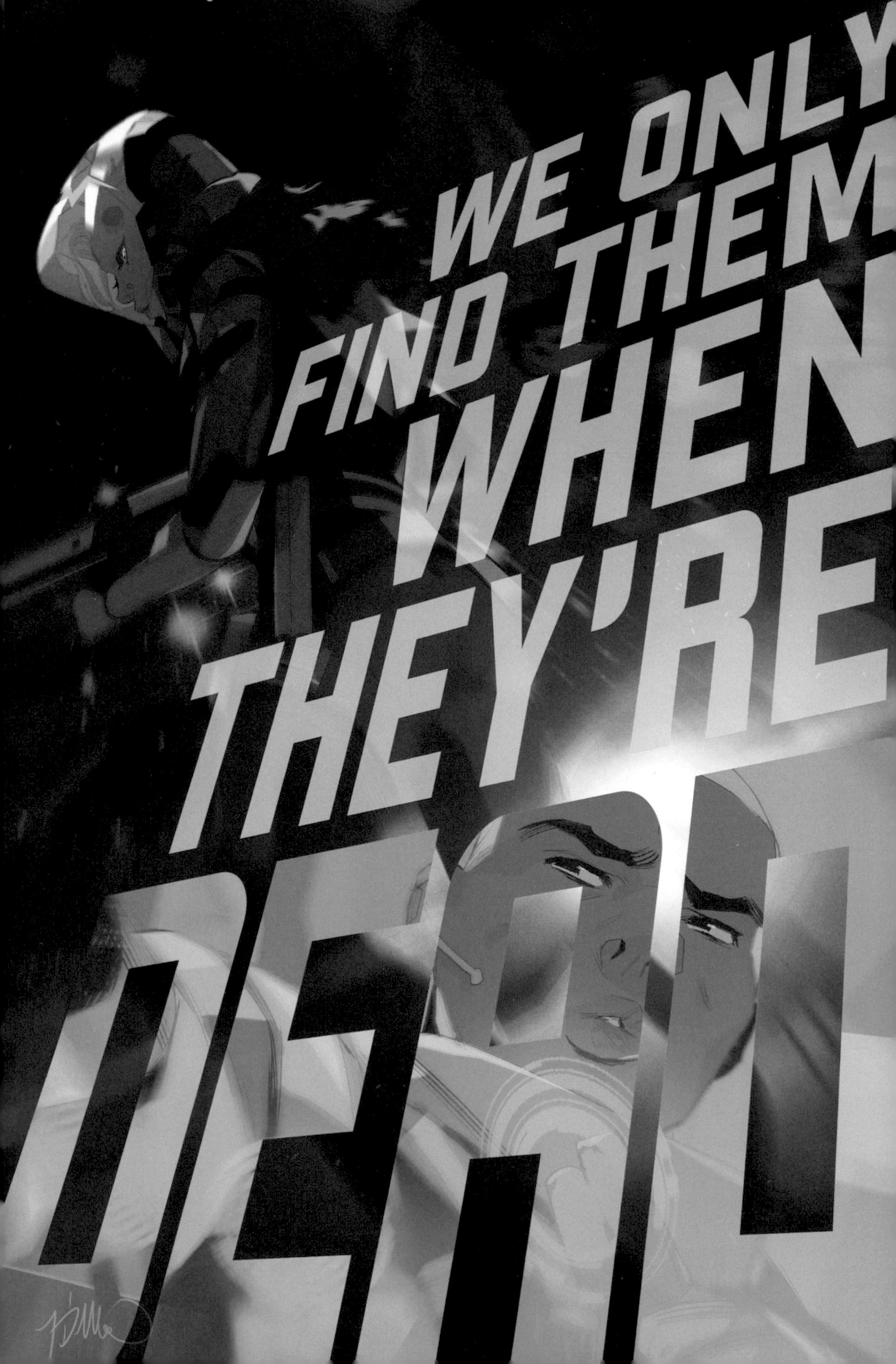
WE ONLY
FIND THEM
WHEN
THEY'RE

Issue Five Cover by Toni Infante

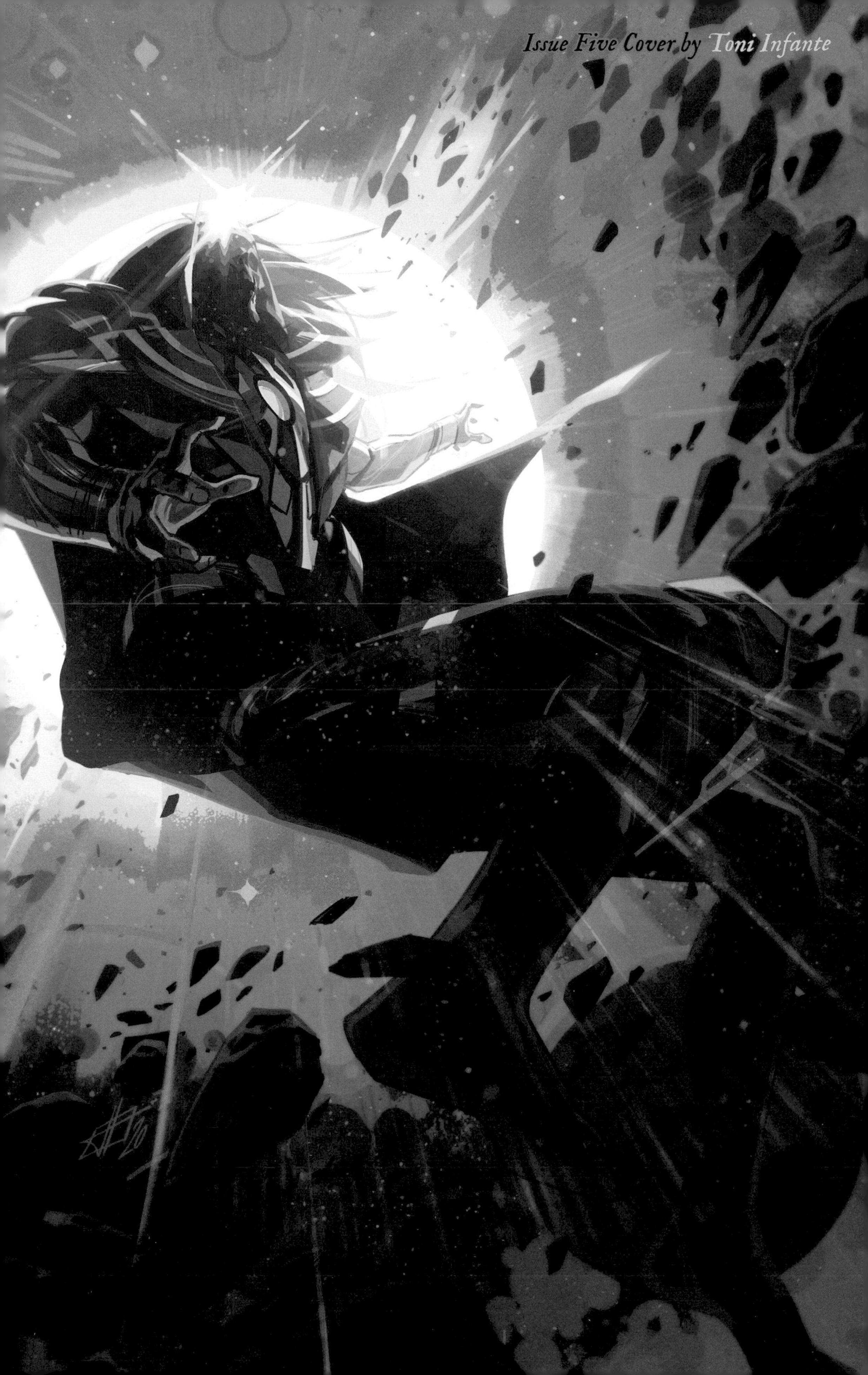

Issue One Cover by ***Christian Ward***

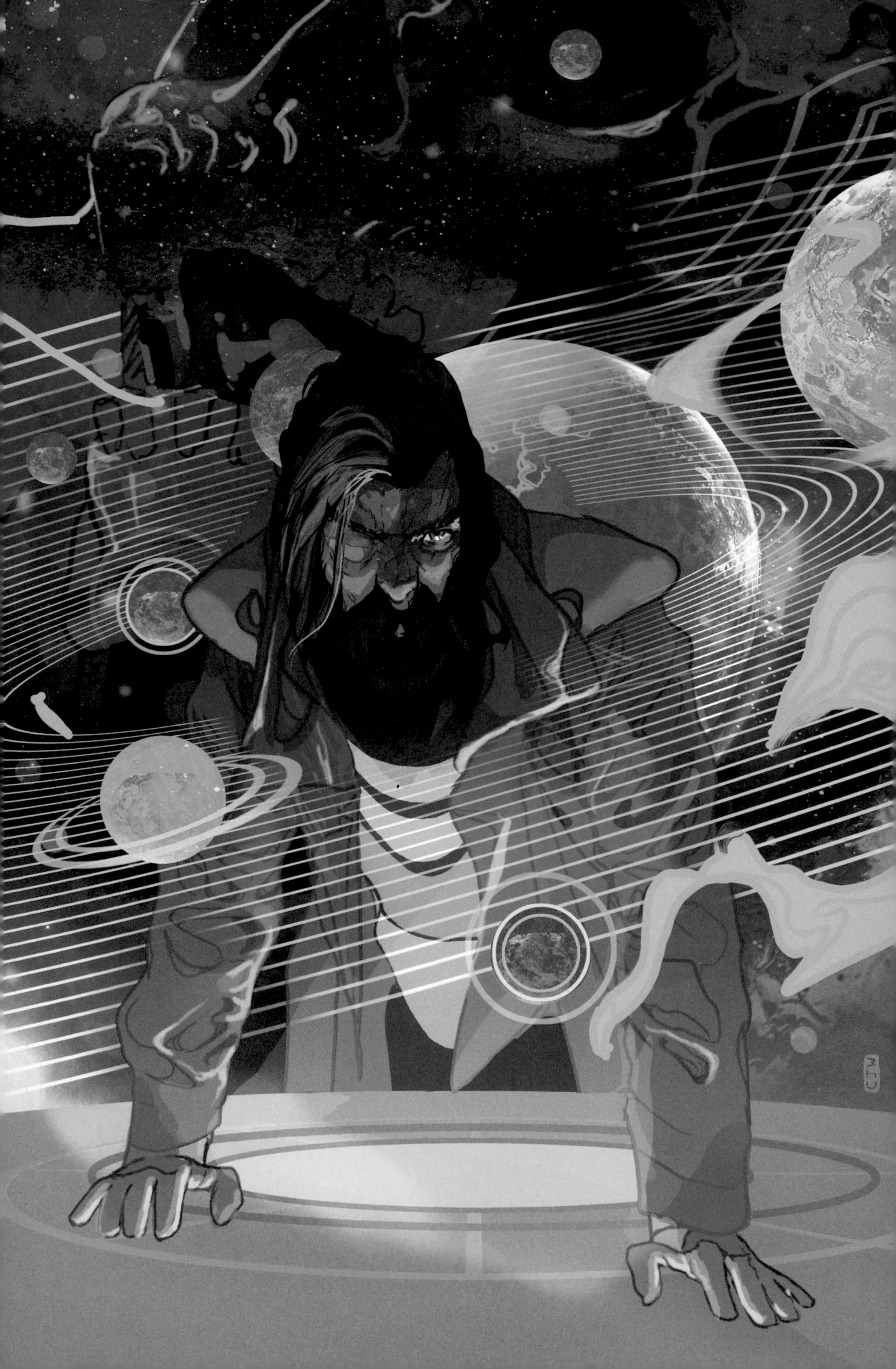

CTW

Issue One Cover by Jenny Frison

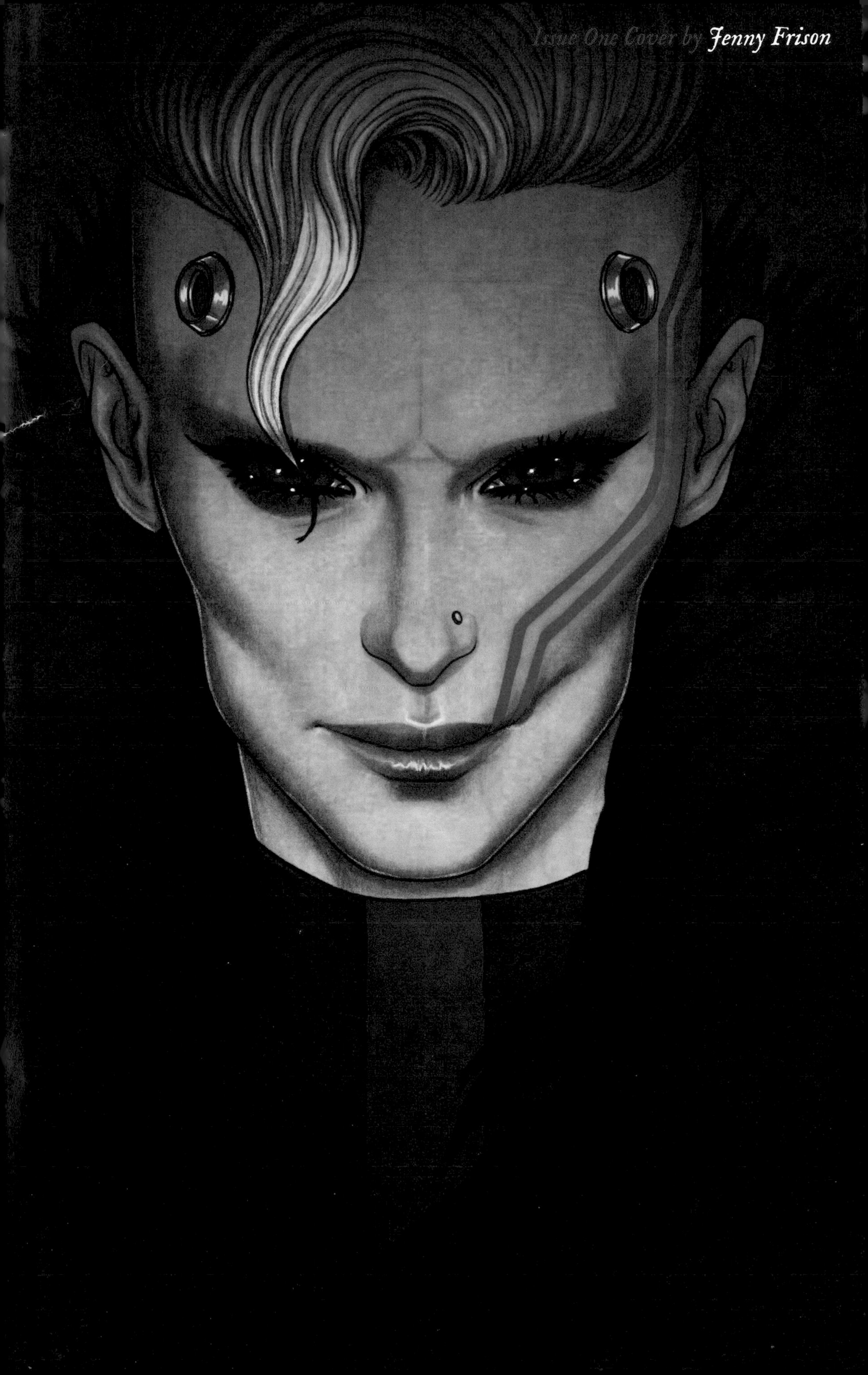

About the Authors

Al Ewing *is best known for his work for Marvel, including writing* Immortal Hulk, Guardians of the Galaxy, Ultimates, Loki: Agent of Asgard, Avengers: No Surrender, *and many more. Other work includes* Judge Dredd *and* Zombo *for* 2000AD *and* Doctor Who: The Eleventh Doctor *for Titan Comics.* We Only Find Them When They're Dead *is his first project for BOOM! Studios.*

Simone Di Meo *is a comic book artist from Italy. He was the artist for the blockbuster* Mighty Morphin Power Rangers/Teenage Mutant Ninja Turtles *and* Mighty Morphin Power Rangers *series at BOOM! Studios. His previous work includes high profile projects at Marvel including* Venom, Old Man Logan, *and* Immortal Hulk: The Best Defense.